THE NEW

CAIRN TERRIER

THE NEW

CAIRN
TERRIER

Betty E. Marcum

HOWELL
BOOK
HOUSE

HOWELL BOOK HOUSE
A Simon & Schuster Macmillan Company
1633 Broadway
New York, NY 10019

Library of Congress Cataloging-in-Publication Data
Marcum, Betty E.
   The new Cairn terrier/Betty E. Marcum.
       p. cm.
   ISBN 0-87605-073-9
   1. Cairn terriers. I. Title.
 SF429.C3M27 1995   95-13520
 636.7'55—dc20   CIP

Manufactured in the United States of America
10 9 8 7 6 5 4 3 2 1

Contents

Ch. Coralrocks Class Act

Foreword

In any discussion of the Cairn Terrier among breeders, judges or just fanciers of these sensitive, intelligent and game little dogs, the name of Betty Marcum and the Cairmar Cairns will always emerge. It is most fitting that this dedicated friend of the breed has taken the time to write about the Cairn Terrier—she is so much a part of its history.

For over twenty-five years, the Cairmar Cairns have had a major influence on the steady progress the breed has enjoyed. That she should author this most complete and thorough treatise on the breed comes as no surprise, as her involvement has been threefold, first as a very successful breeder/exhibitor, eventually as an equally successful professional handler, and more recently judging some sweepstakes around the country.

Over 150 champions have been made up at Cairmar, the large majority being homebred, and owner shown. Four have achieved the highest honor as a Best In Show winner, most notably Ch. Cairmar Cowardly Lion. A host of top producers carry the Cairmar prefix, including the late Ch. Cairmar Fancy Dresser, tied as the all-time top sire with fifty-one champions.

I first became acquainted with Mrs. Marcum after her success at the CTCA National Specialty in 1972, where she handled her first homebred, (Ch) Cairmar Cantie Croftee, to Best Puppy in Sweeps, and Winners Dog from the 6–9 puppy class. That she was already on the right track goes without saying. More recently, I was able to observe her during a "breed seminar" given in California on the Great Western weekend in June 1994. Her presentation was outstanding, displaying her intense knowledge of the breed, its background and unique personality.

When she embarked on this writing project, she did so with my complete support, and the results are worthy of that support. *The New Cairn Terrier* is comprehensive, covering all aspects of the breed, and is researched with unprecedented care and accuracy. It is the first definitive work on Cairn Terriers, and will be a most welcome addition to any Terrier fancier's library.

Dan Kiedrowski

Ch. Copperglen Foxtrot (front) and Ch. Glenmore's Miss Margaue (rear).

Preface

My deepest thanks to my husband, Joe, my best friend for more than thirty years. A strong, loving man, he allowed me to choose my path through life and gave his never failing support and patience when the going got rough.

A very special thank you to Seymour Weiss, my editor, for his unwavering belief in me, that I could do this project and do it well.

The quality and quantity of the research and statistical information contained within these pages has been greatly enhanced by Clarence Vaughn. His vast data base makes available to the reader much more information than I could have gathered on my own. My deepest gratitude for the support provided by Clarence, for the statistics—both for the top producers and for the champions by year—gathered at great cost to him in terms of both money and time. He also provided the lines of descendancy. My greatest thanks go to Clarence for the amount of his own time that he gave so unselfishly, because he wanted this to be a better book.

In researching this book, I drew very heavily on *The Cairn Terrier in America, 1991*, and *1992*, compiled by Clarence F. Vaughn and David Fee, and *The Compendium of British Cairn Terrier Records* by Patricia A. McKinney. Cairn fanciers are fortunate to have such records as these available.

Lynne Nabors and I worked so well together on the Cairn Terrier Club of America (CTCA) publication *Cairn Terrier Grooming Start to Finish*, that I asked her to read this manuscript and make comments. All her comments were of the utmost importance. She sacrificed a lot of time and lost much sleep in order to do this labor of love for the breed.

My thanks also to Don Robbie for his unfailing enthusiasm for this effort, and all his efforts to obtain needed photographs. The many thought-provoking conversations we shared inspired me to work even harder.

Laura De Vincent generously shared her art collection with me, and as a result made this book a much prettier one.

Special thanks to Pam Pettus and Cindy Eli, who are still trying to explain the term *computer friendly* to me, and without whom I fear the computer would have won!

Gary Hess, upon whom I depended very heavily for the early history, and who continually searched for photographs I could use from his own collection.

Ann Priddy, for her drawings. Ann has a gift of knowing just what you want even when you are just formulating the ideas.

Ken Kauffman for his drawings and his many keen observations about the Cairn Terrier.

Carol Kelly for allowing me to use some of her drawings that are so much a part of the history of the Cairn Terrier Club of America and have been used by the club in so many ways over the years. It wouldn't be a Cairn Terrier book without them.

Robert and Diane Williams for sharing the "Williams Collection" with us and allowing reproduction of the materials therein.

Dan Kiedrowski has been unfailingly patient with his help with show statistics, and has provided photographs and negatives from the *Terrier Type* files, all to help make *The New Cairn Terrier* a better book.

Ferelith Hamilton opened the files of the English *Dog World*, and sent photographs that are priceless in historical value.

And my heartfelt thanks to all those Cairn enthusiasts, in the United States, Canada and abroad, who shared pictures, articles, old letters, did photo shoots, and the other fanciers who called and asked how they could be of help.

I feel that all these people pooled their talents and resources to help me create a work that ties together all of the Cairn Terrier's history. This book serves as a bridge to the present from both editions of the late John Marvin's *The Complete Cairn Terrier* and *The New Complete Cairn Terrier*.

I think of this book as belonging to all Cairn fanciers; it is truly a group effort. Many people have contributed, and I cannot name them all, but they are remembered with affection. So many people gave of their time and effort, asking no credit, and willing to give anything that I asked.

I gratefully dedicate *The New Cairn Terrier* to you all.

Chapter One

The History of the Cairn Terrier

As the nineteenth century opened, Sydenham Edwards published his *Cynographia Britannicis* (1800 et seq.). In the chapter titled "The Terrier," published in 1801, the author offers descriptions as follows:

> In Scotland, the use of the Terrier is to kill; and here they breed a fierce race. Great is their courage, they will attack and destroy the largest foxes with which the country abounds, following them into chasms of rocks, where they often perish together.

There is evidence that one of the oldest-known strains of Cairns, or "Short-haired Skye Terriers," as the breed was generally known at the turn of the century, is that founded by Captain Martin MacLeod of Drynock, Isle of Skye. Captain MacLeod was a great Highland sportsman and an enthusiastic otter hunter. He maintained a pack of silver-gray Short-haired Skye Terriers for forty years before emigrating to Canada in 1845. The Drynock strain was kept alive by Mr. John Macdonald, Bridge of Ose Kennels, Isle of Skye. Mr. Macdonald was gamekeeper to the Clan Chief MacLeod of MacLeod, Dunvegan Castle, for more than forty years. In 1917 he wrote that he

Lithograph by N. Currier (before Ives), The First Lesson. Collection of Laura De Vincent.

1

Oil by Van Adam, nineteenth-century English. Collection of Laura De Vincent.

On Guard *by Richard Ansdell.* Collection of Schuler and Linda Nelson.

Mrs. Alastair Campbell with three of her Cairns in 1909.

and his late brother had this Drynock strain for the last seventy years. This strain thus dates from more than 110 years ago.

Captain Macdonald of Waternish, who was born on the Isle of Skye in 1823, took more interest in and knew more about the terriers of his native island than anyone living. He maintained that the short-haired breed was the purest Skye Terrier. He stated that the long-haired type was descended from a "Maltese Terrier" and a "French Poodle" that landed on the west coast of Skye after a shipwreck, and that ladies fancied them as lap dogs and made them fashionable. Another kennel of good Short-haired Skyes was that belonging to the Mackinnons of Kilbride. These terriers were descended from an old breed owned by Farquhar Kelly who lived at Drumfearn, Isle of Skye, in the seventeenth century. All of these strains played an important part in the early lines of the breed pioneers.

Mrs. Alastair Campbell and Mary Hawke were the pioneers of the breed as we know it today. It is due to their persistence the breed was granted recognition by the Kennel Club in 1910.

Lord Hawke and his sisters, Mary and Betty, imported some terriers from the Isle of Skye after a visit there. These all had drop ears and were small. Miss Hawke's kennel was founded on the Waternish strain through Craignish Scarba. Her dogs Bridget,

A view of the Isle of Skye as it appears today. Gary Hess.

Bride and Bruin were, as John Marvin wrote in *The Complete Cairn Terrier,* "Road markers, in the breed's early history, just as their owner was one of the first pioneers of the Cairn."

In the second edition of *The Popular Cairn Terrier* (London, 1929), J. W. H. Beynon writes:

> Mrs. Campbell owned her first Cairn—or "Short-Haired Skye"—when quite a young girl. He came from the kennels of Martin Mackinnon. Some years later she bought Moighan and his mate, the famous old bitch Calla Mhor, from the Nicholsons of Drynock; MacLeod of MacLeod, Doran Bhan and Roy Mhor followed, all of which were destined to play an important part in the progress of the breed. Then came that great pillar, Ch. Gesto, probably the greatest, as he was certainly the most famous Cairn of all times, which was purchased from Mr. Mackinnon as an outcross.

Dandy, 1869, *Gourlay Steell, R.S.A., Scottish, 1819–94, pastel and oil.* Collection of Walter F. Goodman. Photograph Courtesy William Secord Gallery, Inc., New York.

Mrs. Campbell showed her Short-haired Skye Terriers for years. She must have been aware there would need to be background and historical documentation before there could be any serious attempts at separate breed recognition. In witness thereof consider the following:

Tigh-an-Rudha, Ardrishaig. N.B.

Interest in the old and (in my opinion) the original breed of Skye Terriers has very much revived in recent years. Personally, I have a considerable kennel of them and many breeders have asked me to try and get them recognised by the Kennel Club. At present one can only register them as "Skye Terriers," and at the Kennel Club shows only the long-haired breed of Skye Terrier is recognised. I sent two of my terriers to the KC show in Edinburgh in the spring of 1897. They were entered in three classes but only recognised in one viz: the "Brace Class," in which class they were awarded the first or only prize, as they were the only entries. I maintain that this was an admission by the judges that the dogs were, as entered, Skye Terriers. Subsequently the judge of that class of terriers at the show wrote me stating that for twenty years these terriers had not been shown and that, there being no class (Classification) for them, they could not be recognised. I, however, showed again at a Championship Show in October of the same year and got for one dog a "Reserve prize" in Variety Class and VHC (Very Highly Commended) for the others. The judge praised the dogs and urged me to get a class (Classification) for them made, as they were, in his opinion, better than the "West Highlanders." Again at Greenock I showed and won a Third Prize and at Glasgow two VHCs, for two dogs. The fact that these were shown in the Open class implies that the dogs competed against many prize winners. I have written to the Secretary of the KC and he replied that he must have a full history of the dogs before making a place for them but that I could, on writing to the Secretary of any show, have a class made at that show, but the difficulty is this: To show the dogs they must be registered in the KC. As stated above they can only be registered at present as "Skye Terriers" and as such are shown. The breed of Skye Terriers recognized by the KC at present being long-haired, the type in question are not allowed to compete. If I asked a Secretary of any show to make a class for "Old Breed Skye" the KC would raise an objection at once, as my dogs are entered as "Skye Terriers." I am anxious to supply the Secretary of the KC with the history of these terriers from those who have had this breed for a long time. My terriers are from an old breeder, who originally purchased from a breeder who left Skye fifty years ago. Personally, I have only, within recent years, taken a practical interest in the breed, and can only supply the following information:

"The older breed of this terrier was 'blue-grey' and 'lemon' (Cream) and broken-haired, but now they are chiefly brindled and the 'Mackinnon Skye' is black. They are kept for foxes, being very swift

Morning Call, *lithograph by Maude Earl.* Collection of Laura De Vincent.

and having both scent and pluck. Some are prick-eared, others dropped, with small faces. They are mostly to be found in the Isle of Skye and the Outer Islands. Some of these terriers have been crossed with Scotch Terriers and have thus acquired the large heads and limbs and are consequently not so useful."

It seems a pity that this breed, of which so many people are fond, should be allowed to die out. There is nothing like showing a dog to keep up the characteristics of the breed. I propose to endeavor to have them recognised as "Old Breed" or "Sporting Skye Terriers." These terriers are similar to the West Highland (old type) terrier, but not to the "Scotch White Terrier," and I am sure if I am supported by fanciers of the breed, they would soon get a place in the "Doggy World." I have never come back from a show without some reward for these dogs. I shall be glad if you will kindly circulate this letter among any you know who are interested in the breed and oblige me with any information as to the history of the breed, which you may be able to supply. When I have got to-gether sufficient information to enable me to reply to the Secretary's letter, I shall do what I can to have the breed recognised as a distinctive type and to get a proper place for them at the KC shows.

Yours truly,
Ida Alastair Campbell

BREED RECOGNITION

The months between the Kennel Club shows of 1909 and 1910—these shows were run as *The Kennel Club Shows* until after World War II when the Kennel Club acquired from the representatives of the late Mr. Charles Cruft the name and title of Cruft's—were filled with toil and turmoil for the pioneers of the Cairn Terrier. Mrs. Alastair Campbell, who courageously pushed and fought for her beloved Highland Terriers, was not to be denied in attaining breed recognition. Classes for "Short-haired Skyes" were offered at the 1909 Inverness show. The exhibitors were Mrs. Campbell and Mrs. McDonald. The next stop for Mrs. Campbell's terriers was the Kennel Club Show, where there were additional classes listed under the unrecognized breed name of "Short-haired Skyes." Mr. Robert Leighton was the appointed judge and his performance lent credence to the quest for recognition as a separate and distinct breed:

> The ring stewards and one or two exhibitors objected to my paying attention to these unfamiliar dogs, on the plea that there was no such breed, and that "mongrels" ought not to have been admitted to the show. But as the numbers were entered in my judging book, I, of course, resolved to do my duty. A goodly team was entered into the ring—lively, energetic little animals, superficially different from one another, but having a general similarity in type which stamped them as a distinct and genuine breed. Happily—fortunately—I was not a stranger to such dogs . . . and I recognized them at once as the original, unspoiled working terriers of the Highlands. Small, active, game, very hardy in appearance, they were strongly though slimly built. . . . I examined each of them with attentive care, noticing in particular their soundness, their flexible backs and sturdy forelegs, their powerful jaws and strong, even teeth, their clear dark eyes and their sterling terrier character. After the judging, a meeting of the Skye Terrier Club was summoned, and many protests were made.

After the Kennel Club Show of 1909, there was, in the canine press, a heated debate over the origins of this terrier from the Highlands. Not only was the origin of this terrier disputed, but the use of the name "Short-haired Skyes" led to objections from Skye Terrier fanciers. *The Illustrated Kennel News* published an illustration of Mrs. Campbell's dog, Roy Mohr, and captioned it as "Short-haired Skye." Naturally, both sides claimed that their terrier was the original terrier of Skye.

The following text of undated correspondence to *The Illustrated Kennel News* from Miss Hawke's papers will be of great interest.

SHORT-HAIRED SKYES
(To the Editor of *The Illustrated Kennel News*)

Sir: I was somewhat surprised to see in your issue of the 23rd inst. that your frontispiece should be an illustration of "Short-haired Skyes." As secretary of the Skye Terrier Club of England I should be pleased to know of their origin. The Kennel Club, according to their lists, apparently do not recognize such a breed. At Cruft's Show of this year there was provided a classification for "Short-haired Skyes." Being interested in the real Skye Terriers, I especially made the journey to London to view these specimens. I was greatly disappointed to find that there was only one exhibitor of these animals. I therefore concluded the lady must have guaranteed the classes herself. I cannot say that I admired them no more than I admire a very poor Scottie; but irrespective of that, I must raise an objection to their being termed Skye Terriers. One can read in books of Skye Terriers of long length and with long hair as being famous and of noted origin, and being separately bred and distinctive, from the sixteenth century; but in every case there has been unquestionably length of body and hair. So much for the ordinary Skye Terrier. In Mrs. J. Alastair Campbell's celebrated kennel of winners I did not observe at Cruft's Show one of these qualifications. That they may have an origin in Skye I do not doubt; but we have in Cheshire, and I am sure, all other counties, dogs of uncertain origin. With such facts, no doubt we shall shortly see Cheshire Terriers, London County Hounds, and Scottish Borzois. It would, I feel sure, only be in keeping with the Short-haired Skye Terrier.

Regretting troubling you,
James Porritt. Hon. Sec. Skye Terrier Club of England

We have received from Miss M. Grace Collins, of Ashburton, a photograph of two terriers, which bear a strong family likeness to the dogs published on the front page of last issue. Miss Collins writes: "When I was a little girl I was given the two little terriers (whose portraits I enclose) in, I believe, 1884. They were called Aberdeen Terriers, and were bred, I believe, by a keeper in the employment of Mackenzie of Kintail; at any rate, they came from Glen Inwick, Ballater, Aberdeenshire. I think you will be struck by the extraordinary likeness between my little terrier Mae and Mrs. Campbell's Roy Mohr. Mae was silver-grey in colour, with a harsh coat, soft prick ears, of a darker shade. His muzzle, in youth, was almost black, he had a distinct frill, and a gaily carried, scimitar-like tail. Jock was darker—in the photograph he is quite a puppy—but later he developed more frill and a harsher coat. Mae died aged ten, and Jock lived to be thirteen or fourteen; and till today, when my weekly *Kennel News* arrived, I have never seen any dog at all resembling mine. The modern Scottie is quite different. Should Mrs. Alastair Campbell care to see the photograph, I shall be pleased to send it to her to look at.

THE ORIGINAL SPORTING SKYE
(To the Editor of *The Illustrated Kennel News*)

Sir: Mr. James Porritt seems to take great exception because photographs of my terriers (at request) were put in your paper as "Skye Terriers." He and Sir Claude Alexander have, I understand, written to the Kennel Club objecting to my showing these terriers at Cruft's as Skyes, the Kennel Club having refused to take any notice in the matter. If he refers to page 564 in last number he will see it was by mistake the awards in variety classes and others were put in. There were two distinct breeds of Skye Terriers in the island, the long haired pet Terrier called *Measan*, of foreign extraction, the other, a small "Cairn Terrier," used to bolt the otter and fox, and sometimes to kill them; these were called *Abhag*. Mr. Porritt evidently agrees with the old Gaelic-speaking people of Skye, that his terriers came from the old pet terrier, now almost impossible to find. I had always understood that his were a cross between the two, as the show terrier of an early date was not unlike these little "Short-haired working Skyes," or "West Highland Terriers." There is a print of a terrier in Mr. Leighton's *New Book of The Dog* very much resembling my terriers, who are thought to be by many authorities on the Scotch Terriers the original of the present show Scotch Terrier. Sir Paynton Pigott took his from Isle of Skye. They are the same breed as the West Highland White Terrier as he was originally shown. I wish to point out that I did not know that this class had been decided on for Crufts show till a few days before entries closed, otherwise I should have been supported by a breeder of these, who is a winner in the showing of the White Terriers. Mr. Porritt was not the only person who traveled purposely to see these terriers. I am glad to say that in the other cases they won so much approval that I have had many offers from buyers, some of whom breed these terriers. I am not, as he imagines, the only breeder who wishes to get these terriers recognized. We are forming a club of those who wish to keep this breed pure to the old type, some of whom own many terriers, one of these having won a cup at the Crystal Palace a few years ago. These Terriers were not only found on the island of Skye and other Western islands, but at one time were in many numbers on the mainland, where they have now been ousted by their white brothers, or crossed with the later-day Scotch Terrier, but many of the purer of these owe their descent from the old sporting Skye. I beg to say my information is all from breeders in Skye, and the Gaelic-speaking people. The difference between the claim of the two Skyes is this, the short-haired have been known to be bred in Skye from eighty to one hundred years (probably much longer), and the long-haired show type is not to be found here except as a visitor, but I may add we breeders are perfectly willing to re-name them; an authority on these dogs having suggested "Hebridean Terriers" as not interfering with names already appropriated. The Skye Club has no distinctive prefix as the "West Highland White Terrier," and these working Skyes are also drop and prick-eared.

I. Alastair Campbell
Tigh-an-Rudha, Ardrishaig, N.B.

Although the Cruft's Show of 1910 scheduled two classes for "Cairn or Short-haired Terriers," Mrs. Campbell and Miss Hawke drew the controversy into the open by entering their dogs (Cairns) in classes for Skye Terriers. The judge, Miss A. K. Clifton, refused to judge the dogs as Skyes and marked her book "Wrong class." The culmination of this action by the breed pioneers was that the Skye Terrier fanciers demanded a deputation be sent to the Kennel Club to make an official protest that this short-coated terrier should not be called Skye Terrier. It became clear that if the Short-haired Skye Terrier fanciers were to be successful in gaining breed recognition they would have to find a name that was acceptable. The Skye Terrier Club's committee was comprised of Mr. Robert Leighton, Sir Claude Alexander, Mr. James Porritt and Mr. E. R. Sandwich. The meeting between this deputation and the Kennel Club Committee was held on April 6, 1910. The following is an extract from the report given in the *Kennel Gazette*:

> The Committee considered the question of the registration of Skye Terriers. Sir Claude Alexander, in introducing the deputation, informed the Committee that Skye Terrier breeders and exhibitors were much perturbed at the introduction to shows of so-called "Short-haired Skyes." These dogs differed materially from the accepted type of Skye Terrier, but they were accepted for registration in the Skye Terrier Register.

According to Robert Leighton's account of the meeting:

> The question was discussed in Committee as to whether or not these unfamiliar dogs from Dunvegan should be officially recognized, and, if so, under what breed name.

It is well documented that on March 12, 1910, the Secretary of the Kennel Club, Mr. Jaquet, had received a letter from her Excellency the Countess of Aberdeen, in which she suggested that the name "Cairn Terriers of Skye" might be a solution to the matter. Leighton continues:

> Many names were suggested: Otter Terriers, Waternish, Island, Hebridean, West Highland Terriers other than white—anything but Skyes. Finally on my own urging, and on historic grounds, it was decided that they should be recognized as Cairn Terriers. And so they have remained.

After some further discussion and inspection of photographs, the deputation retired. The Committee decided: That the breed (hitherto described as "Short-haired Skye Terriers") shall only be registered as Cairn terriers in the register for British, Colonial and Foreign Dogs, which have no separate classification on the register.

The first Specialty breed club for the Cairn Terrier was formed at a meeting held in Edinburgh, at the North British Hotel, October 1910. The name of the club was to be The Cairn Terrier Club. The object of the club was: To promote the breeding of the old working terrier of Skye, and West Highlands, now known as the Cairn Terrier. To protect and advance the interest of this breed by exhibiting, guaranteeing classes at shows, and offering special prizes at above shows held under Kennel Club rules. The Cairn Terrier Club (CTC) emerged with A. R. McDonald of Waternish, President; McCloud of McCloud, Vice President; and Mrs. Alastair Campbell, Hon. Secretary. Most of the membership was from Scotland at that time. The Cairn Terrier Club formed the hub of worldwide success for the breed.

During the 1911 CTC meeting in Edinburgh, the first "Standard" and "Scale of Points" was drawn up for the Cairn Terrier. Present among the club officers and members were Lady Sophie Scott, Lady Charles Bentinck, the Hon. Mary Hawke, Mrs. Fleming and Mrs. Florence M. Ross. It is believed that the following description of the Cairn Terrier was based on the points of Mrs. Campbell's own Cairns: Roy Mohr, Gesto and Calla Mohr:

Standard of Points

as adopted by
THE CAIRN TERRIER CLUB
and as approved by the Kennel Club on General Appearance
(Original British Standard)

General Appearance (20 points)—Small, active, game; very hardy in appearance; strong though compactly built. Should stand well forward on fore paws, strong quarters, deep in ribs; very free in movement; coat hard enough to resist rain; head small, but in proportion to body. A general foxy appearance is the chief characteristic of this Working Terrier.

Skull (10 points)—Broad in proportion; strong, but not too long or heavy jaw. A slight indentation between eyes; hair should be rather full on top of head.

Muzzle (10 points)—Powerful, but not heavy; very strong jaw, with large teeth; roof of mouth black.

Eyes (5 points)—Set wide apart, large, hazel or dark hazel, rather sunk, with shaggy eyebrows.

Ears (5 points)—Small, pointed, well carried and erect but not too closely set.

Tail (5 points)—About six inches, well furnished with hair but not feathery: carried gaily, but must not curl over back.

Body (25 points)—Compact, straight back, deep ribs, strong sinews, hind quarters very strong.

Legs and Feet (10 points)—Low in leg; good, but not too large bone; fore
legs should not be out at elbow, but fore feet may be slightly turned out;
fore feet larger than hind; legs must be covered with hard hair; pads should
be black.

Coat (10 points)—Coat hard, but not coarse, with good undercoat and head
well furnished; in colour—sandy, grey, brindled or nearly black; dark points
such as ears, muzzle, very typical.

In order to keep this breed to best old working type, any cross with a
modern Scotch Terrier will be considered objectionable.

FAULTS

Muzzle—Undershot or snipey.
Eyes—Too prominent or too light.
Ears—Too large or round at points. They must not be too heavily coated with hair.
Coat—Silkiness or curliness objectionable; a slight wave permissible.

Scale of Points

Skull	10
Muzzle	10
Eyes	5
Ears	5
Body, Neck and Chest	25
Legs and Feet	10
The Tail	5
General Appearance, Size and Coat	30

100

The British Cairn Standard has gone through many changes since the
approval of the original document. Several changes were printed in the
1916 *Cairn Terrier Yearbook*.

The following listing is a brief summary.

1. The word "Shaggy" was added to the beginning section describing General Appearance.
2. In the section describing skull, the description was changed from "A slight indentation between eyes" to "A decided indentation between eyes."

3. The description of the muzzle was clarified with "which should be neither undershot nor overshot"; the description of "roof of mouth black" was deleted.
4. The description of tail was changed from "about six inches" to "short."
5. Under the "body" description, "well-sprung" was added to "deep ribs" and also the first mention was made of a "medium" length back.
6. Description of "shoulders, legs and feet" was amplified by adding that "pads should be thick and strong, thin and ferrety feet are objectionable." The first mention of "a sloping shoulder" and "medium length of leg" was made in this section also.
7. Description of "coat" was amplified to include a description of the "short, soft and close" undercoat. "Open coats are objectionable" was added to this section.

In the section describing faults, "Nose—Flesh or light colored most objectionable," was added and under "muzzle," the wording was changed from "undershot or snipey" to "undershot or overshot."

A section describing the ideal weights was added, which stated that dogs should weigh "about twelve to sixteen pounds," and bitches "about eleven to fourteen pounds."

In 1922 the weight clause for both dogs and bitches was changed to "Ideal weight fourteen pounds."

This early history is very important to present-day breeders. Our dogs are based almost entirely upon British imports, so it is important for us to understand the stratagems (developmental paths) necessary for the emergence of the modern Cairn Terrier.

On May 29, 1912, the Kennel Club Committee gave the Cairn Terrier a separate register. The Cairn could now compete at designated championship shows. All the early club members participated in the rapid growth of this breed. Mrs. Campbell was quite active, breeding, showing and judging. Miss Lockwood, Miss Viccars, Mary Hawke, Mrs. Fleming, Mrs. Ross and Baroness Burton were of great importance. It is interesting to note that Baroness Burton was a fancier of the Keeshond, as well as the Cairn. In 1929, her Keeshond, Dochfour Hendrik, became the first British champion for the breed.

This intriguing photograph is probably of Mrs. Noney Fleming, with an assistant and six Cairns on bath day. Collection of Laura De Vincent.

Ch. Rime and Ch. Fury Out-of-the-West. Collection of Laura De Vincent.

The first Challenge Certificate (CC) winners were Firring Fling and Firring Flora, both owned by Messrs. Ross and Markland. This event occurred in 1912, in Richmond, with Mrs. Alistair Campbell judging. Four shows offered CCs for dogs and bitches in 1912, and in 1913 eleven shows offered CCs. Tibbie of Harris, owned and bred by Lady Sophie Scott, earned her third CC in January 1913, and in so doing became the breed's first champion. Gesto became the first male title holder in April 1913. Firring Frolic, Skye Crofter and Shiela of Harris also earned their titles in 1913.

The foundation for the Cairn Terrier was laid in these early days by breeders and dogs whose names must always be remembered by those who now cherish and safeguard the breed. Many of the greats march through the pages of history during this time period, both breeders and their Cairns.

Mrs. Alastair Campbell's "Brocaire" line was established by Ch. Gesto, and was always considered very pure Cairn type with no trace of Scottish Terrier inheritance. Ch. Gesto, Doran Bhan, Roy Mhor and Calla Mhor were all bred on the Isle of Skye, and formed the foundation for successive generations of Brocaire breeding. Baroness Burton's judicious blending of that breeding produced her own Dochfour line. Ch. Firring Fling and Ch. Firring Frolic were sold by Macdonald of Skye, their breeder, to Messrs. Ross and Markland. Fling was later owned by Baroness Burton, where he

sired Lady Burton's Ch. Rona. The Shearer-McLeod partnership introduced Skye Cottar and Skye Crofter. Both were sired by Ferracher; Cottar
was out of Callac, and Crofter out of Morag. Crofter became a champion,
but Cottar sired more winners, including Ch. Northern Nonpareil, owned
by Miss Lucy Lockwood. Mr. Errington Ross founded his "Glenmhor"
Cairns on the dogs from Macdonald of Waternish. Mr. Ross's kennels are
practically the foundation of the "Harviestoun" strain. Harviestoun Raider
was a direct descendant of the old Glenmhor Cairns, and Ch. Harviestoun
Brigand, Ch. Harviestoun Chieftain, Dochfour Brigand and numerous
others followed. Mrs. Flemings's "Out of the West" kennel was also
founded on the old Skye bloodlines. Her Ch. Fisherman Out of the West
and his sire Doughall Out of the West were important sires in the 1920s.
Mrs. Stephens's "Hyver" kennel also shared this foundation, as she purchased her first Cairn from Mrs. Alastair Campbell, a bitch puppy by Roy
Mhor ex Diana of Harris. Quisaidh of Hyver was the first "Brocaire" bitch
to go to the south of England, and was the foundation of the Hyver
Cairns.

Chapter Two

British Cairns from the 1930s to the Present

Concentration of Harviestoun, Hyver and Out of the West produced the great Ch. Splinters of Twobees (Trashurst Chip ex Sorag of Twobees), who had a tremendous impact on the Cairn. Whelped on January 15, 1933, Splinters won eight Challenge Certificates (CCs) under the leading judges of the era. His most important contribution, however, was his ability to stamp his quality and type on his get, and future generations as well.

Splinters is in the background of such influential dogs as Eng. Ch. Uniquecottage Flycatcher, and all his influential get, in Britain, and in the United States all the descendants down from Ch. Redletter McJoe, sire of Ch. Redletter McRuffie, Ch. Redletter McMurran and Ch. Redletter Fincairn Frolic, among others. These dogs have heavily influenced the American Cairn. Further information is available in the Appendix, Top-Producing Cairn Terrier Sires.

An explanation of the line and family theory is appropriate in this context, since we are discussing some of the most influential dogs in the history of the breed. More information about the influence this concept has upon breeding in the United States can be found in the Appendix mentioned above.

The line and family theories began in the 1890s with Bruce Lowe, who began tracing pedigrees of winning racehorses. He determined that many of the most successful animals could be traced back to a few significant stallions and mares. This theory takes into account only the top line of the pedigree, the stallions, and the bottom line of the pedigree, the mares. This theory was first applied to Cairns by Mr. and Mrs. T. W. L. Caspersz in *Cairn Terrier Records*, published in 1932 and revised about a year later.

This theory has no scientific basis, but great numbers of influential descendants have come from a very few lines and families, and the theory should be studied. The major flaw in the theory is the discounting of the

Ch. Splinters of Twobees.

Pedigree of Eng. Ch. Splinters of Twobees

                                        Eng. Ch. Ghillie of Hyver
                        Ch. Donninton Gillie
                                        Chip of Hardings
        Trashurst Sandyman
                                        Sweep of Frimley
                        Eaton Wendy
                                        Dochfour Flora Ruadh
Eng. Ch. Trashurst Chip
                                        Eng. Ch. Ghillie of Hyver
                        Eng. Ch. Dud of Hyver
                                        Knipton Dian
        Cherry McBryon
                                        Strathblane Chaillean
                        Haggis of Sandiacre
                                        Stew of Sandiacre
                                        Eng. Ch. Harviestoun Brigand
                        Offley Brimon
                                        Canna of Firmle
        Eng. Ch. Quicksand Out of the West
                                        Eng.Ch. Quicksilver Out of the West
                        She
                                        Dderfel Caraid
Sorag of Twobees
                                        Harviestoun Raider
                        Glenmhor Rascal
                                        Sorag
        Mulaidh of Twobees
                                        Harviestoun Raider
                        Glenmhor Coullie
                                        Mulaidh

middle lines of the pedigree, and attributing genetic influence only to its top and bottom lines. In 1933 Mr. and Mrs. Caspersz's completed analysis of Cairn Terrier champions established eleven male lines and fifty families. The basis for establishing a line or family is that the ancestry was traced back to the first dog who had produced at least one champion.

DGS has its origins as follows: The D line traces back to Duan, G to Ch. Gillie of Hyver and later S was added to the DG lines, which indicated all the descendants of Ch. Splinters of Twobees. The SD line traces back to Doughall Out of the West. Line I traces back to Ross-shire Glenara and his son Ross-shire Warrior.

The families are more difficult to trace. The influential ones then were 2, 3, 4, 5, 6, 17, 59 and 80. Others have been added as bitches produced more champions, such as 90, 106 and 109. Offspring from these families include many champions from the kennels of Uniquecottage, Twobees, Oudenarde, Redletter, Lynwil, Yeendsdale, Thistleclose, Treblig, Blencathra, Greetavale and Lofthouse, among others.

I drew some interesting statistical conclusions based on the *The Cairn Terrier in America*. There are some pedigrees in these volumes that do not indicate lines and families, so there are seven dogs and bitches not reflected in these statistics. Without these dogs, in 1992, 67.8 percent of all Cairn Terriers, or ninety-nine, finishing their championships were from the DGS line. Breaking it down further, 17.8 percent, or twenty-six, were descended from Line I, 3.4 percent, or five, were Line GR, and 4.8 percent, or seven, were from Line DR.

To draw a comparison with Great Britain in 1992, eight dogs or bitches completed their championships. Of those eight, seven were from Line DGS, and one was from Line I. In 1991, twelve dogs and bitches completed their titles, and all were from Line DGS.

Redletter

Certainly the most influential breeder of the time was Walter Bradshaw, Redletter Cairns. Mr. Bradshaw was no stranger to dogs when he first entered the world of Cairns. He had been active in several breeds since the 1920s. Shortly after World War II, which slowed all kennel activities in both Great Britain and the United States, Mr. Bradshaw purchased two bitch puppies, Redletter My Choice and Redletter Mayflower. My Choice was bred

Ch. Redletter Elford Mhorag.

Ch. Redletter McMurran.

to Ch. Bonfire of Twobees, and on August 22, 1948, Redletter McJoe was born. McJoe easily became a champion, going Best Puppy at eight months of age at the club show, and claiming his third Challenge Certificate at the same event the following year. McJoe sired nine champions, and many more CC winners. Among them was his son out of Cairncragg Binky, Ch. Redletter McMurran. McMurran won twenty-six CCs and was the first Cairn Terrier in England to capture Best in Show at a championship event. A McJoe daughter, Ch. Redletter Elford Mhorag, out of Foundation Sylvia, and full sister to Ch. Brindie of Twobees, won eighteen CCs during her show career.

McMurran bred to Ch. Redletter Miss Splinters produced Redletter McBryan and Redletter McBrigand. McBryan captured seventeen CCs and sired thirteen champion offspring, including Ch. Redletter Master Mac. Thirteen champion offspring was the breed record until 1984. The record for bitch CCs was held by Ch. Redletter Moonraker (Ch. Redletter Moon Tripper ex Ch. Redletter Marcel) until Ch. Robinson Crusoe of Courtrai broke the record.

Another McBryan son, Ch. Redletter Maestro, was bred to Felshott Araminta and produced Ch. Redletter Twinlaw Melissa and Ch. Twinlaw Blithe Spirit, and most importantly Ch. Redletter Twinlaw Sea Spirit, the second Cairn Terrier to win Best in Show at a championship event in England. This important event occurred at Manchester in 1968. Sea Spirit was purchased by Mrs. Betty Hyslop and continued his winning stride in the United States and Canada.

The Redletter Cairns dominated the British show ring for many years. Mr. Bradshaw died on July 2, 1982, at the age of eighty-six. His last champion was Redletter Martini, to bring the final tally of Redletter champions to forty-two. The Redletter dogs live on in pedigrees in Great Britain, the United States and Canada, and in other countries worldwide. Enough will never be said about this grand dog man and his accomplishments, and his dogs' influence on the history and the future of the Cairn Terrier.

Toptwig

Another British breeder whose dogs have had widespread influence overseas is the late Gladys (Gay) Marsh. Mrs. Marsh has reminisced about traveling by train with her dogs during World War II, and recalled how much the American soldiers on the train enjoyed holding and petting the dogs. Mrs. Marsh was able to maintain enough dogs through the war years to have a nucleus for her postwar breeding efforts. Obviously, Mrs. Marsh bred Cairns for many years before her untimely death on the eve of her long-awaited Cruft's judging assignment in 1975. Eight champions bearing the Toptwig prefix were made up. Among them were Eng. Swed. Int. Ch. Toptwig Tilden, who was exported to Sweden at nine years of age, after Gay's death, to Karen

Ch. Toptwig Tilden. Photo courtesy Maud Montgomery-Bjurhult.

Schmidt, Snorrehus Kennels. Through Karen Schmidt's skill as a breeder, Tilden has exerted considerable influence over the development of the Cairn Terrier in Sweden.

Eng. Am. Ch. Toptwig Fly-By-Night of Oudenarde was made up to his English championship by Ferelith Somerfield after Gay Marsh's death, and then exported to Mr. and Mrs. William Adams in Florida. He was shown successfully in the United States by Don Gates.

One of the early Toptwig exports was Toptwig Fay of Caithness, sent to Betty Stone. Fay is the dam of Ch. Caithness Fay's Falcon, who figures in many American pedigrees.

Eng. Am. Ch. Toptwig Mr. Defoe was exported to Betty Hyslop, and later sold to Judy Brouillette, Crandrum Kennels.

Ch. Duntiblae Top Secret of Toptwig, a Tilden daughter, and Toptwig Wideawake, a Blencathra Brat daughter, were exported to Lynne Nabors, who changed her prefix to "Twigbent" due to the profound influence Mrs. Marsh's breeding exerted over her own theories.

Donald and Grace Lynch imported thirteen Cairns from Toptwig, among them Eng. Ch. Toptwig Miss Defoe. The Lynches took their kennel prefix "Cath-mhor" from a dog they imported, Toptwig Cathmhor, Tilden's sire. Ch. Toptwig Perry sired several champions as well.

Oudenarde

The Oudenarde affix was granted by the Kennel Club to the sisters Helen and Margaret Hamilton. Their brother George later married Diana, and they had a daughter, Ferelith. Helen and Margaret, later Mrs. Temple, owned Smooth and Wire Fox Terriers, Airedales and Pekingese before World War II.

After the war, Sheila Thomas, later Mrs. Tarry, brought Irish Terriers, Japanese Chin and Beagles to Oudenarde. Other breeds fancied were

Ch. Oudenarde Special Edition, Fall. Collection of Mrs. Ferelith Hamilton Somerfield.

Ch. Oudenarde Fair Prospect. Collection of Ferelith Hamilton Somerfield.

Ch. Oudenarde Bold and Free. Collection of Ferelith Hamilton Somerfield. Thomas Fall.

Dalmatians, Border Terriers and English Setters. Diana Hamilton was well respected, in both Great Britain and the United States, and is much missed by the dog fancy.

Today, Diana's daughter Ferelith carries on her mother's Oudenarde bloodlines, as well as being involved with her husband, Stafford Somerfield, and his Boxers. Mr. Somerfield has been very successful in other Terrier breeds as well, having won Best of Breed in both Irish Terriers and Lakelands at Cruft's in 1994. Ferelith is also a writer of considerable renown, and currently holds the position of editor-in-chief for the English weekly *Dog World*.

Ferelith recounts that her mother feared never making up a dog to his championship, as their early successes were all with bitches. Oudenarde Duskie Belle was the first champion to be made up, followed by Joyful Light, Souvenir, Light Melody and many others. The first male champion for Oudenarde was Sandboy, to be followed in quick succession by Special Edition, Fellame Lad, Midnight Chimes, Midnight Marauder, Raiding Light and What Next, the last champion bred by the late Mrs. Diana Hamilton and the late Miss Helen Hamilton. Ch. Oudenarde Wot a Lad, bred by Mrs. Ferelith Hamilton Somerfield, and owned by Mr. Somerfield, was the next champion—carrying on the tradition. Ch. Oudenarde Fair Prospect, pictured here, was considered by many to be one of the best Oudenardes. She was the dam of Ch. Oudenarde Midnight Marauder, who siredEng. Am. & Can. Ch. Oudenarde Sea-Hawk. Imported to Canada by Betty Hyslop, Sea Hawk sired well in North America. Ch. Oudenarde Raiding Light, another Marauder son, became fourth top sire of all time in Britain.

Ferelith remembers her mother as having liked dogs from both Mr. Bradshaw and Mrs. Drummond, and recalls the excellence of both kennels. Diana used studs from both kennels with great success, as did the Misses Hall and Wilson, of the Felshott kennels, although Mr. Bradshaw and Mrs. Drummond themselves did not work together to any great degree.

Ferelith recalls that her mother always thought that Ch. Oudenarde Fair Prospect was the best specimen of either sex produced by her kennel. When asked for the best Cairns ever seen, Diana names Ch. Trashurst Chip and Ch. Merrymeet Tathwell Therese.

Felshott

The Misses Hall and Wilson at Felshott were responsible for some sixteen English champions, most in the 1970s, and the list includes the influential Ch. Felshott Wine Taster, Ch. Felshott Anita, Ch. Felshott Hilarity, Ch. Felshott Honeydew of Rossarden, Ch. Felshott Silly Season of Oudenarde, Ch. Felshott Taste of Honey and Felshott Honey Badger, who sired several champions. Two Felshott bitches have the distinction of each producing four English champions. They were Felshott Anita and Ch. Felshott Bryany.

Rossarden

Miss C. H. Dixon's Rossarden Kennels has met with considerable success over the years and brought much pleasure to many dog fanciers. Miss Dixon, known to the dog fancy as "Charlie," resides in a wonderfully historic rectory, "The Sanctuary." Rossarden has been in existence since the late 1940s when Charlie and her sister Betty began it as a joint venture.

They tried to keep to certain bloodlines that they found to their liking, including Hyver, Mercia and Twobees, to which they added Rhu. Rufus of Rhu bred to Red Devil of Rossarden and produced their first CC winner, Rhoda of Rossarden and their first champion, Rogie of Rossarden. Rhoda's son Riskin sired Ch. Ronaldshay of Rossarden, winner of five CCs. Other lines incorporated into the Rossarden breeding program included Pledwick, Blencathra, Redletter, Felshott, Uniquecottage and Avenelhouse. Uniquecottage Henry Iggins and Iona of Rossarden, a granddaughter of Ronaldshay, produced a litter of four bitches including Drusilla of Rossarden who when bred to Ch. Blencathra Brat produced Ch. Heshe Donavon and Ch. Heshe Izawyche.

Ch. Rossarden Drambuie is by Ch. Robinson Crusoe of Courtrai ex Rossarden Cognac (1982). Miss Dixon has done some close breeding and is satisfied with what she is doing. She is maintaining the type she requires, and the Rossardens are known for their excellent toplines, strong quarters and color, notably the Rossarden "Reds," for many are a beautiful shade of red. This kennel set its sights on the working Cairn, and is a stronghold of vigorous and workmanlike Cairns.

Avenelhouse

Another of the kennels that has exerted strong influence over the years in England and the United States is Avenelhouse. In the early 1950s, Hazel

Ch. Avenelhouse Golden Oriole. Photo courtesy Mrs. Hazel Small.

Uniquecottage Kirk. Photo courtesy Mrs. Hazel Small.

Longmore bred West Highland Whites under the Jollee prefix, later adopting Uniquecottage as a prefix for the Cairns, with her partner, Judy Marshall. Both women later married, Judy becoming Mrs. J. G. Parker-Tucker and Hazel being wed to Major Small. Judy kept on with the Uniquecottage prefix, and Hazel adopted Avenelhouse. The lovely grounds of her kennels are located on the grounds of Avenelhouse Manor, Major Small's family home. Ch. Avenelhouse Golden Oriole is one of many beautiful dogs bred there. Oriole's litter brother, Ch. Avenelhouse Nutcracker, went to Mr. and Mrs. George Gilbert, kennels located in Morrison, Colorado, and was campaigned by Ray Bay with considerable success in the mid 1970s.

I imported several dogs from Avenelhouse, and they have all made their mark in the United States. I spent many hours on the parlor floor with Hazel Small watching me amusedly as I copied old pedigrees. This was in the days before computers could print up a ten-generation pedigree in a few minutes. I went through all her old photographs, and tried to learn about all the dogs behind those I was purchasing.

The Avenelhouse dogs were known for their superior structure. Such sound movers, they typically exhibit excellent layback of shoulder, and hindquarters to match. Avenelhouse is located in the south of England, near Exeter Devon, and with its lovely gardens and greenhouse, it is a very pretty location for the dogs.

Uniquecottage

Mrs. J. G. Parker-Tucker has had great success with dogs in Britain. This woman truly has a sixth sense for which dogs to put together to result in excellent offspring. She is dedicated to her dogs, and works very hard for the success she has. Her kennel is located in Silverton Park Gardens, Silverton, near Exeter, Devon. The kennel is located on charming property that was once a walled garden for a castle. The kennels themselves are lovely, comprised of well-kept individual paddocks with walkways and houses, with two or three Cairns to a paddock, and plenty of grassy areas surrounding, in which many beautiful puppies often play. There are large paddocks bordering the perimeter where adults race and play.

Mrs. Parker-Tucker's devotion to the breed is obvious in the excellent condition of all the animals, and there are quite a few. The puppies are all friendly, and all her Cairns are truly typical.

Her hard work has brought her many great rewards. Many say that Ch. Uniquecottage Sir Frolic was one of the finest of his time. Ch. Earlybird of Uniquecottage is the dam of four champions, quite remarkable within the English system.

Ch. Uniquecottage Flycatcher, who became a champion in 1979, earned fifteen CCs. His son Ch. Uniquecottage Tree Creeper, a champion in 1981, ex Ch. Tweenus Georgina of Uniquecottage, earned fourteen CCs; Georgina won nine CCs. Other champions made up since 1980 include Uniquecottage Brer Fox, Uniquecottage Bristol Bird, Uniquecottage Cara Cara, Uniquecottage Gold Feather, Uniquecottage Gold Kinloch, Uniquecottage Kittiwake, Uniquecottage Little Swift, Seneley Captain Poldark of Uniquecottage, Uniquecottage Snow Lark, Uniquecottage Soleil D'or and Uniquecottage Swallow Lark.

A personal favorite of mine, Ch. Uniquecottage Gold Diver, earned four CCs, and when bred to Uniquecottage Jenny Wren, produced Eng. Am. Ch. Uniquecottage Gold Grouse. This dog was eventually purchased by Charles Merrick III, and successfully campaigned in the United States by Linda More. Gold Grouse later returned home to Mrs. Parker-Tucker to sire winners in Britain as he did in the United States. Mrs. Parker-Tucker's breeding accomplishments—more than thirty English champions plus the many who have gained foreign titles—are truly remarkable. The future holds much more success for this kennel and its outstanding Cairns.

Am. Ch. Uniquecottage Georgie Girl, bred by Mrs. J. G. Parker-Tucker, was brought back from Britain for Mrs. Pauli Christi.

Ch. Uniquecottage Flycatcher, with Mrs. J. G. Parker-Tucker. Photo courtesy Gary Hess.

Ch. Courtrai John Julius, owned by Mesdames Howes and Clark. Anne Roslin-Williams.

Ch. Robinson Crusoe of Courtrai. Photo courtesy Maud Montgomery-Bjurhult.

Uniquecottage Cairns have made their mark in many countries. Breeders fortunate enough to have obtained these bloodlines appear to be doing very well with them, both as winners in the show ring and as producers.

It is interesting to note that Flycatcher and his son Tree Creeper appear in the pedigrees of Ch. Larchlea Take A Chance On Me, thirty-five CCs, Ch. Beaudesert Royal Viking, thirty-three CCs and the bitch, Ch. Corbieha Hazelnut, twenty-nine CCs, the record breakers of the 1990s.

Courtrai

The kennel of Doris Howes and Chrissie Clark summons charming memories of beautiful dogs, outstandingly warm hospitality and two charming women who loved what they were doing. When I met Doris and Chrissie, they were retired and living in a cottage in Buckden (Huntingdon, Cambridgeshire), raising Cairn Terriers. The cottage was very modern, with all conveniences, and a lovely place to do what they were doing. Courtrai was an active kennel from the 1960s through the 1980s. Breeding Cairn Terriers was a form of retirement activity for them. Both retired from full-time nursing as matrons; between them they had spent eighty years in the nursing profession. It was their feeling that many of their colleagues involved with administrative nursing were not happy in retirement, lacking purpose and not coping well with leisure. These two forward-thinking women decided to breed and show Cairn Terriers, to occupy their leisure time. They approached the Cairn Terrier as students, acquiring as many books as they could and talking to those more experienced at every chance. Gay Marsh took an interest in Doris, helping with grooming tips. Before retirement, Doris had acquired a pet from Miss Betty Bentley-Carr (Attic), and continued to visit Miss Bentley-Carr and her mother.

An interesting event that shaped much of Doris's thinking over the years occurred at the Bentley-Carr home, when several exhibitors had been invited for tea after a dog show. Miss Bentley-Carr had a litter of eight-week-old puppies. The sire was Diana Hamilton's Oudenarde Raebrook Merry Cavalier and the dam was Attic Christmas Carol. Mrs. Hamilton had selected a puppy from the litter for herself. Miss Bentley-Carr had selected another, and another puppy was booked as well. Doris admired still another puppy, in spite of the formidable experience amassed there to evaluate one litter of puppies. Mrs. Hamilton overheard Doris commenting to herself and drew her out in conversation as to why she liked the particular pup. Mrs. Hamilton urged Doris to buy the pup after they had both examined her more closely. Doris had many reasons why she could not, but Mrs. Hamilton urged her to follow her instincts. In the end Doris telephoned Chrissie and took home Mary Lou, who would become their first champion. What caught Doris's eye was that the puppy stood so beautifully on her own. Doris learned from this incident that the stance of the dog does much to catch the judge's eye, a lesson that would stay with her always. And indeed, the Courtrai Cairns did catch one's eye, both in the show ring and at home. The Cairn can make itself look better and more elegant simply being itself, than any attempt to pose the dog in an artificial manner could ever achieve.

In the 1970s, Courtrai Nimble Nell was purchased for Mrs. Jerry Robinson by her husband from Mesdames Howes and Clark. Nell was bred to Ch. Heshe Donavon, producing a litter of one dog and one bitch. Doris and Chrissie took the dog, who became Ch. Robinson Crusoe of Courtrai, who earned five CCs and is the breed's top sire in England with eighteen champions. He has held this record since 1984. Crusoe's grandson, Ch. Penticharm Silver Rocket, sired both Ch. Corbieha Hazelnut and Ch. Beaudesert Royal Viking, whose impressive achievements have been described earlier. Other Courtrai champions include Sugarplum, Triella Trudy and John Julius. An interesting tidbit—the Courtrai women always felt it a piece of luck to include the letter U somewhere in the names of their dogs!

Advice Doris and Chrissie would offer to new fanciers, "Enjoy the Cairns, the outings, showing and the people."

Lofthouse

The Lofthouse Kennels of Hilda Manley accounted for some nine champions, among them Ch. Lofthouse Davey, exported to Mrs. Betty Hyslop's venerable Cairndania Kennels in Canada and Ch. Lofthouse Geryon, a Lofthouse Larkspur son exported to the United States to Don Robbie. Geryon was a major influence in American pedigrees, with many successful Cairns showing him in their pedigrees. Others of importance were Ch. Lofthouse Golden, Ch. Lofthouse Rough Tweed and Ch. Lofthouse Larkspur. Another very influential dog was Ch. Lofthouse Geryon of Mistyfell, bred by Mary Simpson and owned by Hilda Manley.

Ch. Craiglyn Crofter, Best in Show at the Terrier Club of New South Wales, 1977, under Ferelith A. Somerfield. Trafford.

Craiglyn

Miss E. Campbell's Craiglyn Kennels was responsible for some lovely dogs, which are behind many Cairn Terriers in many countries. Among the English champions were Cavalier, Commodore, Easter Bonnet, Easter Parade, Morag and Stornoway. Eng. Ch. Craiglyn Caledonian (Craiglyn Commodore ex Craiglyn Christmas Carol) was owned by Mrs. J. G. Parker-Tucker and late in life was exported to the United States to Col. and Mrs. G. W. MacSparran, in Texas. Caledonian finished his American championship at nine years of age, and sired well for the MacSparrans' Littleclan establishment. Ch. Craiglyn Christmas Carol, dam of Caledonian, was imported by Wolfpit Kennels and produced two American champions, Ch. Boysenberry of Wolfpit and Ch. Bayberry of Wolfpit. Mr. and Mrs. A. Cooper owned Craiglyn Cantata. Craiglyn was responsible for seven English champions, and more recent breeders such as Sally Ogle were fortunate enough to obtain some stock from her.

Yeendsdale

The Yeendsdale Kennels were active in the 1950s, and are responsible for seven champions, including Yeendsdale Inspiration, Masterpiece of Yeendsdale and Rob of Yeendsdale. It is interesting to note that a Yeendsdale Cairn appears in Ch. Cairnwood's Quince's pedigree. Lucky Bracken of Yeendsdale is his maternal granddam, and she was sired by Yeendsdale Merry Man ex Nice-Enough of Yeendsdale.

Ferniegair

Walter Craig learned his love of Cairns at his father's knee. His father also had an early interest in Scottish and Fox Terriers, but finally settled upon the Cairn. Mr. Craig describes his youth as "walking, cleaning and breeding—brought up the hard way." Mr. Craig notes that his father started with a very good Yeendsdale bitch and established his own line.

Mr. Craig senior showed a bit and had moderate success, to use Walter Craig's own words. Walter inherited the dogs upon his father's death. He exported several dogs to the United States that were very successful, primarily to Virginia Cadwallader (Ch. Ferneigair Fearnought) and Dr. Grey Newman (Ferneigair Kirstie) among others.

Mr. Craig still owns two Cairns, but has retired from showing. He keeps his interest alive in the breed by helping newcomers with pointers about trimming for show and training.

Foxgrove

Albert James Wilkinson of Foxgrove Kennels retired from the dog fancy in 1981. His wealth of beautiful dogs lives on in the United States, Canada and the United Kingdom. Mrs. Betty Hyslop imported Chs. Foxgrove Jester, Foxgrove Susanella and Foxgrove Jeronimo, all of whom did very well in the showring.

Pictured here is Foxgrove Venus (Ross of Ainsty ex Foxgrove Fascination), dam of Jester and Susanella, and granddam of Jeronimo.

Hearn

Mrs. Patricia Breach's Hearn kennels has been very influential in the United States. She exported several dogs to Don Robbie. He then placed Hearn Thunder Thighs with Martha Brewer, and Hearn Hellbender with Laura De Vincent. One of the greatest that she kept was Hearn Fiddler, who earned two CCs. I greatly admired her Hearn Nickel Nugget, and saw him win the CC in 1980.

More recently Mrs. Breach exported several dogs to Clarence and Susan Vaughn. Among them is Ch. Hearn Primadonna, a beautiful wheaten bitch that finished her American championship with some outstanding wins. Others imported by the Vaughns are Ch. Hearn Man O War, Ch. Hearn Typhoon and Ch. Hearn Helmsman.

Walter Craig (Ferniegair), photographed at age seventy-four.

Foxgrove Venus, dam of Ch. Foxgrove Jester and Ch. Foxgrove Susanella, and granddam of Ch. Foxgrove Jeronimo. She was by Ross of Ainsty ex Foxgrove Fascination.

Heshe Tycho, owned by Frank Edwards.

Ch. Blencathra Sandpiper. Photo courtesy Mrs. Ferelith Hamilton Somerfield.

Heshe

Frank Edwards, who admits to a reluctance to talk about himself, did send some information to me. We were introduced in 1983 at the Windsor dog show, when he was picking up Courtrai Jupiter from Mesdames Howes and Clark, to return to Holland, his residence at the time.

Mr. Edwards first met the Cairn in September 1939, when he was evacuated from his home with his brothers and sisters. They were sent to live at Wolverly Manor Court, owned by Lady Pillingsly who owned a "pack of Cairn Terriers" (Mr. Edwards's wording). This was Frank Edwards's introduction to the breed. He describes living at Lady Pillingsly's manor as very much "Upstairs/Downstairs," and recalls using the servants' quarters with the butler. He also recalls accompanying her ladyship across the estate with the pack of Cairns. Lady Pillingsly carried a whip, which she would crack in the air to get the attention of the pack. Later in life, while serving as the Honorable Secretary of the Southern Cairn Terrier Club, Mr. Edwards noticed the name of Lady Pillingsly as a committee member from the older times.

In 1957, Mr. Edwards acquired his first Cairn, Crowtrees Patience, a dark brindle, bred by the late Mrs. Swire. This bitch was a granddaughter of Ch. Woodthorpe Clansman, and very much like her grandsire. Through the years, Mr. Edwards produced six English champions, and three others that won CCs, and while living in Europe made up another twenty-plus champions.

One of the most influential English champions is Ch. Heshe Donavon (Eng. Ch. Blencathra Brat ex Drusilla of Rossarden), sire of Ch. Robinson Crusoe of Courtrai, top-producing sire in England, with eighteen champions to his credit. One of the more recent Heshe champions is Int. Ch. Heshe Sun Buddy, awarded the Terrier Group at the Winners Show in Amsterdam by Joe Braddon. "Buddy" went on to win Best in Show at this show.

Mr. Edwards looks back at a favorite dog, not from his own kennel, and remembers Ch. Blencathra Brat. Brat's legacy is remembered on many continents, and his influence will be felt for many years to come.

From among his own Cairns, Frank Edwards remembers with exceptional fondness Ch. Heshe Izawyche, sired by Brat, as a beautiful Cairn with very sound movement and great showmanship.

Blencathra

There is a great deal to be said about Mrs. E. H. Drummond and her wonderful Blencathra Kennels. Blencathra produced twenty-five English champions, among them Ch. Blencathra Clivegreen Timothy, Ch. Blencathra Galgate Lady Piper, Ch. Blencathra Elford Badger, Ch. Blencathra Milord and Ch. Blencathra Barrie. Blencathra Derryvale Tara never became a champion but did produce Ch. Blencathra Brat, a very influential stud that appears in many pedigrees today, as do many other Blencathra Cairns, in both Great Britain and the United States.

Dorseydale

Doris Seymour, Dorseydale, bred three English champions, all males, and all of them figure heavily in many pedigrees in the United States, Canada and Great Britain. They were Ch. Dorseydale Tammy, Ch. Uniquecottage Powdermonkey and Ch. Lofthouse Davey. Davey, later purchased by Betty Hyslop, was a good winner for her,

Ch. Blencathra Galgate Lady Piper. Photo courtesy Mrs. Ferelith Hamilton Somerfield.

Ch. Blencathra Stonechat. Photo courtesy Mrs. Ferelith Hamilton Somerfield.

Ch. Blencathra Barrie. Photo courtesy Mrs. Ferelith Hamilton Somerfield.

Ch. Dorseydale Tammy. Photo courtesy Don Robbie.

and quite effective as a stud dog siring twenty U.S. champions. Dorseydale Justeena, dam of both Tammy and Davey, has exerted her influence through her sons in both the United States and Great Britain.

Other British breeders of this era and their dogs figure extensively in the achievements of many American breeding programs.

Another well-respected fancier, Col. H. F. Whitehead was a warm and intelligent person, who was of great help to many on both sides of the Atlantic. A memorable figure was Alex Fisher, a fancier since the early 1920s and co-author, with J. W. H. Beynon, of *The Popular Cairn Terrier.*

SEVERAL IMPORTANT TAIL MALE DESCENDANCIES

From the sound foundation of the kennels just documented, British breeders have moved forward very successfully. Listed below are some "tail male" lines of descendancy that show very well the connection between the history recounted earlier, and the successes of the 1980s and 1990s mentioned in this chapter and the one that follows.

Trace the tail male line of descendancy of Ch. Penticharm Silver Rocket, DGS, whose dam was Penticharm Dark Secret. Silver Rocket when bred to Uniquecottage Fire Fairy produced the formidable winner Ch. Beaudesert Royal Viking. Silver Rocket when bred to Pinetop Nutmeg of Corbieha produced Ch. Corbieha Hazelnut, top CC-winning Cairn Terrier bitch of all time.

Ch. Penticharm Silver Rocket, (sired by)
  Ch. Penticharm Guy Fawkes, (sired by)
    Ch. Robinson Crusoe of Courtrai, (sired by)
      Ch. Heshe Donavon, (sired by)
        Ch. Blencathra Brat, (sired by)
          Blencathra Derryvale Tara, (sired by)
            Ch. Blencathra Elford Badger, (sired by)
              Ch. Blencathra Brochter, (sired by)
                Cairncrag Caesar, (sired by)
                  Ch. Redletter McBryan, (sired by)
                    Ch. Redletter McMurran, (sired by)
                      Ch. Redletter McJoe, (sired by)
                        Ch. Bonfire of Twobees.

Larchlea Take a Chance On Me (Ch. Larchlea Here's Harvey ex Ch. Larchlea's Winner Takes All) 35 CCs, DGS

Ch. Larchlea Here's Harvey, (sired by)
  Ch. Standykes Pete, (sired by)
    Ch. Redletter Moonstruck, (sired by)
      Ch. Redletter Moon Tripper, (sired by)
        Ch. Redletter Michael, (sired by)
          Ch. Redletter Marshall, (sired by)
            Redletter Mr. Frolic, (sired by)
              Ch. Redletter McBryan, (sired by)
                Ch. Redletter McMurran

Here is an influential line of descendancy based on Line I. Cloth of Gold is the sire of Mostly Mary of Tweenus, who is the dam of Tweenus Georgina of Uniquecottage, who is the dam of Ch. Uniquecottage Treecreeper. Ch. Uniquecottage Treecreeper and his sire Ch. Uniquecottage Flycatcher have been very influential studs in England.

Ch. Avenelhouse Cloth of Gold, (sired by)
  Ch. Lofthouse Rough Tweed, (sired by)
    Ch. Lofthouse Larkspur, (sired by)
      Ch. Lofthouse Geryon of Mistyfell, (sired by)
        Ch. Blencathra Redstart, (sired by)
          Ch. Blencathra Clivegreen Timothy

Ch. Lofthouse Geryon of Mistyfell also sired another very influential group of dogs, down through Ch. Dorseydale Tammy, including Ch. Uniquecottage Powdermonkey, Dorseydale Nevah Carlos and Dorseydale Red Admiral. Red Admiral produced Ch. Brucairns Red Robin, Ch. Brucairns Crackerjack and Dorseydale Pitz Palu. Pitz Palu produced Dormerhall Apple Catcher who produced Glenbrae Frumento who produced Uniquecottage Grey Strike, who produced Ch. Uniquecottage Kittiwake and Ch. Uniquecottage Snow Lark.

Chapter Three

The Cairn Terrier in the United Kingdom and Other Countries

The previous chapter led us from the 1930s to the present, and many of the kennels profiled are still very active and successful. Since the late 1970s, however, considerable excitement has been generated in Great Britain by the kennels discussed in this chapter, including new records for numbers of Challenge Certificates (CCs) won by both dogs and bitches. This chapter also includes profiles of three continental kennels—two located in Italy and one in Sweden.

Statistics quoted in this book regarding numbers of CCs won by dogs and bitches from Britain have been taken from *The Compendium of British Cairn Terrier Records* by Patricia A. McKinney (London: Higham Press, 1994).

The British system for obtaining a championship is different from that used in the United States, and attaining a championship in Britain is much more difficult than in the United States. Because of Britain's size, there are fewer shows at which a dog can win a CC. The required CCs can only be won at championship shows, which are much larger than open shows. Open shows do not offer CCs. There are thirty-three championship shows, and five club shows per year in Britain. A club show is one sponsored by a Cairn Terrier Breed Club.

Classes are divided by sex and include minor puppy, puppy, junior, special yearling, maiden novice, tyro debutante, undergraduate, graduate, post graduate, limit and open. The British use the option of multiple entry far more than do American exhibitors. A dog or bitch must win every class in which it is entered to be eligible to compete against the other class winners in its sex for the Challenge Certificate.

Cairn entries at championship shows are usually in excess of one hundred, perhaps closer to 150, and are often much larger than that. One dog and one bitch are awarded a CC at each championship show. There is no

Cairn Terrier in a Red Armchair, *Edwin Douglas, Scottish, 1848–1914, oil on canvas.* Photograph courtesy William Secord Gallery, Inc., New York.

separate class in which champions compete; to win the CC a dog or bitch must win over every entry in its sex. Champions continue to amass CCs, as long as they are being shown and continue to win. Thus, when

The Duke and Duchess of Windsor with two of their Cairns. Photo courtesy Don Robbie.

an outstanding dog or bitch is being campaigned heavily, he or she may win all or most of the CCs being awarded at the time. Competition is very keen, and contenders may be unable to accumulate the three CCs under three different judges that are required in order for a dog to become a champion.

The winning of even one CC, or a Reserve CC, elevates a dog to a new status. Best of Breed goes to one of the two CC Winners, and this dog goes on to compete in the Group, just as it would in the United States. The dogs are awarded beautiful ros-ettes, and it is the custom for the handler to wear the rosette during Group competition.

Britain is a country famous for its beautiful countryside. Their dog shows set in such beautiful terrain are quite remarkable. Particularly attractive is the Windsor show, held in view of the world-renowned Windsor Castle. The shows are impressive not only for the lovely surroundings, but also for the number of terriers entered at each show. Many of their shows resemble our Montgomery County with respect to the depth and quality of the entries.

The British seem much more down to earth in their attitudes toward dog shows. Many routinely undergo physical inconvenience and sometimes even hardship in order to be able to attend the shows. Picnic baskets are often seen, with most shows being benched, leaving plenty of time for visiting and serious study of the dogs. Cluster shows, so popular in North America, are unheard of in the British Isles.

The open shows are often held in conjunction with fairs, and one may be so fortunate as to find a horse show or flower show to attend on the same grounds as the dog show. Vendors often sell interesting items, and local entertainment and contests may also be offered.

MORE RECENT BRITISH BREEDERS

Beaudesert

The Beaudesert affix was selected by Alan and Kathleen Sanders because the area in which they live was once designated as the Royal Beaudesert, and frequented by the Prince of Wales (later the Duke of Windsor), a Cairn patron himself for many years. Princess Elizabeth as a very young child was given a Cairn for a pet by the Prince of Wales.

Alan and Kathleen Sanders have had Cairns as pets for more than thirty years, but it was only seven years ago that they acquired a puppy for show from the Penticharm Kennels. Two years after that they obtained a line bred bitch from Uniquecottage Kennels. After two years, they bred Uniquecottage Fire Fairy to Ch. Penticharm Silver Rocket, producing a litter of six. The Sanders have kept all six, but the outstanding one to date is Ch. Beaudesert Royal Viking. Royal Viking was top Cairn in Great Britain in 1991, 1992 and 1993.

Ch. Beaudesert Royal Viking. Photograph by Michael Trafford.

His record includes thirty-three CCs and thirty Bests of Breed, and he is the first Cairn to win Best in Show at the National Terrier show, in existence for seventy-five years. Viking is also the first Cairn to win Best in Show at the Welsh Kennel Club. The Sanderses state that Liz Hooten, of Penticharm, was among the first to recognize the excellence of this young dog, and that she has presented him for them in competition in lovely condition.

Ch. Birselaw Boomerang. Russell Fine Art.

Birselaw

The Birselaw Kennels began in 1981 with the purchase by Miss Yvonne Cato of Ch. Pinetop Savannah of Birselaw. Her daughter Ch. Birselaw Country Girl produced Ch. Birselaw Boomerang and Ch. Birselaw Countryman. Country Girl was an outstanding show girl and was able to pass on that quality to her offspring.

Boomerang, the top winner for this kennel, was Top Cairn in 1989 and 1990, winning twenty-three CCs and twenty-one Bests of Breed.

Ch. Brindleoak Buck.

Brindleoak

Kevin Holmes was raised with Cairns and was given his first Cairn by his parents. She was mostly of Blencathra breeding, and proved to be an excellent foundation bitch. Mr. Holmes decided to breed her to Felshott Honey Badger, who was ultimately the sire of seven English champions. Keeping the best bitch from this litter, Brindleoak Honey Maid, and breeding her to Eng. Ch. Robinson Crusoe of Courtrai resulted in Eng. Ch. Brindleoak Buck. "Buck" has, in turn, proven himself both in the showring and as a stud, with champion progeny in England, Scandinavia, the United States and Canada.

One of Mr. Holmes's fondest memories is winning Best of Breed at Cruft's in 1982, with Brindleoak Bianca earning her third CC to complete her championship and become Mr. Holmes's first homebred champion, all on the same day.

Mr. Holmes prefers to use line breeding with occasional outcrosses, and his practice of using older, proven stud dogs certainly seems to have served him well. He also exhibits Sealyham and Border Terriers.

Cairngold

In 1964, when she was twelve, Linda Jones showed her first Cairn. "Ricky" was of Toptwig and Vinovium breeding, and did reasonably well in the show ring. Linda's parents were the original holders of the Cairngold prefix. When Linda married Alan Firth in 1975, Ricky came to live with them, and they continued with Linda's family prefix.

Ch. Cairngold Kramer.

In 1978 the Firths acquired a bitch puppy from Mr. and Mrs. Arrowsmith (Thimswarra). The bitch became their first champion, Thimswarra Estelle. The Firths had admired the Redletter stock of the late Walter Bradshaw, and understandably, their Cairngold Candy Floss was bred to Ch. Redletter Moonstruck. This was one of the last litters he sired, and it produced Am. Ch. Cairngold Crackerjack, who was imported into the United States by Jack and Karen Smith.

The first homebred champion for the Firths was Ch. Cairngold Kramer (Ch. Courtrai John Julius ex Cairngold Canoodle), and their second was Ch. Spirecairn Charmer, bred by Mr. and Mrs. Bunting, who had purchased their first Cairn from the Firths. Charmer was also sired by Ch. Courtrai John Julius. Kramer won his title in 1987, and was the Firths' fourth champion. Kramer is the sire of Am. Ch. Pinetop Paperchase, who is producing well in the United States, owned by Jack and Sue DeWitt.

The birth of their daughter Amy Marie in 1987 added to the quality of the Firths' life. Amy is a born Cairn lover and a joy to all who meet her. Linda Firth began awarding Challenge Certificates in 1988 in England. Her career as a judge has taken her to the United States for "plum" assignments in Southern California and Chicago, as well as in Sweden. She has also been invited to officiate in Amsterdam, Denmark and Australia. In 1993 Alan Firth also became qualified to award Challenge Certificates.

Croyanda

Mr. and Mrs. Croyman began showing in the early 1980s, and the first dog they made up was Ch. Pinetop Raffles of Croyanda, purchased from Mrs. Sally Ogle. Raffles has sired two champions for them, Croyanda Carnaby (ex Pinetop Harlequin of Croyanda) and Croyanda Manhattan (ex Pinetop Happy Go Lucky of Croyanda). Happy Go Lucky produced Ch. Croyanda Vienna when bred to Ch. Monary Something Special.

Mrs. Croyman with five Croyanda champions.

Harlequin when bred to Wendanny Carigroyale produced Ch. Croyanda Charleston. All five are shown in the photo above.

Harlight

Mrs. L. Z. Spence's Harlight Cairns have met with considerable success since Harlight's inception in 1974. Her interest in terriers dates from her childhood when she had Scottish Terriers. Her foundation stock came from Mr. Cooper's Greetavale line, among them Greetavale Honey Star. Honey Star produced Honey Bunch, who produced two champions, Ch. Harlight Hilary and Ch. Harlight Heidi. She also produced Ch. Harlight Honeysuckle and several that became champions outside Britain.

Ch. Greetavale Honeydew of Harlight produced Ch. Harlight Hello Honey, Ch. Harlight Hornblower and Ch. Harlight Hooray Henry. Henry was exported to the United States, to Brian and Patricia McKinney. This small but select kennel is noted for its strength in its bitches, and for the lovely heads seen in the stock it produces.

Kinkim

Ron and Brenda Birch began in Cairns more than twenty years ago with "Kim." Today, all the Kinkims (kin of Kim) are descended from her. The Birches have made up seven English champions, and are very active in club work. They try to keep the number of dogs in their kennel to between ten and twelve.

Larchlea

Carole Templeton's Larchlea Kennels, located in Glasgow, is small, comprising only four dogs at this writing. Ms. Templeton's interest in the Cairn began with rescue, and has evolved into a very successful career in

Ch. Harlight Hooray Henry was Reserve Best in Show at the Scottish Breeds event. He is shown here with his breeder-owner Leone Spence, judge Marjorie Arnold and Best in Show judge Ferelith Somerfield. David Lindsay.

the showring. Ch. Larchlea's Winner Takes All, top brood bitch in 1991 and 1992, is the dam of Ch. Larchlea Take A Chance On Me (by Ch. Larchlea Here's Harvey), Top Stud Dog 1992 and 1993. Chance's record includes thirty-four CCs, twenty-four Bests of Breed and several Specialties. Another member of this small kennel is Larchlea Fatal Attraction, sired by Ch. Uniquecottage Gold Diver ex Ch. Larchlea Roar N' Success. Larchlea exports to the United States include Am. Ch. Larchlea Stars and Stripes, Ch. Larchlea From Me to You (a full sister to Chance) and Ch. Larchlea's Obsession, to Martin and Deanna Ogulnick.

Ch. Larchlea Take A Chance On Me.

Monary

The Monary prefix of Mrs. Monica Shuttleworth dates from twenty-five years ago with her first Cairn, "Skipper." From the obedience class the Shuttleworths attended with Skipper, they learned about conformation classes at dog shows, and wanted to know more. They next

Ch. Monary Susanella.

purchased Cricket of Claybrooke, their first show Cairn. The Shuttleworths eventually became very involved with Miss Hunt, moving their printing business and home to Claybrooke Kennels. They maintained a partnership on the Claybrooke prefix for some time. Next they acquired Cairntop Master Simon from Mrs. Sangar, and Simon became their first champion. Simon is the sire of Ch. Saucy Miss of Monary.

The Shuttleworths moved when Claybrooke Kennels was sold, and applied for their own prefix, Monary. They bred Mitchan Dana to Ch. Robinson Crusoe of Courtrai. This was the first litter under the new prefix, and it produced Ch. Monary Roda. Roda bred to Dutch Ch. Heshe Haggis in 1982 and produced Ch. Monary Something Special and Ch. Monary Susanella. Suasanella was Best of Breed at Cruft's in 1984, and won a total of eleven CCs. Ch. Monary Something Special is the sire of eight champions in England, and many abroad. "Saucy Miss" produced two champions,

Ch. Penticharm Silver Rocket.

Ch. Monary Saucy Kristine and Ch. Monary Trudie, both sired by Special, but from two different litters. Trudie is the only English champion exported by Monary, and was sent to Nan Anderson, Knoxville, Tennessee, because of the close friendship that has developed between Mrs. Shuttleworth and Mrs. Anderson.

Monary has made up eleven champions, and two in partnership with other fanciers.

Penticharm

The Penticharm Cairns belonging to Patrick and June Hooten and their charming daughter Liz trace back to their foundation bitch, Avenelhouse Young Charm, bred by Hazel Small in 1972. Charm was by Blencathra Derryvale Tara ex Uniquecottage Gold Charm. The first Penticharm champion was her daughter, Ch. Penticharm Golddigger, a pet for Liz, who handled her to all her wins, starting when Liz was only eleven.

The Penticharm Kennel is fortunate to own two influential stud dogs. Ch. Penticharm Guy Fawkes (Ch. Robinson Crusoe of Courtrai ex Penticharm Calamity Jane) is the sire of nine English champions. Ch. Penticharm Silver Rocket (Guy Fawkes ex Penticharm Dark Secret) is the sire of six English champions, including the top winner Ch. Beaudesert Royal Viking, and the bitch CC record holder, Ch. Corbieha Hazelnut.

Two influential brood bitches are Penticharm Calamity Jane (Ch. Uniquecottage Grey Swift ex Penticharm Hazelnut), dam of three champions, and Penticharm Dark Secret (Ch. Uniquecottage Tree Creeper ex Penticharm Secret Love), dam of four champions.

An example of the staying power of these Penticharms is furnished by Ch. Penticharm Sparkler, who won the bitch CC at Cruft's in 1990 at almost seven years of age. With Liz Hooten representing the next generation, it will be interesting to see what lies ahead for this already successful kennel.

Two young dogs have come to the United States in recent years, Ch. Penticharm Private Eye, exported to Martin and Deanna Ogulnick and Ray Gernhart. More recently, Ch. Penticharm Jack the Lad was exported to American fancier Ann Kerr.

Pinetop

The Pinetop Kennels of Mrs. Sally Ogle is another example of the excellent quality to be found in the United Kingdom.

Mrs. Ogle purchased her first show Cairn, Craiglyn Minstrel Boy of Pinetop (Ch. Blencathra Barrie ex Ch. Craiglyn Morag), from the late Mrs. Bette Campbell in 1971. Craiglyn Curiosity (Ch. Blencathra Brat ex Ch. Craiglyn Easter Bonnet) was acquired about two years later.

Ch. Pinetop Montana.

Mrs. Ogle has won quite well with the Pinetops. She has produced ten British champions, among them, Ch. Pinetop Montana, who won Best Terrier and Reserve Best in Show at Darlington. Montana was top Cairn the same year. Three years later his granddaughter Ch. Pinetop Priscilla won top Cairn as well.

Business pressures have prevented Mrs. Ogle from being as active in the showring for a few years. However, she is now back on the scene, with Pinetop Hotspot, and his litter brother, Pinetop Havana, owned by Mrs. Fiona Cameron.

Pinetop Hot Spot.

Mrs. Ogle's exports to the United States and other countries have met with considerable success as well.

Sandaig

Pat and Jim Jeffrey started in 1959 with a pet Cairn, "a grey streak of fun," to quote Pat, that enriched their lives until 1970. They then went to Felshott Kennels and obtained Felshott Honesty, by Felshott Honey Badger. Honesty, called "Morag," became the foundation of this kennel. Bred to Ch. Blencathra Barrett in 1973, she produced Sandaig Sea Breeze, which had two CCs and one Reserve CC when she

Sandaig Spinner.

died tragically at two and a half years. In direct descent from Morag are the two champions, Sandaig Sula Rhu and Sandaig Salad Days.

The Jeffreys were assisted in the early days by the Misses Hall and Peggy Wilson (Felshott) and Alice Henderson (Twinlaw).

Successful exports for Sandaig include Am. & Can. Ch. Sandaig Spinner, to Doris Willis in Canada, and Ch. Sandaig Spruce to Austria.

KENNELS IN OTHER COUNTRIES

Italy

Giorsal

Int. Ch. Giorsal Groenlandia. PRO-DOG.

Giorsal Kennel, owned by Alberto Tartari and established in 1980, houses Cairns with roots to Uniquecottage, Pinetop, Standyke and Oudenarde. Mr. Tartari then turned his interest to Denmark, importing Ch. Tjeps Gaia Rhea Silvia, out of Ch. Dancairn Tjep. This bitch has produced well for Mr. Tartari. In 1989 Ch. Hjohoo's Hjolly Goodgracious, another that would produce well for Mr. Tartari, was imported from Sweden. Homebred champions for this kennel number twenty-two Italian and nine International. According to Mr. Tartari, his kennel has won the Gold Medal offered by the Italian Kennel Club (ENCI), for first prize as the best kennel of Terriers in Italy for the years 1983 through 1987 and 1990 through 1992.

Solcamp

Mr. Alberto Marengoni was kind enough to send from Italy photographs of his Ch. Solcamp Babette. Babette is sired by Ch. Giorsal Solcampfire ex Ch. Uniquecottage Goldsmudge. It is amazing what a profound influence Uniquecottage seems to exert wherever fanciers have been fortunate enough to be able to obtain breeding stock from Mrs. Parker-Tucker.

It is also interesting that Mr. Marengoni is also a Fox Terrier breeder, having bred Smooths for twenty years, yet being fascinated with Cairns for the entire time.

Sweden

Sarimont

Maud Montgomery-Bjurhult developed a love of dogs during her childhood, which was populated with Dachshunds and Cocker Spaniels. In

1971, she acquired her first Cairn and became interested in showing and breeding, only to discover that her first Cairn was of pet quality. Fortunately, her next addition, "Sara," was to be a foundation bitch, and she still breeds from that line. From a litter by Ch. Brucairn's Crackerjack, three bitches were whelped—all became champions. Ch. Sarimont Savannah was purchased by the Hjohoo Kennel and produced five champions, including the Best in Show winner Ch. Hjohoo's Bear. The bitch retained by Sarimont, Ch. Sarimont Sangria, produced twelve champions. Two of her sons have been good winners and top producers as well. Int. Ch. Sarimont Skallagrim, sired by Snorrehus Merrie, was top-winning Cairn in Sweden in 1982 and 1983. He won the Terrier Group nine times, was Best of Breed thirty-three times and earned a Best in Show in Stockholm in 1983. He was then retired from the showring. He had been purchased as a puppy by Miss Ingela Antonsson, Clayrags, and sired twenty-two champions for her, including three Group winners. He is the grandsire of two Best in Show winners: Int. Ch. Hjohoo's Hjolly Good Fellow and Int. Ch. Hjohoo's I Love Hjo Ye Ye Yeh, a bitch.

Ch. Solcamp Babette.

Mrs. Montgomery-Bjurhults kept Int. Ch. Sarimont Sycamore, which was also a Terrier Group winner, and which sired Ch. Qarnax Dante,

Ch. Sarimont Sundae.

Int. Ch. Sarimont Simon Templar and Ch. Sarimont Smock-Frock, all Terrier Group winners as well. Dante was Terrier and Cairn of the year in 1988.

Simon Templar, owned by Mrs. Kohler, is the top producer in Sweden with nearly thirty champions. Smock-Frock, owned by Mrs. Askenmo, is

Karen Schmidt with Int. Ch. Snorrehus Japonica. Photo Courtesy Maud Montgomery-Bjurhults.

also a Terrier Group winner and dam of Sarimont Sierra Nevada, exported to Judy Irby in the United States.

Interestingly enough, both Sarimont Skallagrim and Sarimont Sycamore were sired by sons of Eng. Ch. Toptwig Tilden.

The chronicle of top producers goes on. The Sangria Daughter, Int. Ch. Sarimont Shelley, also a Terrier Group winner, was the dam of eleven champions, including three Group-winning bitches.

The Sangria daughter, Int. Ch. Sarimont Smart Lady, was also retained by Mrs. Montgomery-Bjurhults and produced seven champions, including Ch. Sarimont Saratoga, top Cairn in Norway in 1985. Saratoga's litter brother, Sacramento, is the sire of Am. Ch. Clayrags Litzie, exported to Bergit Coady in California.

In 1987 Mrs. Montgomery-Bjurhults purchased a son of Simon Templar, Int. Ch. Skean-Dhu Rough Diamond, who has already sired fifteen champions. Again, this is a small kennel, never retaining more than six dogs. Over the years, the stud force consisted solely of the two males: Sycamore and Rough Diamond, one succeeding the other. The story of Sarimont clearly exemplifies the fact that a successful breeding program need not be dependent on a large number of animals to meet its goals.

Mrs. Montgomery-Bjurhults is licensed to judge all Terriers, some Toys and Poodles. She has been honored with the invitation to judge bitches and intersex competition at the CTCA National Specialty in 1995, a highly coveted assignment for any judge.

Chapter Four

Early History in America: 1913–1950

The eventful decade following World War I was of lasting importance to the Cairn Terrier in America. Two especially prominent breeders of this period were Mrs. Henry F. Price, Robincroft Kennels, and Mrs. Byron Rogers, Misty Isles Kennels.

Mrs. Price is remembered both as the first importer of the Cairn in the United States and as a long-time faithful Cairn fancier. She imported two Cairns in 1913, Loch Scolter's Podge and Sandy Peter Out of the West, to establish her kennel in Riverside, Connecticut.

The first Cairn Terriers shown in America debuted in Danbury, Connecticut, in October 1913. Sandy Peter Out of the West was the first Cairn granted American Kennel Club (AKC) registration in 1913. He was assigned No. 173555 in the stud record, and was the only Cairn Terrier registered with the AKC in 1913. The first litter of Cairns was registered in the United States in 1914.

The breed immediately began to achieve popularity, as in 1917, thirty-two Cairns were added to the stud book. On December 18, 1917, the Cairn Terrier Club of America (CTCA) gained membership in the American Kennel Club. The first officers of the CTCA were Mrs. Payne Whitney, president; Mr. William R. Wanamaker, vice president; Mrs. Byron Rogers, secretary; and Mrs. H. F. Price, treasurer. This recognition resulted in added prestige for the relatively new breed. In the early days of exhibition, the Cairn was shown in the Miscellaneous Class at American shows, the normal procedure still followed when a newly introduced breed begins seeking AKC recognition. During these years, the show-giving club could limit the breed classes offered at its show, and all others could only compete in the Miscellaneous Classes. By 1915, the Cairn was being shown in both the Miscellaneous Class and separate breed classes. The first club to offer separate classes for the Cairn Terrier was Ladies Kennel Association of America at Mineola, New York, on June 3 and June 4, 1915, with Holland Buckley officiating.

Eng. Ch. Lofthouse Geryon, Marjorie Cox, oil. From the collection of Don Robbie.

Two Cairns, Fannie Moody. Courtesy Don Robbie.

The members of the CTCA adopted the British Standard almost verbatim. This was done to expressly preserve the old working terrier. Minor differences in wording are noted.

1. The word *Shaggy* was added to the beginning section describing General appearance.
2. Description of eyes was changed from *large* to *medium* in size.
3. Description of tail was changed from *about six inches* to *short*.
4. Under the *body description, well-sprung* was added to deep ribs and also the first mention of a medium length back appeared.
5. Description of *shoulders, legs and feet* was amplified by adding that pads *should be thick and strong, thin and ferrety feet are objectionable.* The first mention of *sloping shoulder* and *medium length of leg* was made in this section also.
6. Description of *coat* was amplified to include a description of the "*short, soft and close*" undercoat.

The section describing faults remained unchanged except for the addition of a statement declaring flesh- or light-colored noses most objectionable. There was a disqualification for dogs weighing more than sixteen pounds and for bitches weighing more than fourteen pounds.

Mrs. Rogers entered the breed after Mrs. Price, and was originally interested in Sealyham Terriers. Mrs. Rogers included Cairns in her kennel, and began exhibiting in 1917. She also wrote the first American book on the breed, *Cairn and Sealyham Terriers,* in 1922. When Mrs. Rogers returned to England in 1924, she was probably the first person to engage in an exportation business by sending Cairns to other breeders in the United States. In 1927 she returned to America, relocating to Bedford, New York.

In 1918, Mrs. Payne Whitney's imported Greentree Ardsheal Gillie Cam became the first Cairn Terrier to become an American champion. In 1920, Mrs. Winans Burnett's Goldthread of Quinnatisset became the first American-bred champion. The first American-bred bitch to become a champion was Tempest's Kiltie of Misty Isles, bred by Mrs. Rogers and owned by Mr. A. U. Whitson.

Prometheus, bred and owned by Mrs. Price, is said to be the first American-bred puppy registered with the American Kennel Club. There is some question surrounding the date he completed his championship. Records vary as to his having finished his championship in either 1921 or 1925. The CTCA official yearbook indicates the year as 1925. Both *Pedigrees of American Bred Cairn Terrier Champions 1920–1933*, compiled by Elizabeth H. Anderson, and Cairn Terrier records indicate the year as 1921.

Other fanciers of the 1920s were Mr. and Mrs. Brydon Tennant (Glenconnor), Mr. and Mrs. Norman W. Ward of Bedford Hills, New York (Cornor), Miss Edith McCausland of North Easton, Massachusetts (Kedron), Mrs. Edward Loomis of Convent, New Jersey (Knocwood), Mr. and Mrs. Henry Slack of New York City (Rosscamac), Mr. and Mrs. Kenneth Harlan of Hollywood, California (Marken), and Mr. and Mrs. Lindsley Tappin of New York City (Tapscot).

It is interesting that during the 1920s and 1930s there is a historical discrepancy about the first Cairn to win a Best in Show in the United States. Jacobi's *Your Cairn Terrier* and Marvin's *The New Complete Cairn Terrier* both relate that the first Cairn to win an all-breed Best in Show was Ch. Jinx Ballantrae, bred and owned by Kenneth Harlan, a widely known movie actor. The dog was handled to the win by his wife, actress Marie Prevost, in Portland, Oregon, in March 1927.

Robert Williams's collection of rare dog memorabilia contains a photo once owned by Mr. Charles G. Hopton, a well-known judge of the time. The inscription on the back of the photo reads: "The first Cairn Terrier to win Best of All Breeds at an American show." This Cairn was Ch. Grosse Point Rags. "Rags" was owned by Mrs. Henry J. Stephens of the Grosse Point Kennels in Detroit, Michigan.

Another Best in Show is recorded in St. Louis by Ch. Gillad of Cairmore, an import owned by Mrs. and Mrs. Richard Stix, in April 1928, under judge Mr. Frank Addyman. Mr. and Mrs. Stix of Cairmore Kennels, of Cincinnati, Ohio, were the first major fanciers located any distance from the traditional East Coast stronghold.

Other noteworthy kennels during this period included Mrs. Amy Bacon's Cairnvreckan Kennels. Mrs. Bacon also maintained an active interest in West Highland White Terriers, successfully breeding and exhibiting both.

Mr. and Mrs. Lindsley Tappin's memorable Tapscot Kennels originated in a spacious apartment on Park Avenue in New York City. For some years the dogs were housed in bedrooms in the Tappin home, and exercised three times a day on lead. Undoubtedly, this regimen contributed to the poise of the dogs in the showring. The Tappins produced forty-five champions, a record at the time. Eventually they moved to Wilton, Connecticut, and their fortunes prospered with many fine exhibits before the kennel was closed in 1943.

During the 1920s, in spite of the breed's growth, imports exceeded American-breds. A total of ninety-one Cairns became champions during the 1920s, only thirty of which were bred in the United States.

The great depression of the 1930s surely slowed the development of the Cairn; however, the devoted fanciers kept the breed going. Among those, Mrs. H. F. Price and her Robinscroft Cairns were still very active, as was Mrs. Amy Bacon, with her Cairnvreckans. Tapscot Kennels also continued strongly.

In 1933, the American Standard was changed. In earlier years the American Standard had been changed to reflect an "ideal weight" of twelve to fifteen pounds for dogs, and eleven to thirteen pounds for bitches. This great disparity in weight is considerable for an animal as small as a Cairn Terrier. It allowed for considerable size difference, and the appearance of too-small, weedy exhibits, with little bone and substance. To remedy this situation, the CTCA changed the weights to fourteen pounds for dogs, and thirteen pounds for bitches. This still applies today.

Other influential fanciers whose interest also dates from the 1930s will be familiar to all active contemporary Cairn enthusiasts. It was at this time Mrs. G. W. Hyslop (Cairndania) became active in the breed. Also becoming active were Mrs. C. Groverman Ellis (Killybracken), Miss Helen Hunt (Shagbark), Mrs. Lillian Wood (Melita), Mrs. R. T. Allen (Craigdhu) and Miss Elizabeth Braun (Bethcairn).

The 1940s saw the first mention of the legendary handler Percy Roberts showing for Mrs. H. Terrell Van Ingen (Pinefair). Other new exhibitors in the 1940s included Mrs. Howard L. Platt (Eastcote), Mrs. Elise Untermyer, Mrs. G. C. Bird (Gildor) and Mr. and Mrs. Charles F. Dowe (Dowesfort). The Dowesfort Cairns were shown to great advantage by Bob Craighead.

At this time several women involved themselves with the breed records, so necessary to the success of today's endeavors. They were Elizabeth H. Anderson (Down East Kennels), Frances R. Porter and Clara M. LeVene (Tana). They spent untold hours compiling all American Cairn champions' pedigrees from 1920 to 1952. Miss Anderson compiled and researched pedigrees from 1920 through 1933, published in 1934.

Frances Porter and Clara LeVene continued with this work through 1952. Miss Porter was also the breed historian for many years, and wrote numerous excellent articles on many aspects of dogs.

Chapter Five

Further Progress
of the Cairn Terrier

At one time, judges were granted breeds within the various groups, based on the relative importance of those breeds. The "key" breeds were assigned first. The balance of the breeds were granted to the judges almost in order to complete the group, and with little thought as to their importance. The Cairn Terrier was in the latter grouping.

Many seasoned exhibitors will recall a puzzled gaze from the Terrier Group judge (which made one think they were wondering which of these minor breeds this little "haystack" was), or else the Cairn was totally ignored in Group competition.

The breeders' tenacity must be applauded, for the Cairn's chances in Group competition have improved considerably. This is also due in part to the perseverance of some of the top professionals of the time: Roberta Campbell on the East Coast, with many of Betty Hyslop's Cairndania exhibits; and Daisy Austad on the West Coast, with Ch. Buckshot of Melita, owned by Doris Harris, and then with Isabel Eckfeld's Ch. Bellacairns Bit O' Scotch. Maxine Beam began

Ch. Cairndania Brigrey's Berry Red is at the center of this famous trio of Cairn fanciers. Handled by her owner, Betty Hyslop, she is shown winning the CTCA Specialty under judge Mrs. R. T. Allen (left) of Craigdhu fame. The trophy presenter is Celeste Hutton, whose Greysarge Cairns were widely known and respected. Evelyn Shafer.

Better known to dog exhibitors today as a judge in high demand, Maxine V. Beam was a handler of rare ability. Her client list included Mildred Bryant, and she is shown here with a young "Milbryan" in a Best of Breed win under Anne Rogers Clark. Don Petrulis.

Ch. Foxgrove Jester, with handler Roberta Campbell, was the winner of three Bests in Show in the United States. Stephen Klein.

winning Groups with several of Mrs. David Bryant's Milbryan Cairns in the Southwest, and later Betty Munden won Groups with several Cairns for Bob and Sally Yancey's "Prestwick Kennels" of Greensboro, North Carolina.

The tenacity of the many owner-handlers in the breed has also greatly benefitted the Cairn Terrier. Some of the most outstanding were Betty Hyslop, Esther Coleman and later her daughter, Lydia Coleman Hutchinson (Wolfpit). Nancy Thompson (Gayla Cairn) won many Terrier Groups in the Southeast with several different Cairns, and Betty Marcum (Cairmar) won consistently with a long line of quality homebreds and imports.

Breeding stalwarts like these had made the Cairn Terrier a force in Group competition in the 1990s.

Killybracken

Some earlier fanciers are no longer breeding or showing, but they were certainly a potent force during their day, and their bloodlines still exert an impact upon the breed. Notable among them are Mrs. C. Groverman Ellis and her daughter Mary Jane, of the Killybracken Kennels.

The Ellises, their Cairn Terriers and Irish Wolfhounds were an integral part of the fabric of the dog fancy in the Chicago area. The CTCA annual national Specialty was held for years in Chicago, at the International Amphitheater, the day before the Chicago International show in April.

Exhibitors competed fiercely for the privilege of staying at the Stock Yards Inn, next door. The name implies much. This was a historic old hotel built to accommodate cattlemen and ranchers who needed convenient lodging. The Stock Yards Inn was the property of the Ellis family, and the Cairn fancy always had preferential treatment.

The Killybracken Kennels became involved with Cairns in the early thirties. Irish Wolfhounds had been on the scene since 1928, and were always a love of Mrs. Ellis and her daughters. Killybracken pro-

Ch. Braemuir Raffan II, owned by Mildred Bryant and handled by Maxine Beam, shown in a Best of Breed win under Dr. Harold L. Huggins. Blicks.

duced well over thirty Cairn champions in its day, and obedience was an interest as well. *The New Complete Cairn Terrier* indicates that Ch. Tam Glen of Killybracken may have been the first Cairn to earn a Tracking degree. Mrs. Ellis imported from Mrs. Alistair Campbell, Brocaire Crisp-Jura, among others. Red Magnet of Mercryd was purchased in 1937 at the Crystal Palace show. Red Magnet was a double cross on Moccasin Magnet, which provided Killybracken with a strong influence from Harviestoun Raider. Later, Mrs. Ellis added Cairnvreckan Trian. Mrs. Ellis thought Chs. Trip, Spray and Alex were among the best of the Killybrackens. Alex won two Groups, and went Best in Show at Kalamazoo in 1957. The Ellises usually handled their own dogs, but occasionally used the professional ser-

Ch. Whistlegate Red Falcon winning the Terrier Group at the Sacramento KC under judge Phil Marsh, handler Phyllis Greer.

vices of Virginia Hardin. Mrs. Ellis was also very active in the affairs of the International Kennel Club of Chicago for many years.

There were many other significant breeders and kennels during this important period of development. Among them were the Shagbark kennels of Miss Helen Hunt and in Canada, the Melita Kennels of Mrs.

Ch. Bonnie Bairn of Wolfpit (left), with handler Jimmy Butler, and Ch. Heathcairn Cuthbert with Martha Brewer at the International Kennel Club, circa 1956. Photo courtesy Lydia Coleman Hutchinson.

Melita Wood and Mr. and Mrs. Mark W. Alison, who used their family name as their prefix. Mr. Alison was quite a successful owner-handler who was very active in the affairs of the CTCA for a number of years. The Catescairn Kennels of Mr. and Mrs. H. B. Stewart Jr. from Ohio were quite influential. Bairdsain, the kennel of Charles and Audrie Norris, was very successful in the 1960s. Ch. Baird's Thorn was Best of Breed at the 1963 national Specialty, and his litter brother, Ch. Baird's Bramble, did the same the following day at Westminster. These two were from an all-champion litter of four, the other litter mates being Baird's Shaldar's Boy and Baird's Thicket. This quartet was sired by Ch. Heathcairn Cuthbert ex Shaldar of Rossarden.

Greysarge

Also prominent were Celeste Hutton and her wonderful Greysarge Cairns, Chs. Greysarge Flare and Greysarge Naughty Marietta among them. Celeste served as president of the CTCA, and was very active with the Baltimore SPCA, located in what had been a water treatment facility. Several CTCA board meetings were held in a spacious home also on the property, and tours of the SPCA were provided. Celeste kept donkeys and other large animals at her home, and was very apt to rescue any animal of any species that she believed was not being well treated. An invitation to partake of the dog show lunch served on the tail gate of Celeste Hutton's custom Cadillac station wagon was prized by all, and an event to be remembered.

Badenoch

Jim MacFarlane was keeping Cairns about 1920 in Scotland. Due to business pressures this effort was eventually abandoned. After relocating to Canada, Jim and his wife, Kay, purchased Badenoch Cubbie of Kenten. Jim's uncle, the redoubtable Col. H. F. Whitehead, was able to trace Cubbie's pedigree and discovered that she traced back to one of his early favorites, Ch. Guynach Eachunn, the colonel's first champion. This bitch produced Badenoch Foxy Sue, by Ch. Redlettter McRuffie, and her name is seen in many pedigrees of today. Mr. MacFarlane died in 1981, and the kennel was closed. There was the also the Braemuir, kennels of Mr. and

Mrs. Philip Thompson, who obtained their stock from Cairn-vreckan bloodlines.

Isabel Eckfeld from California bred a number of good Cairns including Ch. Bellacairn's Bit O' Scotch, best remembered for his Best in Show victory at the Kennel Club of Beverly Hills in 1968, beautifully shown and conditioned by Daisy Austad.

The interest of the late Betty Stone dates from 1926, when she purchased a Cairn while in Scotland and registered Caithness as her prefix. Mrs. Stone had Setters and Dalmatians as well, but in the late 1940s, the Cairns began to claim more of her attention. Mrs. Stone imported several dogs, among them Eng. Ch. Thistleclose MacGregor, Ch. Uniquecottage Mr. Tippy of Caithness, Toptwig Fay of Caithness and Foundation Moss Rose of Caithness. Mr. Tippy and Moss Rose produced Ch. Caithness Briar Rose. Briar Rose when bred to Ch. Cairndania's McRuffie's Raider produced a litter that included Chs. Rosette, Rosalie, Rosemary and Rufus.

Rufus won the 1964 CTCA Specialty from the puppy class under Elise Untermyer, and continued his winning ways throughout his illustrious show career. He

Ch. Caithness Rufus, owned by Betty Stone, was one of the breed's all-time greats. Evelyn Shafer.

Ch. Cairnwoods Golden Boy. Photo courtesy Laura De Vincent.

was retired from the showring to allow Mrs. Stone to show his son, Ch. Cairnwoods Golden Boy. Golden Boy was eventually sold to Mr. John Honig, a well-known Collie breeder and multiple Group judge, who also bred Cairns under the Accalia prefix.

An important historical note is taken from the comments Mrs. Untermyer wrote for *Pure-Bred Dogs—American Kennel Gazette*, in September 1964, after judging the CTCA national Specialty in Chicago. Mrs. Untermyer comments that a good entry was there, with entrants from California, Texas, Kentucky, Georgia, Missouri, and the Northeast and Canada being represented in force as usual. Mrs. Untermyer struggled with the diversity of type, as we do today, thirty years later. She specifically mentions weight and body proportion, type and expression. Also of concern to her were poor fronts and bad mouths, still a concern today. Rufus forged his way to Best of Breed from the puppy class at age seven months. Regarding the choice of Rufus for Best of Breed, she wrote:

> He was alert and interested all the time in the ring, never let go even when relaxed; his head and tail never down. He moved beautifully and showed with the poise of a veteran. With a specials class of fifteen, it took a good deal of soul-searching and very careful observation of the many qualified contenders to put a puppy over the champions, but on that day he was outstanding.

What a lovely memory. I wish I had been there; Rufus was a favorite of mine, and he is behind many of today's great winners and producers. His influence lingers to this day, being fifth top-producing Cairn Terrier sire of all time.

Topcairn, owned by Girard A. Jacobi and William R. Chatham, Spring Valley, New York, was very successful for a number of years. Kennel activity was discontinued following the death of Mr. Jacobi in 1983.

Moving forward into the seventies, some breed stalwarts maintained their position, and indeed progressed in different areas. Mary Jane Ellis, Killybracken, judged for a number of years, and is very well respected. Miss Ellis was approved by the American Kennel Club to judge all Terriers and several of the Hound breeds.

Mrs. R. T. Allen, well known for her Craigdu Cairns, was also a contributor for several dog publications. The last dog she campaigned was Ch. Alison's My Tup Bruaria, shown by George Ward and bred by Mr. and Mrs. Mark W. Alison.

Eleanor Finkler, another longtime breeder, obtained some foundation stock from Melita Wood. She has consistently produced champions over the years, and the total American champions bearing her prefix number over seventy.

Martha Baechle wrote many articles for *Terrier Type* and *Pure-Bred Dogs—American Kennel Gazette*, was very active in the organization of first the Cairn Terrier Club of Southern California, and then that of Northern California, and served ten years as show chairperson for the Santa Clara Valley Kennel Club.

Mrs. Mildred Bryant, after many years as a successful Cairn breeder, has turned her hand to judging, and is currently approved to judge all Toy, Terrier, Non-Sporting and Herding breeds, in addition to several Sporting and Working breeds. The occasional four-footed friends still figure in the Bryant lifestyle, in spite of Mildred's heavy judging schedule. Her love for Cairns, Doberman Pinschers and Dachshunds continues. Her last Cairn was a rescue that became her husband David's dog, and happily lived out her life with them.

THE BEST IN SHOW WINNERS

The roster of Best in Show (BIS) winners since 1980 reads like a who's who in Cairn Terriers.

1980	Ch. Rogerlyn Sea Hawk's Salty Sam - 1
	Ch. Coralrocks's Boney Maloney - 1
1981	Ch. Rogerlyn Sea Hawk's Salty Sam - 2
	Ch. Cairmar Call to Arms - 1
	Ch. Lakewood's Snapshot Studley - 1
1982	Ch. Foxgrove Jeronimo - 2
1984	Ch. Wee Gaelic Todd Cairndania- 1
1985	Ch. Brigadoon's Tough Guy - 1
1986	Ch. Tidewater Master Gold - 1
1987	Ch. Tidewater Master Gold - 6
	Ch. Sharolaine's Kalypso - 1
	Ch. Whetstone Jack Tar - 1
1988	Ch. Tidewater Master Gold - 8
1989	Ch. Uniquecottage Gold Grouse - 2
	Ch. Cairmar Cowardly Lion - 1
1990	Ch. Cairmar Cowardly Lion - 7
1991	Ch. Dees Comanche - 1
	Ch. Terriwood's Best Dressed - 1
1992	Ch. Caledonian Berry of Wolfpit - 4
	Ch. Foxairn Tinman - 2
	Ch. Goosedown's Tailor Made - 1
1993	Ch. Caledonian Berry of Wolfpit - 1
	Ch. Tigh Terrie's Hello Dolly - 1
	Ch. Foxairn Tinman - 1
	Ch. Chesapeake Rising Son O'Scot - 1
	Ch. Coach's Watch Those Sparks - 1
1994	Ch. Foxairn Tinman - 5
	Ch. Chesapeake's Rising Son O'Scot - 2
	Ch. Dee's Dust Devil - 1
	Ch. Car O'Mik Tata Ouija Wytch - 1

Throughout this listing, we see again some of the most influential names within the breed. Betty Hyslop and her Cairndanias continue as a formidable presence while Lydia Hutchinson, daughter of Taylor and Esther Coleman, carries on the Wolfpit tradition with great distinction. Betty Marcum's Cairmar dogs, especially "Call to Arms," shown by his owner, and "Cowardly Lion," shown by Judy Webb, are part of this ill-ustrious company. Nancy Thompson, one of the breed's most success-ful owner-handlers, and her Gayla Cairn Kennels, and Charles Merrick III, who continues to have success in the ring, also have a place in this compilation. The latter's "Master Gold" and "Gold Grouse," shown by Linda More, are particularly memorable. Molly Wilder with "Jack Tar," shown by Judy Webb; Jamie and Bob Abhalters' Ch. Coralrocks Boney Maloney, shown by Pete Clay; and Nell Stumpff, an owner-handler with Ch. Lakewood's Snapshot Studley, are yet additional examples. It is also delightful to note the many names new to the BIS Winners Circle. Among these fanciers are Susan and Clarence Vaughn, with their Ch. Dees Comanche shown by Bill Trainor, and more recently Peter Green with Ch. Dees Dust Devil; Tom and Karin Godwin; Pat Hassey, breeder of Ch. Goosedown's Tailor Made; Lyn Hickey, breeder of Ch. Tigh Terrie's Hello Dolly; Pam Pettus and Marilyn Rhodes, breeders of Ch. Chesa-peake Rising Son O'Scot; and Jan Cherry, whose Coach's dogs are shown by Bill and Georgia Harris.

The professional handlers who had a major role in these success stories include Roberta Campbell, Pete Clay, Linda More, Peggy Beisel McIlwaine, Judy Webb, Robert Peebles and Craig Osborne, William Trainor, Bill MacFadden and Christi McDonald. These people have greatly benefitted the breed by showing their Cairn charges to Bests in Show. It is such a thrill to see this breed being recognized in this fashion. At one time this kind of winning was virtually unimaginable for Cairns. Today an all-breed Best in Show win by a Cairn Terrier is not unusual.

NATIONAL SPECIALTY BEST OF BREED
WINNERS SINCE 1980

1980	Ch. Cairnwood's Quince
1981	Ch. Foxgrove Jeronimo
1982	Ch. Foxgrove Jeronimo
1983	Ch. Chasand's Yankee Peddlar
1984	Ch. Cairnlea's Robson
1985	Buccaneer's Iris at Terratote
1986	Ch. Whetstone Halston
1987	Ch. Copperglen Fame N Fortune
1988	Ch. Tidewater Master Gold
1989	Ch. Ollie North of the Highlands
1990	Ch. Goosedown's Tailor Made
1991	Ch. Goosedown's Tailor Made
1992	Ch. Glenarden Debut Attraction
1993	Ch. Tigh Terrie's Hello Dolly
1994	Ch. Foxairn Tinman

WESTMINSTER BEST OF BREED
WINNERS SINCE 1979

1979   Ch. Rogerlyn Sea Hawk's Salty Sam
1980   Ch. Rogerlyn Sea Hawk's Salty Sam
1981   Ch. Rogerlyn Sea Hawk's Salty Sam
       Group Third
1982   Ch. Foxgrove Jeronimo
       Group Third
1983   Ch. Cairndania Sam's Sundew
1984   Ch. Cairndania Sam's Sundew
1985   Ch. Gaelic Haggis MacBasher
1986   Ch. Gaelic Haggis MacBasher
1987   Ch. Cairndania Sam's Sundew
1988   Ch. Tidewater Master Gold
       Group First
1989   Ch. Tidewater Master Gold
1990   Ch. Sharolaine's Kalypso
1991   Ch. Mapleleaf Farm Sir Gallahad
1992   Ch. Goosedown's Tailor Made
1993   Ch. Foxairn Tinman
1994   Ch. Foxairn Tinman
1995   Ch. Tigh Terrie's Hello Dolly
       Group Third

Betty Hyslop's dominance of Cairn Terriers at Westminster continues with thirteen of the last sixteen Best of Breed winners coming from her venerable establishment.

Chapter Six

Prominent Cairn Terrier
Fanciers of Today

Cairndania

Certainly the strongest influence on the Cairn Terrier in North America is the Cairndania Kennels of Betty Easton Hyslop.

Cairndania is located on a bluff overlooking the St. Lawrence River near Brockville, Ontario, Canada. From this lovely setting, among towering trees, far off the beaten path, the Cairndanias have made their place in breed history for more than sixty years. The home itself is of rough-hewn granite, nearly two hundred years old. This wonderful, enduring structure could well represent the steadfast concern and dedication demonstrated by Mrs. Hyslop toward the dog fancy in general, and Cairn Terriers in particular, during her long tenure.

A view of Betty Hyslop's Cairndania Kennels.

The name "Cairndania" is derived from Mrs. Hyslop's interest in Great Danes as well as in Cairns. However, since the late sixties, the Cairn Terrier has achieved preeminence in this kennel. Mrs. Hyslop has imported many great dogs and it has always been her practice to make the stud dogs at Cairndania available to all. This policy has greatly benefited the entire breed over the years.

Mrs. Hyslop's interest in Cairns began in 1928 with the purchase of

Ch. Redletter McRuffie. Rudolph
Tauskey.

*Ch. Foxgrove Susanella, winning Best of Breed
at the 1974 CTCA Specialty at Montgomery
County under judge Diana Hamilton.* Evelyn
Shafer.

Placemore Peekaboo, an English import from Mrs. Bird. Peekaboo was
joined soon after by Ch. Seaworthy Out of the West and Moccasin Mercy.
Mrs. Hyslop first entered her homebreds at Westminster in 1931, and has
dominated Cairns at this great show ever since, winning Best of Breed
more than forty times! There have been three Westminster Terrier Group
placings for Cairndania, the first in 1952 with Ch. Kiltie's Foxglove of
Cairndania, and more recently, both Ch. Foxgrove Jeronimo and Ch.
Rogerlyn Sea Hawk's Salty Sam have placed third.

Mrs. Hyslop has most recently captured the breed with Ch. Foxairn
Tinman in both 1993 and 1994. His sire, Ch. Sharolaine's Kalypso, was
best Cairn at Westminster in 1990.

One of Mrs. Hyslop's early winners and important dogs was Eng. Am.
Ch. Divor of Gunthorpe, followed by Am. & Can. Ch. Tinker of Tapscot
and Pimpernel of Mercia. These were all in the 1930s. The 1940s and
1950s saw still more great Cairndania Cairns making their influence
known both in the showring and as top producers. Among these are Ch.
Chunk of Crockshed, Ch. Kilmet of Cairndania, a Chunk son, Ch. Tam's
Grey Girl of Cairndania, Ch. Kindon Saucy Sue, Ch. Kiltie's Foxglove of
Cairndania and the influential Ch. Redletter McRuffie.

McRuffie, a Group winner, captured the national Specialty three times,
and is one of the all-time top sires, with twenty-five champions. McRuffie
claims the most extensive line of champion descendancy of any stud dog in
North America.

Ch. Rogerlyn Sea Hawk's Salty Sam was Best of Breed from the classes at the CTCA Specialty at Montgomery County, 1977, under judge Jim Reynolds. John Ashbey.

Am. & Can. Ch. Cairndania Smartie's Sandell, owner-handled to Best of Opposite Sex at the Greater Detroit Cairn Terrier Club, under Mrs. Linda Firth of the Cairngold Kennels, England. Martin Booth.

Ch. Redletter Miss Splinters was another great one, and is also the dam of Ch. Red-letter McBrig and, a Best in Show winner, and Ch. Cairndania McRuffie's Splinter.

The 1960s saw the Cairndania dogs garnering the elusive Best in Show with more regularity. Ch. Cairndania McBrigand's Holbrig, Ch. Unique Cottage Mr. Bradshaw and Ch. Cairndania McBrigand's Brigrey all earned all-breed Bests in Show. Brigrey won a Best in Show in 1965, and sired sixteen American champions. Ch. Lofthouse Davey (Eng. Ch. Geryon of Mistyfell ex Dorseydale Justeena) was a wonderful addition to Cairndania, as was Ch. Redletter Twinlaw Seaspirit, both Best in Show winners as well. Ch. Cairndania Brigrey's Berry Red was a tremendous show girl, richly deserving of her many honors, including a Best in Show in the United States and five in Canada. Ch. Vinovium Errol Flynn and Ch. Tammy of Mistyfell rounded out the 1960s for this kennel in terms of Best in Show honors. Many of these dogs are very influential in the pedigrees of a large cross section of the Cairns being exhibited today.

Additional standard bearers from this prestigious kennel moving forward into the 1970s include Chs. Foxgrove Susanella, Rogerlyn Sea Hawk's Salty Sam, Foxgrove Jester and Foxgrove Jeronimo. Susanella won one Best in Show in the United

States and seven in Canada, and was Best of Breed at the CTCA Specialty with Montgomery County in 1974. These dogs were shown by Mrs. Hyslop and Roberta Campbell and all have impressive records, in both the United States and Canada, accounting for many Specialty and all-breed Best in Show wins.

Betty Hyslop is a dominant figure in the showring herself, a fierce competitor and formidable challenge to all as she continues to enter the ring in the eye-catching blue outfits that have become her trademark. Her pert attitude is wonderful to behold; however, she will not give any quarter in the ring. She is a true competitor till the last ribbon has been awarded.

The 1980s saw many more Cairndanias in the showring, among them Ch. Gaelic Jagger Cairndania, Ch. Gaelic Haggis MacBasher and Ch. Cairndania Todd's Hot Toddie.

Ch. Sharolaine's Kalypso, shown with handler Peggy Beisel, was Best of Breed at the Cairn Terrier Club of Southern California under judge Alvin Krause. Elaine Eschbach was the breeder and co-owner with Mrs. Hyslop of this noted winner. Joan Ludwig.

In 1984, Roberta Campbell, long associated with Cairndania, retired from handling and took a position with the American Kennel Club. She is currently the Administrator of Performance Events. The early 1990s saw two spectacular bitches shown, Ch. Cairndania Smartie's Sandell and Am. & Can. Ch. Cairndania Todd's Sparkler.

Mrs. Hyslop used Elliot Weiss as a handler for a number of years upon Roberta Campbell's retirement. In the mid-1980s Peggy Biesel McIlwaine began to show some of the Cairndanias. This relationship has become mutually very successful. The first topper for the Hyslop/Beisel McIlwaine combination was Ch. Sharolaine's Kalypso, bred by Elaine Eschbach. Kalypso, sired by Ch. Cairndania Targon's Thomas out of Recless Kiley of Sharolaine, was a topnotch example of the breeding complement between Mrs. Eschbach's Sharolaine Kennels and Cairndania. Kalypso amassed a record of twenty-two Group firsts and a Best in Show, plus many other Group placements and five Specialty Bests. The number of champion get for Kalypso currently stands at twenty-five.

The next major player for the Hyslop/Beisel McIlwaine team would be the Kalypso son, Ch. Foxairn Tinman. Tinman was from an all-champion litter of four, the dam being Ch. Foxairn Little Miss Marker. Tinman finished his championship by going Best of Winners at the Detroit Cairn

Ch. Foxairn Tinman, handled by Peggy Beisel for owner Betty Hyslop, is a multiple Best in Show and Specialty winner. Alex Smith.

Ch. Cairnlea's Robson. Martin Booth.

Specialty in 1990, and attracted the attention of Betty Hyslop, who purchased him at that time.

Tinman was Number 1 Cairn all systems for 1992, and Number 10 Terrier on the *Terrier Type* system. This dog is still being campaigned as this book goes to press. His show record stands at six Bests in Show, sixty Group firsts and numerous other Group placings. Tinman has also garnered three Canadian Bests in Show. As of 1993, he has sired seven champions with many more in the ring.

Foxairn

The Foxairn Kennels of Sanderson (Sandy) and Margaret (Peggy) Beisel McIlwaine was established in 1980. Mr. McIlwaine's interest in the breed began with his purchase of a Cairn in 1968. Sandy's first homebred was Ch. Mac's Maggie Mae. Maggie's daughter, Ch. Thornwood's Foxfire by Ch. Woodmist Grey Cavalier, was res-ponsible for Peggy and Sandy meeting. Foxfire was being shown by George Ward at the time while Margaret Beisel was employed as an assistant to Mr. Ward. After their marriage, they adopted the kennel name of Foxairn. The Foxairn prefix relates to their interest in Wire Fox Terriers and Cairns. The last litter of Foxairn Wires was born in 1991, as the McIlwaines plan to concentrate on Cairns in the future. Thornwood's Foxfire died an untimely death, starting Sandy on a search for a new foundation bitch. In time, he purchased Woodmist Cluny II (Ch. Cairnlea's Robson ex Ch. Woodmist Penelope) from Virginia Cadwallader. Cluny became the foundation bitch for Foxairn. Bred to Ch. Ugadale Hallmark, she produced Ch. Foxairn Little Miss Marker, who produced the top-winning Ch. Foxairn Tinman. As previously stated, Tinman is from an all-champion litter of four, which included Chs. Foxairn Wizard (E. Skellett), Foxairn Scarecrow and Foxairn Double Trouble (Geis and Anderson).

Other noteworty Foxairn winners include Foxairn Maid Marion, Best of Winners, 1992 CTCA Specialty, and 1993 CTC of Greater Detroit Specialty and Ch. Foxairn LaBamba, Winners Dog and Best in Sweepstakes 1989, CTCGD. Foxairn Kalliope, a newcomer for the McIlwaines, got her career off to a nice start at the Cairn Terrier Club of Greater Detroit Specialty in 1994, advancing from the puppy class all the way to Winners Bitch under Alf Arrowsmith, from England. Kalliope is out of Ch. Ziegfield's Rok Moninoff ex Foxairn Karousel.

Before Tinman and Kalypso entered the showring, however, Peggy McIlwaine was privileged to handle another great one. Ch. Cairnlea's Robson was also purchased from Virginia Cadwallader, but bred by Janet Sternberg. Robson (Pete) was shown for three years, topping the breed at the CTCA national Specialty at Montgomery County in 1984, and amassing a record of twelve Group Firsts plus many other placings and Specialty Bests. "Pete" also has twelve champion offspring to his credit.

Wolfpit

Wolfpit Kennels was established in 1939 when Esther and Taylor Coleman

Ch. Thornwood's Foxfire. Martin Booth.

Ch. Foxairn Maid Marion was Winners Bitch at the 1992 CTCA national Specialty at Montgomery County enroute to her championship. The judge was Patricia Breach of Hearn Kennels, England; the trophy presenter was Marilyn Joachim. John Ashbey.

Ch. Quince's Spunky of Wolfpit, first of Quince's fifty-one champion offspring, and dam of Ch. Dapper Dan of Wildwood. William Gilbert.

Ch. Razzberry of Wolfpit. Kernan.

were given a black Cairn puppy bitch, whom they named Kiltie of Wolfpit. A daughter, Lydia, was born to the Colemans shortly afterward. Kiltie was bred once to Ch. Buff of Eastcote, from Mrs. Howard Lee Platt's kennels. This litter produced Foxie of Wolfpit, who produced Wolfpit's first champion, Mister Mulroonie of Wolfpit who finished in 1950. Young Lydia attended shows in 1949, and her parents bought Shagbark Misty Betts from Helen Hunt for Lydia to show. Misty Betts completed her title in 1951.

The number of champions owned and/or bred by Wolfpit stands at 113 at the end of 1993. Most of the Wolfpit dogs have been owner-handled. Esther Coleman was active in the showring from 1949 to 1979, and Lydia continues strongly with the family interest in the Cairn Terrier that has flourished since 1949.

In addition to being a highly successful Cairn breeder, Lydia enjoys national popularity through judging. She has been judging since July 1964, and is currently approved for all Terriers, a number of the Toy breeds as well as Poodles and both the Welsh Corgis.

Wolfpit was the home of Ch. Cairnwood's Quince (1968–84), acquired at an early age by Esther from the Cairnwood Kennels of Luanne Craco and Jane Dalger. Quince held the top producing record for years, but in 1994 was tied by his great-grandson, Ch. Cairmar Fancy Dresser. The breed siring record is fifty-one champions. Quince also holds the unique distinction of having won the national Specialty four times, three in succession—1971, 1972, 1973—and at almost thirteen years young in 1980. Two other top producing studs have emerged from this kennel, Ch. Persimmon of Wolfpit, by Ch. Vinovium Caius ex Ch. Easter Bonnet of Wolfpit (a Quince daughter), with twenty-seven champions, and Ch. Gadget's Gimmick of Wolfpit, with twenty-three champions, by Persimmon out of Ch. Sunnyland's Gadget of Wolfpit.

Wolfpit Kennels is strengthened by the number of top producing bitches it has housed over the years. Some are:

Ch. Caledonian Berry of Wolfpit, bred, owned and handled by Lydia Coleman Hutchinson, established a strong win record in the early 1990s. Chuck Tatham.

Ch. Bayberry of Wolfpit (Quince ex Ch. Craiglyn Christmas Carol), nine champions; Ch. Bonnie Hoyden of Wolfpit (Ch. Mac Loganberry of Wolfpit ex Ch. Bonnie Vamp of Wolfpit), dam of eight champions; Ch. Razzberry of Wolfpit (Ch. Ramblewood Barney Brehannon ex Ch. Sherry Berry of Wolfpit), six champions; Ch. Bonnie Whirligig of Wolfpit (Gimmick ex Hoyden), six champions. Whirligig is also the dam of an all-champion litter of four.

Over the years, there were other judicious purchases that strengthened the breeding program at Wolfpit. Cairndania Foxglove's Adelaide was acquired in 1952 and produced Bonnie Bairn of Wolfpit, which produced an all-champion litter of three.

Lofthouse Veleta, a full sister to Eng. Ch. Lofthouse Rough Tweed, was imported in 1967. Veleta made her contributions to Wolfpit in the whelping box, being the dam of Ch. MacMurrich of Wolfpit, a Quince son, which sired Ch. Dapper Dan of Wildwood, which sired Ch. Cairmar Fancy Dresser. MacMurrich also sired Ch. Sunnyland's Gadget of Wolfpit, dam of Gimmick.

Craiglyn Christmas Carol (Ch. Blencathra Brat ex Ch. Pledwick Drusilla) was imported from Scotland in 1975 at five years of age. Carol whelped two litters in Scotland, from one of which came Eng. Am. Ch. Craiglyn Caledonian. Caledonian was owned by Mrs. J. G. Parker-Tucker, and is behind many of the Uniquecottage Cairns of this day. Caledonian was later imported to the United States by Colonel and Mrs. MacSparran. Carol produced Ch. Bayberry of Wolfpit and Ch. Boysenberry of Wolfpit for Lydia Hutchinson.

Ch. Tidewater Master Gold, shown in his historic Group First at the 1988 Westminster show under noted Cairn Terrier authority Mildred Bryant. Linda More handled Master Gold for owner Charles Merrick III. John Ashbey.

The current standard bearer for Wolfpit in the show ring is Ch. Caledonian Berry of Wolfpit (Ch. Pinetop Paperchase ex Ch. London Berry of Wolfpit). His current record through 1993 includes five All-breed Bests in Show, eighteen Group Firsts and numerous other placements.

Tidewater

The Tidewater Kennels of Mr. and Mrs. Charles Merrick, in Cockeysville, Maryland, has housed many truly superb Cairns. The Merricks have long been discerning importers, bringing in only dogs that seem to blend beautifully with their own stock to produce one good one after another. The epitome of the Tidewater accomplishments thus far is Ch. Tidewater Master Gold. The breed's top winner to date has won sixteen Bests in Shows, fifty-six Group Firsts and 302 Bests of Breed. This dog was ably piloted by Linda More, who is now building a career as a respected judge. "Eddie" won the Terrier Group over an outstanding field at Westminster in 1988 under breeder-judge Mildred Bryant. This was the first time this honor has ever gone to a Cairn, and it was an exciting moment for Cairn Terrier fanciers everywhere.

In recent years, Tidewater has imported several influential dogs from Uniquecottage Kennels in the south of England. One, Ch. Seneley Captain Poldark of Uniquecottage, finished his American championship handily and has sired nicely for Tidewater. The bitches Ch. Uniquecottage Platypus and Ch. Uniquecottage Phainopepla have been successful additions to the kennel as well. Two Phainopepla offspring, Ch. Tidewater Cloth of Gold (by Poldark) and Ch. Tidewater Fairway Gold (by Ch. Tidewater Black Gold), have also made the grade for the kennel. Ch. Tidewater Fairway Gold is the dam of Ch. Tidewater Royal Gold by Ch. Tidewater Master Gold.

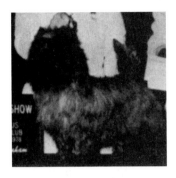

Ch. Gayla Cairns Gregor McKim, bred, owned and handled by Nancy J. Thompson, a Best in Show winner. Earl Graham.

After the rewarding campaign of Master Gold, Mr. Merrick imported Ch. Uniquecottage Gold Grouse, which is both an English and an American Champion. Gold Grouse was also shown by Linda More, and did very well in the show ring, amassing twenty-one Group Firsts and numerous other placings. In a historic move, Gold Grouse was allowed to return to his breeder in England after his successful American campaign. His sire Ch. Uniquecottage Gold Diver had died, and Mrs. Parker-Tucker needed the bloodline back in England. It is fortunate that Grouse sired some lovely puppies in the United States before he returned to his homeland.

Gayla Cairns

In 1954, Nancy Thompson finished her first bitch, Ch. B. Cube's Spunky, which she co-owned with Dr. and Mrs. B. B. Bagb Jr. of the B. Cube's prefix. Since then her very successful kennel, Gayla Cairns, based in Black Mountain, North Carolina, has accounted for more than 130 homebred champions. The topper for Gayla Cairn has been Ch. Gayla Cairn's Gregor McKim, with a record of ten Bests in Show and fifty-three Group Firsts. Nancy and Greg were the 1 team for Cairns in all systems in 1979. One of Nancy's earlier successes was Ch. Gayla Cairn's O'Tilly, which won two Bests in Show and twenty-four Group Firsts. "Tilly" was owner-handled to all of her wins, at a time when Cairns seldom placed in or won Groups and Cairn bitches were rarely campaigned.

Ch. Gayla Cairn's Davey (Ch. Pledwick Lord Frolic ex Ch. Gayla Cairn's Hope), is one of the breed's top all-time producers, with twenty-nine champions, while his great granddaughter, Ch. Gayla Cairn's Nora (Ch. Gayla Cairn's Grey Knight ex Ch. Gayla Cairn's Forget-Me-Not), holds the breed record for top producing bitches, with twenty-two

Ch. Woodmist Legacy, owned by Virginia Cadwallader. Kurtis.

champion offspring. And indeed, Ch. Gayla Cairn's Hope (Ch. Tartan of Melita ex Ch. Gayla Cairn's Little Lynda), Davey's dam, is the fourth all-time top producing bitch, with twelve champions. Hope is sired by Ch. Tartan of Melita ex Ch. Gayla Cairn's Little Lynda. Gayla Cairn has exerted a truly potent influence upon the breed with intense quality continuing to emerge from Nancy Thompson's successful efforts on behalf of the breed.

Woodmist

The Woodmist Kennels of Virginia Cadwallader began in 1963. Her first dog show was an instant success, as her Balkaren Dickie Duff O' Bel-Jay went Best of Breed over specials, and on to Fourth in the Group.

On her first venture to Chicago, where the national Specialty was held at the time, the aforementioned Betty Stone volunteered to help the novice Mrs. Cadwallader groom her Cairn.

Virginia has come a long way since that time. She has had so many good ones that it is hard to chronicle them. More than forty Cairn champions have graced the kennels of Woodmist.

Her most influential dog would have to be Ch. Wyesider Grey Knight (Eng. Ch. Lofthouse Geryon of Mistyfell ex Lordly Greyling). Grey Knight was also a grandson of Eng. Ch. Blencathra Milord. Grey Knight when bred to Ch. Caithness Lyric, a Rufus daughter, produced Ch. Woodmist Grenadier, and in a later breeding, Ch. Woodmist Moonpenny Daisy. Grey Knight bred to Ch. MacLadds Thistle produced Am. & Can. Ch. Woodmist Talisman.

Grey Knight also produced Ch. DeWinters Duncan, owned by Mrs. Cadwallader. His dam was Bel-Jays Belinda Belle. Duncan produced several lovely animals bearing the Woodmist prefix, among them Ch. Woodmist Grey Wren, owned by Mr. and Mrs. James Huber, Ch. Woodmist Willow and Ch. Woodmist Meadow Hawk. Hawk's dam was Ch. Woodmist Morning Glory. Hawk's son, Ch. Woodmist Grey Cavalier, was by Ch. Woodmist Grey Heath. Cavalier, when bred to Ch. Woodmist Morning Glory, produced Ch. Woodmist Vixen. Other noteworthy Duncan offspring were Ch. Woodmist Penelope, Ch. Woodmist Scarlet Star, Ch. Woodmist Meadow Lark and Ch. Woodmist Willow. Duncan sired a total of seventeen champions. Mrs. Cadwallader never kept a son of Dun-

can, finding that his bitches were bet-
ter; however, I kept a Duncan son, Ch.
Cairmar Call to Arms, a Best in Show
winner and sire of fifteen champions.
Cairmar Chandra Te was Call to
Arms's dam, and she was by Ch.
Tradorohgs Dunstan Claymore ex Ch.
Cairmar Stormie Dawn, a Ch. Caith-
ness Barnabas daughter out of Ch.
Tradorohgs Connamarah. Jamie
Abhalter also kept a Duncan son out
Ch. Woodmist Replica of Echo,
Ch. Coralrocks Boney Maloney, which
also earned a Best in Show and has

Ch. Cairmar Cantie Croftee, bred and owned by Betty Marcum. Morry Twomey.

sired nine champions. Echo was a granddaughter of both Ch. Cairnwoods
Golden Boy and Ch. Wyesider Grey Knight.

Mrs. Cadwallader did some very successful line breeding, using Grey
Knight as the foundation. Grey Knight died in 1981 at the age of sixteen.

In 1980 at the CTCA national Specialty at Montgomery County, Mrs.
Cadwallader saw Ch. Ferniegair Fearnought. She found him to be a beautiful animal, and she sent Vixen to him for breeding. Vixen produced Ch.
Woodmist Polly Flinders and Ch. Woodmist Tiger Lily. Woodmist Gillyflower, when bred to Fear-nought, produced Ch. Woodmist Bold Badger.

In the late 1980s Mrs. Cadwallader bred Ch. Woodmist Legacy (Ch.
Woodmist Bold Badger ex Ch. Woodmist Tiger Lily) to a Duncan grandson, Ch. DeRan A Call to Excellence. Call to Excellence was by Ch. Cairmar Call To Arms ex Ch. DeRan Heat of the Moment, a Ch. Whetstone
Halston granddaughter. The result of this breeding was Ch. Woodmist
Highland Falcon. Falcon was then acquired by Susan and Rudy Millward,
and is siring very nicely for them at the time of this writing. To the breed's
benefit, the Woodmist tradition and quality is being carried on.

Cairmar

Like many other people, I wanted a Cairn the first time I saw one. A
friend of mine, Yvonne Pomaineville Sage, had been given one as a gift,
purchased from Mildred Bryant. The first significant Cairns purchased by
my husband and myself were Ch. Tradorohg's Connamarah, already the
dam of three champions, purchased from Mildred Bryant, Caithness Periwinkle and Caithness Barnabas, purchased from Betty Stone. My significant interest in the Caithness bloodlines began after seeing Cairnwood's
Margaree, owned by Molly Wilder, in the ring. Margaree had the head
piece that I think is representative of a quality Cairn, broad top skull,
deep-set eyes, short broad muzzle and small well-placed ears.

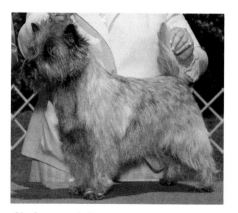

Ch. Cairmar Call To Arms. Cott/Francis.

Ch. Cairmar Bobby McLin. Missy Yuhl.

It was not until I purchased Caithness Periwinkle that I was able to put a point on a dog, competing with the commanding figure of Maxine Beam, who was showing dogs for both Mildred Bryant and Bertha Rae Lain. When I finally beat her under Lee Murray, it was the finest day of my life! I regard Maxine Beam with great affection today and respect her as much as any person, but she is the one person in dogs who has the capacity to reduce me to the equivalent of a quivering jellyfish!

Ch. Tradorohg's Connamarah, "Stormy," when bred to Bertha Rae Lain's Ch. Croftee of Raelain, produced the first Cairmar homebred, Ch. Cairmar Cantie Croftee. "Happy" was Winners Dog at the CTCA national Specialty in Chicago, in 1972, from the six to nine months puppy class, under the late Ann Stevenson. This was a great thrill for me. When I called home and told my husband that we owned the Winners Dog and Best Puppy in Sweeps at the parent Specialty, he asked me which dog I had bought!

Ch. Caithness Periwinkle, who carried Dorseydale and Uniquecottage blood, among others, became the dam of eight champions.

Barnabas produced thirty-three champions. This gave us a good start. Connamarah produced twelve champions—six by Barnabas, three by Ch. Caithness Colonel, one by Croftee, and two by Am. & Can. Ch. Tradorohg's Dunstan Claymore, CDX.

It is said that the strength of a kennel is in its bitches, and this was certainly so with Cairmar. Ch. Cairmar Miss Chance (Ch. Croftee of Raelain ex Milbryan Colonel's Lady) produced three outstanding champion sons, Ch. Cairmar Chance Quest, a Group winner, whom we kept, Ch. Cairmar Grand Chance (Ackerson and Fulkerson) and Ch. Cairmar Fighting Chance, a Best in Show winner, owned by Kitten Cary. These dogs were from two different litters, both sired by Dunstan Claymore.

Connamarah, bred to Barnabas, produced Ch. Cairmar Stormie Dawn. Her daughter Chandra Te, by Dunstan Claymore, outcrossed to Virginia Cadwallader's Ch. DeWinter's Duncan, produced Ch. Cairmar Call To Arms. I put a Best in Show on "Charger" in April 1981 at the Memphis KC. After that win, I gave "Charger" to Judy Webb for a time, and she won several more Groups with him. "Charger" bred to Ch. Cairmar CoCo Chanel, a litter sister to Ch. Whetstone Halston, produced Ch. Cairmar Courtesan,

Ch. Cairmar Cowardly Lion. Kohler

which when bred to Ch. Cairmar Bobby McLin, bred by JoAnn McLaughlin, produced Ch. Cairmar Cowardly Lion, the top winner to date for this kennel. This line has produced all the Cairmar house dogs, and we intend to keep this going! Because Dorothy Higgins had such an interest in obedience, her Tradorohgs Cairns were known for their sensitivity and intelligence. This continues with each successive generation, so that they and their offspring are always a joy to live with.

After the acquisition of Barnabas, I was influenced by the book *Planned Breeding*, written by Lloyd Brackett. This book began as a series of articles written for *Dog World* by this famed breeder of the Longworth German Shepherd Dogs. It espouses the theory "let the sire of the sire be the grandsire on the dam's side." These articles were so well received that they were bound in paperback form, and are cherished today by those lucky enough to possess a copy.

I employed Mr. Brackett's theory in my own breeding program. After the successes with Barnabas, I began looking around for a suitable stud for Barnabas's get, and the next generation as well. I settled on Ch. Tradorohgs Dunstan Claymore, CDX; Barnabas was a Ch. Caithness Fay's Falcon grandson, and Dunstan Claymore was a son of Falcon.

Barnabas was the correct size, a little straight behind, and a little steep in shoulder, but very well balanced. Dunstan Claymore was a bigger dog, with more reach of neck, length of leg, better shoulder layback and rear angulation, but both possessed exceptional balance. The two stud dogs complemented each other, so I felt sure the cross would be a good one, and it was! Dunstan Claymore produced fourteen champions, eleven bearing the Cairmar prefix, and twelve having been homebred.

Our move to Mississippi due to my husband's business put us in a spacious new home with the potential for me to breed and kennel as many Cairns as I could take care of. I decided to turn my attention to professional handling, having been licensed by the American Kennel Club to show dogs for others.

I had a very good run as a handler with many clients putting a great deal of faith in me, and I finished more than fifty Cairns for other breeders. I took it as a genuine mark of faith for other breeders to trust their stock to me and always tried my best to be worthy of that trust.

The week of May 21–27, 1978, was a great one for Cairmar Kennels. We had sent Ch. Cairmar Fighting Chance to Kitten Cary in California, to be shown by Doug Rodwell, and Ch. Cairmar Fancy Dresser had gone to Mr. and Mrs. Barnes in Texas, to be shown by A. J. Tremont. Fancy Dresser went Best in Show on May 21 at the Nolan River KC, under Anne Rogers Clark, and again on May 27 at the Baton Rouge KC, under Nial Koonts; Fighting Chance took a Best in Show in the middle of the same week in the Northwest.

We also imported several bitches from England, breeding them to both Call To Arms and Halston and then crossing the resulting offspring with good results. Among the imports were Ch. Avenelhouse Plain Jane and Ch. Greetavale Golden Vow of Courtrai. Golden Vow was a Robinson Crusoe daughter ex Eng. Ch. Greetavale Super Honey, and Jane was by Bankfoot Devoran (Ch. Redletter Moonstruck ex Ch. Delia of Bankfoot) ex Avenelhouse Tumbler. We also imported Caryshader Seriema (Uniquecottage Bush Chat ex Avenelhouse Lotus Bird), which we later sold to Mike and Cathy Hebert of Ariel Kennels. Seriema was Winners Bitch at the national Specialty in Louisville in 1983, under Edd Bivin. Seriema was bred to Halston and produced the lovely bitch Ch. Ariel Amadan O'Cairmar, who I purchased. She has produced very well and her offspring include Ch. Cairmar Talk Of The Town, owned by Cricket Hendricks; Ch. Cairmar Tara O Wilde Oaks, owned by Mary Lou Wilde; Ch. Cairmar Take No Prisoners, and his sister Cairmar Steel Magnolia; and Ch. Cairmar First Mate.

In 1987 Cairmar returned home to Texas from Mississippi. Cairmar Cowardly Lion had been born and was to become the standard bearer into the 1990s, garnering eight Bests in Show, fifty-one Group Firsts and numerous other Group placements. "Leo" was shown by both Bobby Peebles and his partner Craig Osborne, in 1988 and 1989. Judy Webb then showed Leo to seven Bests and thirty-five Group Firsts in 1990, her final year as a handler, and Leo's last year on the campaign trail.

Cairmar Kennels has bred more than 130 champions. The twenty-five years I have been associated with Cairn Terriers have been great fun for me and my husband, Joe. We have met many wonderful people and dogs along the way, and I wouldn't have missed all those experiences for anything.

Whetstone

Whetstone Cairns have followed the Wilder family life from Kansas to California to Missouri to their present location in Virginia. Molly Wilder's first Cairn was purchased from Betty Stone, Caithness. This was the aforementioned Cairnwood's Margarec. "Maggie" was shown by Vic Boutwell, a successful handler in the Midwest at the time, and now a well-respected judge. The Wilders' next Cairn, Solo of Highhedges, was purchased from Jim and Kay McFarlane. Solo did his winning on personality, always shown on a swivel lead to keep from tangling himself into oblivion. Solo finished very quickly, and all his life wanted to go to the dog show anytime the car was loaded. "Maggie," far prettier, was not easy to finish, since she did not particularly like dog shows.

Ch. Cairmar Connecticut Yankee, owned by Molly Wilder, was Best of Winners and Best Opposite Sex at the Trinity Valley Specialty under Betty Hyslop, handler Betty Marcum. Maurice McGinnis.

Maggie needed only a major to finish when the family moved to California, and Molly entered her in the Northern California Specialty, which was to be judged by Mildred Bryant. Molly's fondest dog show memory is of Maggie being selected from the large group of open bitches, put into a corner and finally Molly realizing that this was indeed, "the good pile." Eventually Maggie went on to win five points, owner handled.

Molly's first homebred champion was Woody MacRuff of Highhedges (Solo ex Maggie). Then she contacted Cairmar in her search for an additional bitch. Upon receipt of photos of three available puppies, she

Ch. Whetstone Jack Tar (Ch. Karengary's Wind Spirit ex Ch. Whetstone Wild Heather). Cott/Daigle.

Ch. Whetstone Fair 'N' Warmer was Best of Opposite Sex at the Trinity Valley Specialty under Girard A. Jacobi. She was owner-handled by Lynne Nabors for breeder Molly Wilder. Pegini.

Ch. Pinetop Piccadilly (Craiglyn Minstrel Boy ex Craiglyn Curiousity), owned by Molly Wilder. Pegini.

put them on the kitchen counter and allowed her children, Andy and Beth, to select the new puppy. They picked the little black one!

Soon to be Ch. Cairmar Connecticut Yankee, "Cindy" was sired by Ch. Cairnwood's Quince ex Ch. Milbryan Killarney O'Cairmar. I would have never sold this bitch to anyone else, but in Molly's letter she mentioned that she was looking for something that went back to the Caithness bloodline. Since the moment I first saw her Margaree, I really found the type I sought, so I was very sympathetic to this request. In this time frame the family moved to St. Louis. "Cindy" was specialed for a short time, garnering numerous group placements, handled by me, and winning the Texas Specialty under Elise Untermyer.

Cindy was also a producer, with eight champions to her credit including the all-champion litter of four by Ch. Cairmar Fancy Dresser. Molly first saw "Danny" when I asked her and Beth to take him to the CTCA national Sweepstakes in Louisville, when I was unable to attend. Molly really liked this youngster, and later bred "Cindy" to him. The four were Ch. Whetstone Halston (Marcum); Ch. Cairmar CoCo Chanel (Marcum); Ch. Whetstone Miss Dior (LeClair); and Ch. Whetstone Annie Hall (Nita Anderson Haas). These littermates all did well in the showring. Miss Dior also finished her championship with Winners Bitch at Montgomery County, at the CTCA national Specialty, under Louis Auslander.

Another outstanding offspring of "Cindy" was Ch. Whetstone Fair 'N' Warmer, CD, by Ch. Rockwell's Little Chap. Sonny was owner-handled by Lynne Nabors to Winners Bitch at the Trinity Valley Cairn Terrier

Club Specialty (Texas) under Girard Jacobi, to Winners Bitch at the CTCA Specialty in Chicago, and Best of Opposite Sex at the CTCA in Louisville, under Edd Bivin.

Halston won the Specialty in 1986, under Sandra Goose Allen, from the Veterans' class, handled by me. He was co-owned with Dr. Álvaro T. Hunt, of New Orleans. This Veterans class included Ch. Cairnlea's Robson, Ch. Foxgrove Jeronimo and Ch. Coralrocks Clancy Maloney, among others. It was delightful to watch this class of great older gentlemen, all of whom had had good show careers and were exerting their influence over the breed as forceful stud dogs.

Molly's daughter Beth showed Cindy that day in the Brood Bitch class with Halston and Fair 'N' Warmer as her get. Truly, it was a day of the best kind of memories. Cindy will long be remembered for the type and showmanship she stamped on her get.

This kennel also has a Best in Show winner, Ch. Whetstone Jack Tar, handled by Judy Webb.

Ch. Brehannon's Graylan Drummer, a noted winner during the 1980s, was owned and handled by Ken Kauffman throughout his distinguished career. Cott/Francis.

Jack Tar is out of another good homebred bitch, Ch. Whetstone Wild Heather (Ch. Cairnwoods Fiver ex Ch. Cairmar Connecticut Yankee). Her other two champions are Ch. Whetstone Sportin' Life (Rogers) and Ch. Whetstone Sailor's Delight (Nita Anderson Haas). Whetstone imported from Sally Ogle Ch. Pinetop Picadilly, shown going Winners Bitch at the National Specialty held in Dallas, under Barbara Keenan, handled by me. Molly is currently approved to judge Cairns and West Highland White Terriers.

When asked about great dogs outside her kennel that had influenced her thinking, Molly mentioned Ch. Cairnwoods Quince and Ch. Cairnwoods Golden Boy.

Ken Kauffman at Montgomery County.

Brehannon

The Brehannon Kennels, of Ken Kauffman and Jack Freidel, is located just north of Philadel-phia, and was established in 1975 with the purchase of Lord Duffer McBriar Rose and Heather's Misty Morn from the Moonstar Kennels of Jeannie Shellheimer. Both were sired by her English import Ch. Redletter Moonstar Turn.

The male, "Duffer," did not turn out to be of show quality, but he and Mr. Kauffman did establish themselves in the obedience ring, a little-known fact about Ken Kauff-man, who is now making himself known as a Terrier judge. Duffer earned his American CD, CDX and a Canadian CD, with five Highs in Trial. This is quite a feat for a Cairn Terrier, considering the breed's independent nature! Duffer, owned and handled by Ken Kauffman, was the top Cairn in obedience in the United States for the years 1976 and 1977.

"Heather," when bred to Marianne Ham's Ch. Maricairn Apollo's Casper, produced the first homebred Brehannon champion, Ch. Brehannon's Wee Bit Of A Brogue.

In 1977, Brehannon acquired Ch. Cairmar's Leslie, and in the same year brought into the kennel Ch. Ramblewood Stormy O'Moonstar. Both bitches finished handily and proved themselves in the whelping box as the foundation for the Brehannon Cairns to follow.

Leslie, bred to Ch. Cairncrest Tuffy, produced Ch. Brehannon on the Rocks, Winners Dog at the Potomac and Housatonic Cairn Terrier Club Specialties in 1980. Stormy was bred to Ch. Caithness Barnabas, and pro-duced Ch. Ramblewood Barney Brehannon. "On the Rocks" was bred to Gray Newman's Scottish import, Ferniegair Kirsty, and produced Ch. Brehannon's Graylan Drummer. "Drummer" was Winners Dog, Best of Winners at the CTCA national Specialty in 1982 and Best of Breed at Montgomery County the following year. Drummer went on to become 1 Cairn in 1983 and 2 in 1984 on the *Terrier Type* system. Drummer's record stands at seven Group Firsts and thirty-three other Group placements. Best of all, Drummer was always owner handled.

Drummer's daughter, Ch. Brehannon Codbank Pizazz, produced littermates Ch. Brehannon's Demon Drum and Ch. Brehannon's Barefoot Boy. "Demon" also established himself as a winner, finishing his championship with three five-point wins, all at Specialties, Potomac, Housatonic and CTCA at Montgomery County, in 1985. He returned to win Best of Breed in 1986 at the two regional Specialties, Potomac and Housatonic.

In 1982, Ch. Marywilf Held Ramsom, bred and co-owned with Mary Desloge, brought Foxgrove and Oudenarde lines into the Brehannon establishment. This bitch produced Ch. Brehannon's Marywilf Mac, Ch. Brehannon Ransom Paid and Ch. Brehannon's Tuff Guy, as well as Chs. Brehannon's Marywilf A'Hellin and Brehannon's Marywilf Hellion. Hellion was Winners Dog at the CTCA national Specialty held in Atlanta, and also at the Potomac Specialty. Ransom Paid was bred to Ch. Brehannon's Hi Stakes Gambler, producing Chs. Brehannon's Mista Rhett and Miss Scarlet, the standard bearers for the Brehannon prefix at this writing.

Brehannon has produced more than twenty champions since its inception, and has consistently ranked among the toppers in Group competition. Drummer has sired fifteen champions at this stage in his career as a stud dog.

Mr. Kauffman is among the talented Cairn breeders who are also trying their hand at judging. He is currently approved for sixteen Terrier breeds, and is demonstrating the same expertise in the judging ring that he has already proven in breeding and showing Cairns.

Mr. Kauffman holds the belief that part of his contribution to the Cairn Terrier breed will be seen in the aspect of grooming. He believes that trimming the Cairn into a more stylized look, while still maintaining the general rough outline, has helped the Cairn in competition at the group level. Mr. Kauffman's exceptional wins in the strong eastern competition, owner handled, certainly gives credence to his comments. The fact that he is also a very talented artist underscores his aesthetic perceptions.

Copperglen

Charles and Carol Ackerson's small but select kennel began in St. Louis, Missouri, in 1970 with the purchase of two puppies. Huck Finn Here We Go Again completed his championship in 1972, with a Best of Breed, handled by the Ackersons' young son, Mark. As with most beginners, the Ackersons set out to educate

Ch. Cairmar Barberry Lass. Carrier.

Ch. Copperglen Fame N Fortune.

Ch. Bold Oaks Maxwell MacGregor, owned by Susan Dees Vaughn. Fox & Cook.

themselves about this breed, studying type, temperament, balance and movement.

They obtained Cairmar Barberry Lass, "Bobby," from me. This bitch quickly obtained her championship and became the cornerstone for Copperglen. Bobby was bred to Ch. Cairnwood's Golden Boy, and produced Copperglen's Caper. "Caper" did not enjoy the showring, but she was a quality producer. Bred to Ch. Cairmar Grand Chance, she produced Ch. Copperglen Tartan Tweed. Bred to Ch. Whetstone Halston, she produced Ch. Copperglen British Sterling, Ch. Copperglen Cinnabar and Copperglen Charlie. "Charlie," when bred to Ch. Cairmar Devil's Advocate, produced Copperglen Willing N' Able, the sire of Ch. Copperglen's Fame N Fortune, the top winner of this kennel to date. Fame won five Group Firsts, several Specialties and was Best of Opposite Sex for all three shows on the Montgomery weekend in 1986. In 1987 Fame was Best of Opposite Sex at Devon and Hatboro, and Best of Breed at Montgomery County. She was 1 Cairn bitch in 1987 and 1988.

Fame went on to produce well for the Copperglen banner. Bred to Ch. Cairmar Scot Free, she produced Ch. Copperglen Great Attraction, who, when bred to Ch. Foxairn Tinman, produced Ch. Glenarden Debut Attraction, co-owned with Denny and Arlene Vinson, and Ch. Copperglen Claim To Fame, "Cally." When bred to Ch. Cairland Brycairn Leg-acy, Cally produced Ch. Copperglen Simply Sinful (Rebecca Stamps) and Ch. Copperglen Silhouette (Carter and Ackerson). Fame was next bred to Ch. Sharolaine Kalypso, and produced Ch. Copperglen Foxtrot, co-owned with Louise Hooper. Foxtrot followed in her dam's footsteps with numerous Group and Specialty wins and was the 1 Cairn bitch in the United States 1991 and 1992.

The breeding to Kalypso also produced Ch. Copperglen Lindy (Buesing and Ackerson) and Ch. Copperglen All That Jazz (Scherbarth and Ackerson). A second breeding to Kalypso has produced Ch. Copperglen Windwalker, co-owned with Mr. and Mrs. William Ham. Windwalker completed his championship on the Montgomery weekend in 1993. In 1994 he captured the breed at the Potomac Specialty under breeder-judge Ken Kauffman, and Best of Breed at Old Dominion, under breeder-judge Molly Wilder.

Dees

Susan and Clarence Vaughn are carving out quite a niche in the Cairn Terrier fancy. Until his retirement, William Trainor presented the Dees Cairns at shows all over the Northeast, and the

Ch. Dees Comanche (Ch. Bold Oaks Maxwell McGregor ex Ch. Dees Miss Kilbride), a Best in Show winner bred and owned by Susan and Clarence Vaughn. Tatham.

handling skills of the Vaughns augmented those of Mr. Trainor, resulting in many successes. The Vaughns now use Peter Green as their handler. The days of the large kennels are almost gone. It is nice to see the Vaughns able to maintain the number of dogs necessary to constantly maintain a string of good ones in the showring.

Susan started by obtaining Lady Brandilere in 1971 from Venita and Donald Ross. This bitch is the foundation of the kennel and appears in many of its pedigrees today. This kennel is a stronghold of English imports, with judicious additions of American dogs. The Vaughns are establishing a very strong type, which is a combination of much of the best from both countries. The Vaughns have in recent years imported from Lynwil, Uniquecottage, Hearn and other prominent English kennels. Several Cairns are producing well for them, including Ch. Bold Oaks Maxwell MacGregor, sire of seven champions. The English import Ch. Lynwil Cavalier has sired eight champions, and the kennel also houses Ch. Dees Just Call Me Angel, dam of eight champions.

During the past five years there has been a Vaughn-sponsored Cairn in the top ten every year. Ch. Dees Comanche won a Best in Show in 1991, and Ch. Dees Dust Devil won a Best in Show in 1994.

Dees is responsible for thirty-four homebred champions since its inception in 1971, and remarkably, twenty-nine of those were finished between 1988 and 1993.

Ch. Lakewood's Snapshot Studley, owned by Dr. and Mrs. B. E. Satterwhite and handled by Nell Stumpff, was a Best in Show dog during the early 1980s.

Lakewood

The Lakewood Kennels, located in Warner Robins, Georgia, began with Nell Stumpff's interest as a child in the family pets. She recalls that they taught her much more than she taught them. The idea of someday breeding dogs stayed with Nell through the years of raising three children. Finally, with the acquisition of Ginger Mist of Merriwood from June Streibel, the dream began to come true. Her first litter by Ch. Cuttie Sark Scotch Whisky produced Ch. Lakewood's Grey Boy, Ch. Lakewood's Tiger Tank and Ch. Lakewood's Raggedy Ann.

Nell next decided to use our Ch. Caithness Barnabas. The Ginger-Barnabas breedings provided Lakewood with nine champions, including Ch. Lakewood's Barnstormer.

Next Nell imported from Mr. Walter Bradshaw, Redletter Moonbeam, alias "Willie." Willie was top producing sire in 1980 and his kennel mate, Ginger Mist of Merriwood, was top producing dam for the same year.

Over the years, Nell has continued to combine the bloodlines of Melita, Caithness, and Redletter, with some considerable success. To date, Nell has bred well in excess of ninety champions, and many have earned foreign titles as well.

Nell's son Jim competed in junior showmanship and put a CD on Lakewood's Indian Legend, again proving that the dogs can provide sport for the entire family.

Lakewood has produced several Group winners, among them Ch. Lakewood's Buffalo Bill, Ch. Lakewood's Constellation and Ch. Lakewood's Satellite. The Best in Show winner for this kennel to date is Ch. Lakewood's Snapshot Studley, owned by B. E. Satterwhite, D.V.M.

Chapter Seven

The Cairn Terrier in North America

THE UNITED STATES

Annwood

In 1967, Susie Armstrong purchased a Cairn Terrier for her ten-year-old daughter, Bitsy, and Annwood Cairns began. As Susie's involvement with Cairns grew, Bitsy became her student, then her partner, and ultimately her heir.

Annwood has remained small, so that all the Cairns could live as family pets. Cairn fanciers who helped Susie included Martha Brewer, Betty Hyslop, Audrie and Charles Norris, and Nell Stumpff.

Susie imported Am. Ch. Oudenarde Flying Flirt (Eng. & Am. Ch. Toptwig Fly-By-Night of Oudenarde ex Oudenarde Sea Romance) and Redletter Honeymoon (Eng. Ch. Redletter Moon Tripper ex Ch. Redletter Midsummer), and set out to combine the wonderful qualities of these two outstanding kennels.

Flirt was first bred to Ch. Lakewood's Sir Echo, a dog carrying a strong Redletter influence. This breeding produced Ch. Annwood King's Highwayman, the first homebred champion. Flirt was then bred to her half brother, Eng. Ch. Oudenarde Sea Hawk, owned by Betty Hyslop. From this breeding she retained Annwood Jenny

Ch. Annwood Quicksilver (Annwood Knolly's Knave ex Redletter Honeymoon) with Susie Armstrong. Thacker.

Ch. Benway State Of The Art, owned by Patsy Wade. Sara Nugent.

Ch. Bold Oaks Play It Again Sam (Ch. Sulinda Samson of Worrindale ex Eldomac Moon Mist), owned by Bill McFadden. Lewis Roberts.

Kiss'd Me, which was outcrossed to Ch. Whistle Gate Glen Fiddich, producing Ch. Annwood Memerlin, CD. Merlin has sired seven champions, is obedience-titled and also excels at working terrier trials.

Mrs. Armstrong's declining health curtailed activities at Annwood in the mid-1980s, and she died in December 1989. However, the line has been continued by Bitsy, through Annwood Moonspinner and her daughter Annwood Ain't She Sweet.

Benway

Jack and Patsy Wade acquired their first Cairn, Ch. Dugan Aberystwyth of Benway, in 1978. Next they added Ch. Chelsea of Raelain and Ch. Cairmar Party Crasher. They then acquired the English import, Am. Ch. Avenelhouse Sixpence, who I imported from Hazel Small and later sold to Patsy. Sixpence, when bred to Dugan, produced Ch. Benway State Of The Art. This truly remarkable bitch won her first Group at six months of age, in 1984. She went on to win multiple Groups and Specialties and was No. 1 Cairn bitch, all systems, 1986, and also ranked No. 4 and No. 5 in the intersex systems for the year.

State Of The Art received an Award of Merit at the 1992 CTCA national Specialty from the Veteran Bitch class. This was the first year in which these awards were given.

Patsy Wade has devoted her considerable talents to the art of handling. She and Judi Hartell have shown a number of winners, not confining themselves to Terriers.

Bold Oaks

Bill McFadden's interest in Cairns dates from 1971, when his mother purchased two Cairns as pets. Bill's interest in dog shows dates from his high school days. He purchased two Cairns from Eldomac Kennels of Eldon and Erliss McCormack, who were professional handlers, located in Yakima, Washington, Bill's home town. The McCormacks showed Cairns for Melita Wood, among others, and bred those bloodlines, which Bill then acquired.

Eldomac Moon Mist was bred to Am. & Can. Ch. Sulinda Samson of Worrindale, owned by Bill and Stella Newby. Three of this litter of four finished their championships including Am. & Can. Ch. Bold Oaks Play It Again Sam, Bill's first big winner. "Sammy" won three Bests in Show in Canada and eleven Groups in the United States. One of his best offspring was Ch. Bold Oaks Booker T, shown by his eleven-year-old owner Michelle Stump to Best of Breed at the Cairn Terrier Club of Northern California Specialty and many other noteworthy victories. Sammy produced three champion daughters, Ch. Howdy's Serendipity Lil Mo, Ch. Howdy's Serendipity Wee Win and Ch. Col-Cairns Ruffy Righinn. These three bitches account for many champion descendants.

Bill owned Lil Mo, and when bred to Ch. Coiltrag Master MacGregor, she produced Ch. Bold Oaks Maxwell MacGregor, later sold to Susan Dees Vaughn. Bold Oaks has been responsible for thirteen champions, but has curtailed breeding activities, since Bill's very successful handling career now takes so much of his time.

Bill showed many dogs for the late John Green (Loch Katrine) and successfully specialed Ch. Karengary's Indian Giver for him. Later, Bill specialed Susan Dees Vaughn's Ch. Bold Oaks Maxwell MacGregor. He followed with Ch. Goosedown's Tailor Made. Tailor was co-owned by Bill and Pat Hassey and Lyn and Frank Hickey. Tailor's daughter, Ch. Tigh Terrie's Hello Dolly was the next and won very well for the Hickeys.

Bramblewood

The Bramblewood Kennels of Ken and Chris Carter started with the acquisition of Roylaine's Bramble Bee, purchased in 1981. Bramble was descended from Clanranald and Glenmacdhui breeding. Bramble produced two champions from her first litter by Ch. Cairmar Fancy Dresser, Ch. Bramblewood's Cat Dancing and Ch. Bramblewood's Kit Kat. Kit Cat finished her championship in 1994, to be the fifty-first champion for Fancy Dresser. Cat Dancing went to Janet Brady in Arizona, and Kit Kat remained in Colorado with the Carters. Although both Cat Dancing and Kit Kat did finish their championships, Bramblewood's Bob Kat was the first

Ch. Bramblewood's Kit Kat, handled by seven-year-old Taylor McFadden. Missy Yuhl.

Ch. Copperglen's Sparrow Hawk (Ch. Copperglen Windwalker ex Ch. Copperglen Simply Sinful), owned by Chris and Ken Carter and bred by Carol Ackerson and Chris Carter. Cott.

homebred to finish. "Little Bob" finished from the puppy class, with several nice Specialty wins. He won a Group at fifteen months of age, owner handled, and placed in many other Groups as well.

The Carters were very impressed with the Ch. Cairmar Fancy Dresser's bloodlines, and concentrated on those lines for some time. Fancy Dresser, "Danny," was sired by Ch. Dapper Dan of Wildwood ex Ch. Cairmar Fancy That. They were also attracted to the Copperglen Cairns, and purchased a co-ownership in a daughter of Ch. Copperglen Fame N Fortune, Ch. Copperglen Claim To Fame. A grandson of Claim To Fame, Ch. Copperglen Sparrow Hawk, a striking young dog, is starting to make his mark in this extremely competitive family.

Bramblewood has produced fourteen champions, including two Group winners. Ch. Bramblewood's BMW, when bred to Ch. Fillkatom's Pride And Joy, produced Ch. Coach's Watch Those Sparks, a Best in Show Winner. "Sparky" was bred by Jan Cherry and shown by Bill and Georgia Harris.

Brightridge

The kennels of Mrs. T. C. Fritz, of Kingsport, Tennessee, began in 1964 with the birth of the first Brightridge litter. The dam was Dustee of Templand, linebred on Mrs. R. T. Allen's Craigdhu line. Dustee's sire, Ch. Craigdhu Spoofer, traces back to the Tapscot line. Dustee was bred to MacDuff of Hemlock, and the first litter produced Mr. Chiquapin of Brightridge and Cindy Lou of Brightridge. Bernice Fritz then purchased Woody's Warbler of Melita, from Melita Wood in Canada, who became the first Brightridge champion. Cindy Lou was bred to Ch. Caithness Chervil, a half brother to Ch. Caithness Rufus, and this breeding produced Brightridge Amber.

Mrs. Fritz combined Amber, Warbler and Wee Acre Judy for her foundation stock. Judy traces back to the Blarneystone line in Scotland. Amber was the granddam of Brightridge Bonny Lad's Caper, Best Puppy CTCA

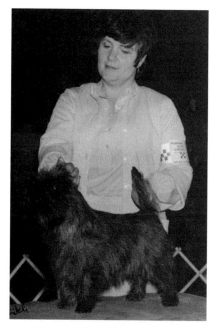

Ch. Chairmar Fancy Dresser, owned by Mr. and Mrs. William T. Barnes, and shown with breeder Betty Marcum. Van Sickle.

Chasands Yankee Peddler. Earl Graham.

Sweepstake 1971 in Chicago under Betty Hyslop. Both Amber and Caper produced five champions.

The acquisition of Ch. Chasand's Yankee Peddler in 1980—a Fancy Dresser grandson that also claimed Ch. Tammy of Mistyfell as his great-grandsire on the dam's side—was a good decision on the part of Mrs. Fritz. "Yankee" was Best of Winners at the CTCA Specialty at Montgomery County in 1980. In 1983, Yankee won the national Specialty in Louisville, Kentucky, under Edd Bivin.

Cairland

Cairland Kennels, owned by Glenna Barnes, was established in 1978 with the acquisition of the aforemetnioned Ch. Cairmar Fancy Dresser. Danny was very capably shown by A. J. Tremont to two all-breed Bests in Show, five Group Firsts and numerous other placings. Danny has proved his outstanding value to the breed through his contribution as a stud dog. His record of siring fifty-one champions to date ties the all-time record of his great-grandsire, Ch. Cairnwood's Quince. Danny has also produced a Best in Show son, Ch. Terriwoods Best Dressed.

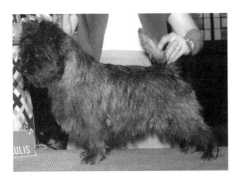

Ch. Chasands Mighty Avenger, owned by Glenna Barnes. Petrulis.

Danny also produced two all-champion litters of four, one out of Ch. Cairmar Connecticut Yankee, owned by Molly Wilder, and the other out of Ch. KiKu's Bouncing Bonnie, owned by Tom and Karin Godwin. In 1989, a Danny great-grandson, bred by Betty Race, Ch. Ollie North of the Highlands, was Best of Breed at the CTCA Specialty in an entry of two hundred!

In February 1981, Cairland acquired Ch. Chasands Mighty Avenger (Ch. Foxgrove Jeronimo ex Ch. Whetstone Miss Dior). "Mikie" finished his champion-ship under the guidance of Dora Lee Wilson, was campaigned for two years, and earned more than ten Group Firsts. He was No. 1 Cairn Terrier in 1984.

Sadly, Mikie died young, but sired nine champions, among them Ch. Cairland Airtight Alibi, Ch. Highland Chatter, Ch. Cairland Blaze Of Glory and Ch. Cairland Brycairn Legacy, "Alfie," which also died at an early age.

Ch. Cairland Fast Talker, bred by Jan Epting, was purchased by Betty Baker and campaigned extensively by Gary Doerge. "Graucho" won thirty Group Firsts, and many other Group placings.

Cairncroft

Michael and Sandra Murray began showing Irish Setters in 1966, and after having a family, turned to the Cairn Terrier as a small, manageable dog that the children could also show. The Murray family purchased their first Cairn in 1979. Betty Cooper, a longtime Scottish Terrier breeder, helped them import Pinetop Gold Dust in 1982 from Sally Ogle. "Dusty" became an American champion easily, and has gone on to produce well. All Cairncroft champions learn to hunt and earn Certificates of Gameness from the American Working Terrier Association. Cairncroft Iron Horse won the 1992 CTCA Sweepstakes under Carol Ackerson.

Cairnwoods

The Cairnwoods Kennel originated in 1961. It is owned by sisters Luanne K. Craco and Jane K. Dalger. Luanne and Jane purchased their first bitch in 1961 from Elizabeth Horton of Crofters Kennel. Their second bitch, Crofter's Heidare Jarre Sue, was purchased in 1964. This bitch, bred to Ch. Caithness Rufus, produced Ch. Cairnwoods Golden Boy, a lovely show dog and sire of eighteen champions. During these early years, a growing friendship began between the two sisters, Luanne and Jane, and Verna Carlisle and Betty Stone. This friendship enabled the Cairnwoods breeders to purchase from Betty Stone Caithness Gracenote, a double Rufus daughter. Gracenote bred to Golden Boy produced Ch. Cairnwoods Quince, sire of fifty-one champions. This breeding also produced Ch. Cairnwoods Jamerson, Ch. Cairnwoods Margaree and Cairnwoods Ayrdrie. Ayrdrie, when bred to Virginia Cadwallader's Ch. Wyesider Grey Knight, produced among others Ch. Cairnwoods Fiver. Fiver enjoyed much success in the showring, but again,

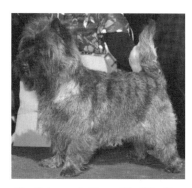

Ch. Cairnwoods Fiver (Ch. Wyesider Grey Knight ex Cairnwoods Ayrdrie), owned by Jane K. Dalger and Luanne K. Craco. Ashbey.

he was more influential as a stud dog. Producing eighteen champions, and bred to only fifteen bitches, his influence is still felt in the breed today. Noteworthy descendants include his daughter, Ch. Tigh Terrie's Buttons 'N Bows (ex Ch. Col-Cairns Ruffy Righinn) and her daughter, Ch. Tigh Terrie's Hello Dolly, by Ch. Goosedown's Tailor Made, bred by Lyn and Frank Hickey, who was Best of Breed at the national Specialty at Montgomery County in 1993. Another noteworthy descendant is the grandson Ch. Whetstone Jack Tar, by Ch. Karengary's Wind Spirit ex Ch. Whetstone Wild Heather, bred and owned by Molly and Beth Wilder, a Best in Show winner.

Chesapeake

Pam Pettus's first show Cairn came from the kennels of Mary Desloge in Virginia, in 1986. She was named Chesapeake Mary Wilf Rand (Ch. Mary Wilf Radiant Ray ex Mary Wilf Ms. Elizabeth Taylor). Chesapeake was adopted as a kennel name since "Chessie" was born on Chesapeake Bay. Attending her first Specialty, the Potomac Cairn Terrier Club, as a spectator in 1987 was the start of something big for Pam. She was fascinated with the dogs and how they were presented, and enjoyed meeting other people who loved Cairns.

In June 1987, following a move to Iowa, Pam and her partner, Marilyn Rhodes, decided to look for another bitch. This time they acquired Cairmar

Ch. Chesapeake Rising Son O'Scot, a noted multiple Best in Show dog handled by Christi McDonald. Petrulis.

Bobby's Girl (Ch. Cairmar Bobby McLin ex Ch. Cairmar Kitten on the Keys).

Both bitches finished in the spring of 1989. "Chessie" was bred to Ch. Cairmar Scot Free. Ch. Chesapeake Bit O'Scot resulted from that breeding and was retained by his breeders. "Doc" has been quite a winner for the Chesapeake banner. In March 1991, at the Trinity Valley Cairn Terrier Club under breeder-judge Ken Kauffman, Doc was Best of Winners and his littermate Chesapeake Sassi Kassi was Winners Bitch. Kassi is owned by Edd and Cathy Miller. Both were five-point wins, and the other littermate, Chesapeake Black Velvet, owned by Kay Boyett, also won her class. Kassi was Winners Bitch under breeder-judge Jack Smith, at the Cairn Terrier Club of Denver, May 1992, and Doc was Best of Opposite Sex at the same Specialty. Doc earned a Specialty Best under Betty Moore at the Sumac Cairn Terrier Club Specialty in 1993.

Bobbie was bred to Ch. Cairmar Winston O'Lincairn, producing Ch. Chesapeake Rendition In Red, owned by Helen Hislop in California. Bobby was then bred to Ch. Cairmar Scot Free, and produced Ch. Chesapeake Rising Son O' Scot, a multiple Best in Show winner.

Coralrocks

Jamie Abhalter received a Cairn Terrier as a twenty-third birthday gift, and has been with the breed ever since. Some ten years later, Jamie and Bob Abhalter moved to Florida and acquired another Cairn Terrier. Jamie tried showing this puppy, with little success, and decided to breed her to Virginia Cadwallader's Ch. Woodmist Grenadier. This breeding produced the first Coralrocks champion, Sparky Maloney. Jamie practiced her grooming on her first Cairn, trying many different looks until she managed to set her own grooming style. During this period, Jamie also purchased Woodmist Replica of Echo. Replica was twice bred to Ch. DeWinter's Duncan, and produced Ch. Coralrocks Bonnie Maloney, a Group placer and dam of five champions. Replica also produced Ch. Coralrocks Boney Maloney and Ch. Coralrocks Georgia Bell. "Boney" was destined to win a coveted all-breed Best in Show and many Terrier Groups. He ranked in the top ten in 1979, 1980 and 1981, and was also a top producer. Replica, when bred to Ch. Cairnwood's Fiver, produced Ch. Coralrocks Clancy Maloney, another successful campaigner, and Ch. Coralrocks Mike O Ragamuffin.

Ch. Coralrocks Boney Maloney (Ch. DeWinter's Duncan ex Ch. Woodmist Replica of Echo) enjoyed a successful show career and became a Best in Show winner guided by handler Pete Clay. Earl Graham.

Ch. Coralrocks Bonnie Maloney produced Ch. Coralrocks Kiti Maloney and Ch. Coralrocks Pippin Maloney. These were by Ch. Cairnwood's Fiver. Pippin, when bred to Ch. Woodmist Bold Badger, produced an all-champion litter of three, Ch. Coralrocks Miss Tiffany and Chs. Blaircairn Coralrocks Rory and Tory, co-owned with Ann Shuler Blair. Rory and Tory also competed as a brace and were twice Best Brace in Show. Rory was campaigned and ranked in the top ten for three years.

Cragcastle

Jennie Willis purchased her first Cairn, Rogue Rob Roy, from a pet shop, and together they earned his CDX degree. While Jennie was showing in obedience, she met Nancy Thompson, Martha Brewer and later Virginia Cadwallader; all were willing to share their considerable breed knowledge with Jennie.

Jennie then purchased a bitch from Nancy Thompson, Gayla Cairn's Cutty Sark, who when bred to Ch. Admiral Hornblower of Melita produced Ch. Cragcastle Tartan, CD, who lived to be twenty years of age.

Later, Jennie purchased Woodmist Persimmon, who earned her championship title, and produced well for Jennie.

Jennie showed and bred less as her two sons grew. When she again became active, she turned to Cairmar Kennels, using the Best in Show winners Ch. Cairmar Call to Arms and Ch. Cairmar Cowardly Lion, as well as the top producers Ch. Whetstone Halston and his son, Ch. Cairmar Scot Free. The Cragcastle bitches niched very well with the Cairmar studs, and produced well for Jennie. Cragcastle Queen Elizabeth, a Halston daughter, has eight champions to date, with others nearing their titles. Ch. Cragcastle Great Scot, the first Group winner for this kennel, and his littermate, Ch. Cragcastle Royal Scot, are by Ch. Cairmar Scot Free ex Queen Elizabeth.

Feldspar/Old Orchards

Feldspar was established in 1972 with the acquisition of Ch. Woodmist Grey Heath (Ch. Woodmist Talisman ex Kamidon Mariposa), purchased from Virginia Cadwallader. This bitch produced several champions, and provided the foundation for Feldspar.

Ch. Old Orchard's Big Shot (Ch. Cairngorm's Adonis ex Ch. Jiminy's Ima Pistol of Bonnieview), an influential stud, was a Ch. Cairnwood's Golden Boy grandson out of a bitch who claimed Eng. Ch. Lofthouse Geryon of Mistyfell as a fifth generation

Ch. Feldspar's Destiny, bred and owned by Susan Vertz-Millward. Booth.

grandparent four times, through Ch. Wy-esider Grey Knight and Loft-house Columbine. "Big Shot" became a beloved house pet after becoming a champion and has produced ten champions.

With the acquisition of Am. & Can. Ch. Woodmist Highland Falcon (Ch. DeRan A Call To Excellence ex Ch. Woodmist Legacy) from Mrs. Cadwallader in 1992, Rudy and Susan Vertz Millward's small kennel comes full circle. Falcon, who claims Ch. Wyesider Grey Knight as his great-great-grandsire and is twice the great-grandson of Am. & Can. Ch. Ferneigair Fearnought, continues the legacy of the Woodmist Kennels.

Gamac

In 1964 Ann McDonald purchased a dog with Milbryan bloodlines to establish her Gamac Kennels. Ann next obtained Ch. Gamac Mr. Tuffy of Milbryan from Mildred Bryant, who subsequently exerted a strong impact on her breeding program.

Three obedience Cairns came along next, Gamac Peach Brandy, Milbryan Heathertip and Ch. Milbryan Mr. McTippy. "Mr. Tuffy" was a Ch. Caithness Colonel son, and sired Gamac Weebita Scotch, dam of Ch. Gamac A. Percynality, a multiple Group winner, shown by A. J. Tremont. A 1978 move to Houston limited breeding activities until 1986, when the McDonalds returned to the Dallas area.

Since returning Mrs. McDonald has produced Ch. Gamac Wind Dancer, which shows much promise.

The Gamac Cairns have been handled to a great extent over the years by Ann's daughter, Christi. Christi spent several years apprenticing with Bobby Peebles and Craig Osborne, and is now handling on her own.

Ch. Gamac Wind Dancer, owned and bred by Ann McDonald. Luis Sosa.

Glenarden

Dr. Dennis and Arlene Vinson's Glenarden Kennels, located in Springfield, Illinois, began with the 1990 purchase of Flickwynds Devoted Dr. Watson, who found his niche in obedience competition. The next acquisition was Ch. Copperglen Great Attraction (Ch. Cairmar Scot Free ex Ch. Copperglen Fame N Fortune), co-owned with breeder Carol Ackerson. Eventually, this bitch was bred to Ch. Foxairn Tinman and produced Glenarden Debut Attraction, "Aggie."

At six months, Aggie was Winners Bitch at the CTCA

national Specialty, 1991, handled by Carol Ackerson. The judge was another well-known breeder, Molly Wilder. At the Chicago Suburban Cairn Terrier Specialty in June 1992, she won Best in Sweeps under the author in a lovely entry, and Winners Bitch under still another breeder-judge, Lydia Coleman Hutchinson.

Aggie finished at sixteen months, becoming the first homebred Glenarden champion. At nineteen months of age, she went on to win Best of Breed at the CTCA national Specialty, held with Montgomery County in 1992, under Mrs. Patricia Breach, handled by Arlene Vinson. This was Aggie's first show as a special.

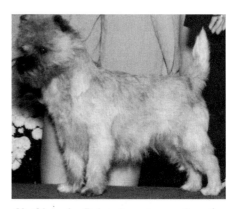

Ch. Glenarden Debut Attraction was Best of Breed at the CTCA Specialty held with Montgomery County, 1992, under Patricia Breach, Hearn Kennels, England. It was "Aggie's" first show as a champion and she was handled to this good win by Arlene Vinson. Asbey.

Glenmore

Bob and Louise Hooper started with Great Danes. Louise stated that her efforts in Danes were based on trying to breed up from average stock. She feels that the first Cairn they purchased, Ch. Cairmar Shadow Box Image, was a good start. She finished her championship with some nice wins, and then produced six puppies in two litters. Five of the six were owner handled to their championships. Three earned Winners Dog or Winners Bitch at regional Specialties. These

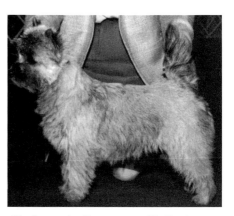

Ch. Copperglen Foxtrot, owned by Louise Hooper. Kohler.

included Ch. Glenmore Michael Angel O, Ch. Glenmore Heaven Sent, Am. & Can. Ch. Glenmore Rusty Angel, Am. & Can. CDX, owned by Susan Ensley and Ch. Cairmar Rhikki of Glenmore, owned by Pat deNeui, all by Ch. Cairmar's Infernal Angel. She also produced Ch. Glenmore Betsy McCall, by Ch. Whetstone Halston.

The Hoopers then added Skerryvore Kiera, by Am. & Can. Ch. Jodian's Tar Macadam ex Am. & Can. Ch. Skerryvore Ceilidh O'Kaird, CG to their kennel, and later Ch. Copperglen Foxtrot, by Ch. Sharolaine's Kalypso ex Ch. Copperglen Fame N Fortune. Foxtrot is co-owned with Carol Ackerson. Both finished their championships easily, and Foxtrot went on to some very nice wins, including five Group Firsts, twenty-five other Group placings, seventy-five Bests of Breed, four Specialty Bests of Breed and four Bests in Sweepstakes as a puppy.

Goosedown

The Goosedown Kennels of Bill and Pat Hassey began in 1986. There have been truly remarkable accomplishments from this kennel in such a short time. The Hasseys bought one Cairn for companionship. This first Cairn, later a champion, The Goose's Gus, was purchased from Marcella Cobb, Misty Meadow Kennels. Pat also recalls learning from Kay Dunham, Clan Makaw's, Marilyn Swearingen, Meriwynds', and Julia Hague, Kisncairn.

By 1987, the Hasseys finished Gus under a breeder-judge at the Southern California Specialty. They had also acquired Ch. Joywood's Elegant Elsie, and were co-owning Joywood's Tiger Lily with Barbara McNamee, Joywood. Tiger Lily was bred to The Goose's Gus. This breeding was repeated in 1988, producing Ch. Goosedown's Tailor Made, the first Goosedown homebred champion. Tailor came from a litter of six, and showed considerable early promise. He fulfilled that promise by finishing his championship at only ten months of age in Texas on the Trinity Valley CTC Specialty weekend. In June 1989, under English breeder-judge Mrs. Linda Firth, Tailor was Best of Breed at the CTCSC, and repeated the win the next day at the KC of Beverly Hills.

Since it was now apparent that Tailor was indeed special, Bill McFadden, a Cairn breeder and now a successful professional handler, worked out a partnership for the Hasseys with Lyn and Frank Hickey. Under Bill McFadden's guidance, Tailor won three national Specialties, eight regional Specialties, several Groups, numerous placements and was retired at the Santa Clara Valley KC with a Best in Show victory.

Tailor has also been proving himself as a stud dog, with eleven champion get so far, and more enroute. His daughter, Ch. Tigh Terrie's Hello Dolly, followed in his footsteps with an impressive string of wins since her campaign began in 1992, including Best of Breed, CTCA, at Montgomery County in 1993.

Ch. Goosedown's Tailor Made, owned by Bill and Pat Hassey.

Happicairn

In 1969, Susan Wofsey perused the dog books in Bloomingdale's and then went to a pet shop in her Manhattan neighborhood to order a Cairn Terrier. "Angus the Pooh" suffered five seizures the night he was purchased, but survived this early rough start in life, and eventually obtained a CD. In 1972, Susan attended Westminster, and there met Betty Hyslop. In April of that year, she purchased Cairndania Brigrey's Dorcy, who became her first champion in 1974. Dorcy bred to Ch. Caithness Reginald produced Ch. Happicairn Nutmeg, and Happicairn Cinnamon, CD, who went on to a career in advertising as a model, earning national recognition as the first "Kibbles 'N Bits" TV and print dog.

Ch. Foxgrove Mutt, imported and owned by Susan and Jack DeWitt. Gilbert.

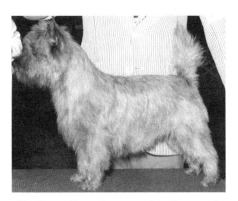

Ch. Pinetop Paperchase, owned by Susan and Jack DeWitt. Chuck Tatham.

Susan, under the Happicairn banner, has finished sixteen champions and earned three CDs. In 1980, she married Jack DeWitt who is well known for his Rhapsodale Wire Fox Terriers. With Jack's support, Susan purchased Ch. Foxgrove Mutt, imported by Peter Shea. "Mutt" has sired fourteen American champions. In 1986, the DeWitts imported Pinetop Melissa from Mrs. Sally Ogle, and in 1987, Pinetop Paperchase. Both these imports finished their American titles in style, and Chase has sired eight champions to date. These include Ch. Caledonian Berry of Wolfpit, a multiple Best in Show winner, and Ch. Dees Dust Devil, a multiple Group winner, with a Best in Show in 1994.

The DeWitts recently acquired Avenelhouse Just Joey from Hazel Small's final litter before her retirement.

It is interesting to note that the Happicairn/Rhapsodale Kennels and the Foxairn establishment share an interest in the same breeds. The DeWitts run Cairn and Wire Fox Terrier puppies together for exercise in supervised paddocks, and enjoy the interaction between the two.

Ch. Hearn Thunder Thighs with Martha Brewer.

Heathcairn

When Carl Brewer gave his wife, Martha, a Cairn Terrier puppy for Christmas, his gesture brought them both into a whole new world. The Cairn was selected because it is such a natural breed—no tail docking, no ear cropping and no overly involved grooming. "Tiny Tim" went to a few dog shows, and then was retired to pet status. Soon afterward the Brewers purchased Catescairn Conquest, who had just gone Winners Dog at Westminster. The Brewers and Heathcairn were on the way to becoming one of the strong but select kennels of the time. Their Heathcairn Cuthbert won the Terrier Group at the International Kennel Club of Chicago. Cuthbert was the first Cairn to win the Group at this show. At the time, the International was one of the largest shows in the United States and, understandably, this win is one of Martha's favorite memories.

One of the best bitches to come from this kennel was Ch. Heathcairn Charlie. Heathcairn also acquired Ch. Hearn Thunder Thighs, imported by Don Robbie. This magnificent dog produced well. Mrs. Brewer currently maintains one dog in her home, Ch. Heathcairn Jennifer, a Thunder daughter, and a granddaughter of Charlie.

Those who were fortunate enough to be present in 1983 at the national Specialty in Louisville were entertained at Martha Brewer's elegant country estate with tremendous amounts of food and the music of an antique steam calliope.

Holemill

Of the kennels of interest to pedigree enthusiasts, one of the foremost must be that of Don Robbie. Mr. Robbie, a renowned designer of mens' fashion apparel, has traveled extensively and has a wealth of Cairn Terrier knowledge to share. His frequent travels to England in the early 1960s gave him the opportunity to learn from many respected breeders. Over the years, Mr. Robbie has consistently demonstrated his eagerness to share this knowledge.

Mr. Robbie's first import was Redletter Miss Choice, the last daughter of Eng. Ch. Redletter McJoe, out of Eng. Ch. Uniquecottage Sir Frolic's litter sister, Redletter Miss Muffit. He then imported Am. Ch. Pledwick Lord Frolic, who later went to the Arringtons, in Georgia, and Pledwick Lady Frolic, by Eng. Ch. Redletter MacBryan. Then came Lofthouse

Velvet, Am. Ch. Sunnybrook Lee Tarquin, Am. Ch. Hearn Thunder Thighs, who went to Martha Brewer, Am. Ch. Petersden Bright Spark and Ch. Hearn Hellbender, who lived with Laura De Vincent and Ch. Hearn Bourbon, who went to Mr. and Mrs. Ray Clarke. Later came Glenbrae Appleson, co-owned with Mary Andregg and Glenbrae Pioppo.

In 1961, in Mr. Robbie's second litter came Holemill Easterly Haar, who won the CTCA Sweepstakes under the highly respected Colonel Whitehead of Scotland. A win of this magnitude seems to ensure continued interest, and such is certainly the case with Mr. Robbie, as he continues to import today, more than thirty years later.

Don Robbie with three Holemill Cairns.

Mr. Robbie also bred Ch. Holemill Velvet Blazer, a grand dog, twice Best of Breed at Westminster. Mr. Robbie was able to use a different concept from that of many breeders. Due to his frequent trips to England, he kept several bitches there and had them bred to the best studs, the resulting progeny being imported to the United States. Among these were Am. Ch. Holemill Applejack and Apple Pie, by Dormerhall Applecatcher. Some of his favorite crosses include using get tracing back to Ch. Blencathra Sandpiper and Ch. Uniquecottage Sir Frolic.

Joywood

Joywood Kennels of Barbara and Larry McNamee is located in Milwaukie, Oregon. The McNamees began with the purchase of Ch. Graystone Fairborn Flame, "Reggie," in 1980. Within a year they co-owned Ch. Meriwynd's Twink with Marilyn Swearingen. Reggie is a grandson of Ch. Oudenarde Sea Hawk on his sire's side, with lines to Ch. Cairnwood's Golden Boy and Ch. Wyesider Grey Knight on his dam's side. "Twink" was tightly bred on lines going back to Eng. Ch. Redletter McJoe, through Eng. Ch. Craiglyn Cavalier, and also Ch. Blencathra Elford Badger. In the first litter produced by these two was Ch. Joywood's Molly McGee. Molly, when bred to Ch. Bold Oaks Booker T, produced Joywood's Abigail McTavish. Abigail was bred back to her grandsire, "Reggie," and produced Ch. Joywood's Tiger Lily, co-owned with Pat

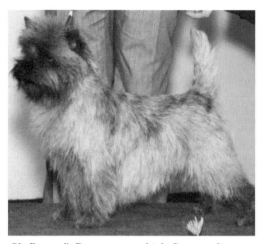

Ch. Joywood's Donovan, a multiple Group and Specialty winner and a successful sire. Callea.

Hassey, and the dam of Ch. Goosedown's Tailor Made. Molly bred to Ch. Gadget's Gimmick of Wolfpit produced Am. & Can. Ch. Joywood's Donovan, Am. & Can. Ch. Joywood's Merry Noel and Ch. Joywood's Elegant Elsie, owned by Pat and Bill Hassey. Donovan was campaigned by Bill McFadden in the late 1980s, and was a top-ten Cairn for two years. He is a multiple Group winner, and won the CTC of Northern California in 1990. Donovan has produced fourteen champions to date. This small but select kennel has had a considerable impact on the breed.

Karengary

Karen and Gary Wilson bred both Irish Setters and Airedales before becoming interested in the Cairn. Their first Cairn, Ch. Strike Up The Band of Wolfpit, was Winners dog at the CTCA Specialty in 1978. The Wilsons established a very good relationship with John Green of Loch Katrine Kennels, who purchased Ch. Karengary's Indian Giver. Indian Giver became an important winner in the hands of Bill McFadden and

Ch. Karengary's Indian Giver, owned by John Green and bred by Gary and Karen Wilson, established a strong record in all-breed and Specialty Competition and was also a successful sire. Mike Lidster.

also proved to be a successful stud dog, having sired eleven champions. The Loch Katrine efforts were ended with the untimely death of John Green in 1989, but his dogs' bloodlines have been maintained by Linda Cooley, Snorkis Kennels, among others.

Karengary's Wind Spirit sired Ch. Whetstone Jack Tar, a Best in Show winner, thereby establishing another achievement for the Wilsons. Karen is yet another Cairn breeder trying her hand at judging, and is currently approved for Airedale, Cairn, Soft Coated Wheaten and West Highland White Terriers. She judged Cairn dog classes at Montgomery County in 1992, a highly coveted honor.

Kishorn

Anna Lee Rucker's Kishorn prefix is taken from the name of a lake in Scotland, "a spot so beautiful it takes your breath away." Ms. Rucker established a considerable niche for herself by matching her feisty, tightly bred Ch. Ymir's Kris Kringle of Kishorn (Ch. Cairnwoods Quince ex Ch. Scot's Heather of Ymir) and the talents of an excellent handler, Judi Hartell. Kris and Judy had several years of winning for Ms. Rucker. Next Judy showed Ch. Kishorn's Rush Hour. "Rusty" was later shown by Bobby Peebles.

After Kris and Rush Hour were retired, Ms. Rucker approached the author about a dog to campaign. The ensuing partnership resulted in the very successful campaign of Ch. Cairmar Cowardly Lion, from 1988 through 1990. Later we would team up to campaign Ch. Chesapeake Rising Son O'Scot during 1993 and 1994, in conjunction with his breeders Pam Pettus and Marilyn Rhodes.

Maricairn

Marianne G. Ham began her Maricairn Kennels in the early 1970s with Red Robin's Holly Berry, who carried Caithness bloodlines. This bitch was bred to Ch. Redletter Twinlaw Seaspirit to produce Ch. Maricairn Apollo's Casper, the first homebred champion. Marianne's interest during this time period lay with the Caithness and Redletter bloodlines.

Marianne was fortunate to acquire in 1985 Ch. Nightfalls Encore. Easily finishing her championship, this bitch went on to earn fifty Bests of Breed. "Cory" was Best of Opposite Sex at the CTCA national Specialty in 1989, 1990 and 1991, thereby retiring the Eng., Am. & Can. Ch. Redletter Miss Splinters Memorial Trophy, offered since 1976. Cory's strong win record earned her the ranking of No. 1 Cairn bitch in the United States for the years 1990 and 1991.

Ch. Maricairn Curtain Call, a Cory daughter, has continued in her dam's winning ways.

Maricairn acquired a co-ownership on Copperglen Wind Walker in 1993, and it will be interesting to follow his career in the ring and his impact on the Cairn Terrier gene pool. He is being shown by Bergit Coady.

Ch. Nightfalls Encore, owned by Marianne Ham. John Ashbey.

Ch. Copperglen Wind Walker, owned by Marianne Ham. Chris Meneley.

Ch. Mary Wilf Apache Fancy Dancer, owned by Mary W. J. Desloge. Dave Ashbey.

Mary Wilf

The Desloge family has loved Cairns since 1960, when they were living in London and owned Inisfail Lass. After a few false starts, the Desloges purchased Cairndania Sea Hawk's Hendy from Betty Hyslop. Mary Desloge showed Mary Wilf Jeronimo's Moon Rock, "Raymond," to his championship herself, an enjoyable time in her life. "Raymond" was then bred to Hendy and produced Ch. Mary Wilf's Radiant Ray, "Randy."

A Randy son, Ch. Mary Wilf Apache Fancy Dancer went Best of Winners at the three Shows, on the CTCA Specialty weekend, Devon, Hatboro and Montgomery County in 1991. The last time this "hat trick" occurred on Montgomery weekend was in 1979, when Ch. Fox-grove Jeronimo scored the same impressive wins. Significantly, Fancy Dancer is a great-grandson of Jeronimo, so the achievement has even more meaning.

Mary Desloge is a dedicated breeder with the tenacity that is typical of "earth dogs" and their people. When appropriate, she has used top handlers such as Peter Green and Peggy Ozorowski Browne with great success.

Nightfalls

The small, select kennel of Judy Irby began in 1972. One of her early standouts, a Ch. Caithness Rufus granddaughter, Ch. Nightfalls Minute Maid, finished owner-handled with a five-point win. When "Molly" was bred to Ch. Cairnwood's Quince, she produced an all-male, all-champion litter.

A Minute Maid son by Ch. Cairmar Chance Quest, Ch. Nightfalls Chance Encounter was Nightfalls Prime Time's grandfather. Prime Time, when bred to Ch. Annwood Memerlin, produced an all-champion litter of three bitches, Shine On, Tulsa Time and Merrily. She is also the dam of Finale and Encore, and produced a total of six champions. Her sister, Nightfall's Cool Change, made a difference for Roberta Perry with her Glen-Ayr Kennels. Cool Change produced several champions including Glen-Ayr Carbon Copy, Winners Bitch at the CTCA Specialty at Montgomery County, 1989.

Judy Irby had early experience with horses—hunters and cutting horses. Obviously this background has given her a deep appreciation for the tremendous importance of good, clean, driving movement, for it is seen in all her stock. She expects her Cairns to be keen and energetic, with good temperament and good health. Judy is particularly aware of the importance of good fronts, and how easy it is to lose them.

Of the Highlands

Betty Race began her kennel in Kansas in the late 1950s. Mrs. Race also bred German Shepherd Dogs at the time. The kennel became inactive in the late 1960s, and surfaced again in 1979, with the purchase of Ch. Cairland Bobby Dazzler, a Fancy Dresser son. Betty's most successful exhibit was Ch. Ollie North of the Highlands, Best in Sweepstakes, CTCA, 1988, and Best of Breed, CTCA national Specialty, 1989. Betty co-bred occasionally with Jonathan Jeffrey Kimes, who used the Whipshe prefix. Mr. Kimes has recently become approved to judge Cairn Terriers.

Ohioville

Ohioville, owned by Ralph and Ellie Buesing, is yet another small kennel that houses a number of outstanding Cairns. Among them are Ch. Ohioville Hooper and his son, Ch. Ohioville Rooster, both top-tenners. The Buesings were drawn by the rough-and-tumble attitude of the Cairn, and thought it would fit their lifestyle. Their dogs are all pets and enjoy hunting and being Cairns. The Buesings breed by the look of the dogs, at this point, considering that better for their program than attempting to limit themselves to pedigree only.

Recless

Lester and Sylvia Selcer began their kennel in 1969 with a combination of Blencathra, Redletter, Ugadale and Foxgrove. Their goal was to breed a good working-type Cairn. The Selcers fondly recall a conversation they had with the legendary Walter Bradshaw, in which they were told, "Cairns don't walk on their heads, that's why balance is so important. A good head is like the frosting on the cake." To enhance their

Ch. Ohioville Rooster, owned by Ralph and Ellie Buesing. John Ashbey.

breed knowledge, the Selcers spent three four-week periods in England studying the ancestors of their dogs and pedigrees back as far as possible. Much of this was accomplished with the help of Peggy Wilson.

The Selcers' kennel strength was in its bitches. Their top brood bitch was Ch. Ugadale Futurist, producing Ch. Recless Fantasia and Recless Kyle, the dam of Ch. Sharolaine's Kalypso, thus figuring in many current American pedigrees.

The Selcers retired to Florida in 1985 and, unfortunately, Les Selcer's death in 1988 brought about the closing of the kennel.

Redcoat

Although the first Cairn acquisition for the Redcoat Kennels of Jack and Karen Smith was an American-bred dog, Ch. Ragtime's Smitty Smith, bred by Elois Roll Renner, their foundation stock came from Great Britain. In 1981, the Smiths traveled to England, and after a meeting with Walter Bradshaw, were introduced to Linda Firth. As a consequence, the Smiths were able to acquire Cairngold Crackerjack. Crackerjack was one of the last dogs sired by Ch. Redletter Moonstruck. "Cracker" carried on the Redletter tradition in the United States by siring fifteen champions for the Smiths. Cracker's name can now be found in many American pedigrees. Also on this trip the Smiths acquired from Mrs. Hazel Small Avenelhouse Katy Darling and Avenelhouse Golden Harvest. "Harvest" was by Uniquecottage Bush Chat ex Eng. Ch. Avenelhouse Acrobat Bird.

Bergit Coady, the well-known California-based Terrier handler, imported Ch. Clayrig's Litzie from Sweden. She was bred to Ch. Cairmar Winston O'Lincairn. The Smiths co-owned Winston with Dr. H. J. Hislop and the author, and he was campaigned by Bergit Coady for two years. The Winston ex Litzie breeding produced Ch. Reanda's Britta at Redcoat, a lovely, sound, Group-winning bitch that was shown to many good wins in 1992 and 1993.

Two of the Smiths' great English favorites were Uniquecottage Gold Feather and Avenelhouse

Ch. Cairngold Crackerjack, owned by Jack and Karen Smith. Joan Ludwig.

Kings Guard. They saw them in the ring together in England, and have attempted to recreate this line in the United States. Ch. Redcoat's Harvest Moon and Ch. Redcoat's Moonlight Bandit are two of their successes.

The Smiths have recently imported another Cairngold dog, Cairngold Captain Jack. This dog claims as great-grandsires, Uniquecottage Treecreeper, Uniquecottage Bush Chat, Heshe Sun Buddy, Cairngold Kramer and Courtraé John Julius.

Ch. Reanda's Britta at Redcoat, owned by Jack and Karen Smith. Missy Yuhl.

Shin Pond

Laura De Vincent's kennel name, Shin Pond, comes from a lake of the same name upon which Verna Carlisle had a summer home.

Laura De Vincent was influenced by Kenneth MacBain, a Terrier handler. Mr. MacBain had read Verna Carlisle's articles about Cairns. He suggested Laura contact Verna, and eventually the two met. Verna owned a granddaughter of Eng. Champion Uniquecottage Sir Frolic.

Eventually Mrs. De Vincent met Don

Ch. Shin Pond Target, owned by Laura De Vincent.

Robbie who was importing dogs from England, his mentor being Hilda Manly of Lofthouse. She learned from Mr. MacBain and Mrs. Carlisle to concentrate on English bloodlines, particularly that of Ch. Dorseydale Tammy. From such greats as Ch. Hearn Thunder Thighs, Ch. Hearn Bourbon, Crondall Lovely Run, Hearn Hellbender and others comes the concentration on Tammy, which has produced such lovely animals as Chs. Shin Pond Rhodes, Tradition, Target, Cedric Devlin and Tradition Reflexion.

TangleVine

The TangleVine Kennel established by Carolyn Myers in Franklin, Tennessee, gathers its strength from a bitch purchased in 1986 from Nancy Thompson, Gayla Cairns Ura Dilly, "Pickles."

Pickles has produced Ch. TangleVine's PTO and Ch. TangleVine's Song and Dance, sired by Ch. TangleVine's Doug Flutie. PTO, or more familiarly "Crawford," won four Group Firsts, numerous other placements and forty-three Bests of Breed while being shown by Gary Doerge. Her next litter was by Gayla Cairns Perfect Blend, and all became champions.

Ch. Gayla Cairns Supercharge (Ch. Cairmar Call To Arms ex Gayla Cairns Loose Wheel), owned by Carolyn Myers.

They were Chs. TangleVine's Sydmonton, Johnny Rotten, Twisted Sister and Skyeclad. Skyeclad is owned by Nancy J. Thompson.

Carolyn then bred Gayla Cairns Loose Wheel to Ch. Cairmar Call To Arms, and got Ch. Gayla Cairns Supercharge. He finished his championship handily with several nice wins, including a Best of Breed over a large specials entry under breeder-judge Mildred Bryant. True to his name, this dog also demonstrated his aptitude in advanced obedience classes and agility.

Terriwood

Tom and Karin Godwin established their Terriwood Kennels in 1984 with the purchase of a bitch puppy from Kay Magnussen, Kiku Kennels. Kiku's Bouncing Bonnie, shown by Sara Osmonson, went on to become an American and Canadian champion, and produced very well for the Godwins.

While learning about pedigrees and the breed in general, the Godwins came to admire pictures of Ch. Cairmar Fancy Dresser, owned by Glenna Barnes. Eventually, a breeding between "Bonnie" and "Danny" was arranged.

This all-champion litter of four would be Danny's last. The litter included Ch. Terriwood's Best Dressed, winner of one Best in Show and eight Groups, and Terriwood's Artful Dresser, a Canadian Best in Show winner and winner of two Groups, owned by Joyce A. and Curt W. Whall. The others in this litter were Ch. Terriwood's Dressed In Style, owned by Malcolm and Joyce Sharp, and Ch. Terriwood's Dressed In Lace, owned by the Godwins.

The Godwins then acquired Ch. Cairland Brycairn Legacy from Mrs. Barnes. "Alfie" was by Ch. Chasands Mighty Avenger ex Cairland Party Doll, a Fancy Dresser daughter. Alfie was a grandson of Am. & Can. Ch. Foxgrove Jeronimo.

Bonnie and Alfie produced Am. & Can. Ch. Terriwood's Mighty Legacy, Am. & Can. Ch. Terriwood's Lasting Legacy and Ch. Terriwoods Texas Legacy.

Ch. Terriwood's Best Dressed, a Best in Show winner, owned by Tom and Karen Godwin.

Tigh Terrie

Lyn and Frank Hickey began in Cairns in the 1960s. Frank had a pet Cairn before the two married, and in 1966 he convinced Lyn that a Cairn Terrier would be the ideal addition to their home. Lyn had never owned a dog up to that time! Lyn bred this bitch a couple of years later, and enjoyed raising the puppies so much that she determined to do it again at the appropriate time in her life. To date, Tigh Terrie has bred twenty-five champions, and there are many more in the wings.

In 1979, Frank convinced Lyn to purchase a Westie. This one was from someone who showed and talked to them about showing dogs and put them in touch with Bill McFadden about getting a show-quality Cairn bitch. Bill whelped Col-Cairns Ruffy Righinn and sold her to the Hickeys. Ruffy had a successful show career, obtaining both her American and Canadian championships, and is currently ranked No. 3 top producing Cairn bitch of all time, with fourteen champion offspring. Ruffie's first breeding was to Am. & Can. Ch. Sulinda Samson of Worrindale. This produced six champions in a litter of seven. The second litter was by Ch. Foxgrove Mutt and produced four champions from a litter of six.

When bred to Ch. Cairnwood's Fiver, she produced Ch. Tigh Terrie's Buttons and Bows, "Scooter." Scooter won five-point-majors at the roving parent Specialty in Atlanta and at the CTC of Northern California. She was bred to Ch. Goosedown's Tailor Made; this breeding worked well for the Hickeys. It also fostered a serious interest in Tailor, resulting in a partnership between the Hickeys and the Hasseys to campaign him. Scooter's first litter included Ch. Tigh Terrie's Hello Dolly, the Best in Show standard-bearer for the Hickeys. Campaigned well, Dolly won the national Specialty in 1993, under the highly respected Anne Rogers Clark, and two regional Specialty Bests plus numerous Group placements.

I remember the first time I saw Tailor Made. Jim Reynolds, a longtime friend of Betty Hyslop and a Canadian all-rounder, told me that he had seen a spectacular young dog out with the veteran Terrier handler Denis Springer and asked if I had seen him. I hadn't, but I did see the dog on the Texas circuit in March 1988, and he was everything that I had been told. I looked at that dog at that time, and felt sure that if all remained well with him, he would forge his way to a CTCA

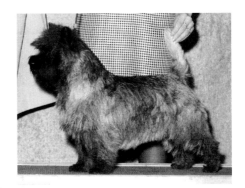

Ch. Tigh Terrie's Hello Dolly, a multiple Best in Show winner owned by Lyn and Frank Hickey. Luke Allen

Ch. Tweedsmuir's Piper's Tattoo, owned by John and Virginia Blankenhorn.

Specialty Best at Montgomery County under Edd Bivin in 1990. And he did.

Tweedsmuir

Virginia Blankenhorn had a very early start in the world of showing dogs. Her father, Dr. Frank Porter Miller, all-breed judge and president of the Kennel Club of Pasadena for fifty-four years, saw to that. He bred several breeds, including Airedale and Wire Fox Terriers, and introduced Virginia to the showring as a child. When Virginia was old enough to select a dog of her own, she decided on a Cairn. Dorcia Nutmeg was purchased from Frances Fertig, Dorcia Kennels. A great-grandson of Eng. Ch. Splinters of Twobees, Nutmeg had his greatest moment when he won Best of Breed at the prestigious Los Angeles Kennel Club show (now the KC of Beverly Hills) in 1941. The show was then held on the grounds of the Ambassador Hotel, was benched and had many movie stars in attendance, which provided a tremendous aura of glamour. Officiating on the day was Alva Rosenberg, one of the greatest dog judges that ever lived. Nutmeg's last show was at Palm Springs, on December 7, 1941. Virginia writes, "that infamous date put a halt to everything."

John and Virginia took time out after the war to raise children, but still maintained a Cairn her father had purchased for her while judging in New England.

For their return to showing dogs, the Blankenhorns selected Ch. Brigadoon's Marvelous Marty in 1983, as a small puppy. Marty finished his championship in six weeks, won the CTCNC Specialty, was in the top ten for two years and never left the state of California.

Marty sired Ch. Brigadoon's Binnie McBean, which, when bred back to her grandsire, Ch. Brigadoon's Pied Piper, produced the outstanding littermates Ch. Tweedsmuir's Piper's Tattoo and Ch. Tweedsmuir's John MacNab. Both these Cairns have won very nicely for the Blankenhorns, with prestigious breed wins at Beverly Hills and other equally important shows, and both have numerous Group placings including Tattoo's Group First under John Honig, May 2, 1992, at Mensona KC.

Whistle Gate

Whistle Gate Kennels was founded in 1957 by Commander Margaret Magee and was based on Ticehurst and Cairnvreckan lines, with the two dogs Ch. Ticehurst McEvan and Ticehurst Marsali.

McEvan was purchased at four months of age and was an immediate success at the start of his show career. Among his noteworthy wins was Best of Breed at the 1958 CTC of Southern California Specialty. When he was bred to Ticehurst Marsali, a dog and a bitch were kept from the resulting litter. These became Ch. Piper Dan of Whistle Gate and Ch. Whistle Gate Scouping Shoon, the foundation of six generations of Whistle Gate champions.

In 1972, Ch. Caithness Fay's Falcon (Ch. Cairnwood's Golden Boy ex Toptwig Fay of Caithness) was acquired from Betty Stone. Commander Magee refers to him as a dog she "could not resist." Falcon won two Specialties, and sired sixteen champions for Whistle Gate. Today his name appears in pedigrees across America and in other countries as well.

Falcon was bred to Ch. Whistle Gate Mairi Ban Og, a Rufus granddaughter. This breeding produced, among others, Ch. Whistle Gate Glen Fiddich II, purchased by Dr. Maxwell Krasno. Glen Fiddich II sired fourteen champions. Another champion from this breeding was Ch. Whistle Gate Red Falcon, who won three Specialties.

Another Falcon son was Am. & Can. Ch. Tradorohgs' Dunstan Claymore, CDX, which caught my eye. I persuaded Dorothy Higgins, Tradorohgs', to allow "Dusty" to live at Cairmar for a while, and he sired very well for me. The sire of fourteen champions, he was owner-handled to Best of Breed at the CTCA Specialty in 1975.

Falcon was the grandsire of Ch. Caithness Barnabas, the dog Betty Stone elected to send to me. Barnabas sired thirty-three champions for Cairmar, leaving his strong mark on the breed.

Wildwood

Bob and Diane Williams became interested in Cairn Terriers in the early 1970s. Both were very active in many sides of the breed. The Williamses handled their own dogs in the ring with great skill. They believed in linebreeding and in starting with excellent foundation stock from an established family and going forward. Therefore, they purchased a Quince daughter, Ch. Quince's Spunky of Wolfpit, and bred her to Ch. MacMurrich of Wolfpit, a Quince son. That breeding produced Ch. Dapper Dan of Wildwood. "Dandy," as he was affectionately known, was never campaigned as a specials dog, but gained enough attention from the classes so that he was modestly used at stud and became the sire of ten champions. His greatest contribution as a sire, which established him as a "Road Marker" in the breed's history, came when he was bred to Ch. Cairmar Fancy That. This breeding produced Ch. Cairmar Fancy Dresser.

Bob Williams greatly admired Ch. Milbryan Killarney O'Cairmar. He assisted Esther Coleman when Killarney was bred to Quince. At the time he expressed an interest in Killarney, if I should ever want to sell her. I eventually did place her with the Williamses. The repeat breeding to

Ch. Dapper Dan of Wildwood, owned by Robert and Diane Williams. John Ashbey.

Quince produced Ch. Tagalong of Wildwood. "Tessie" made her show debut going Best Puppy in Match at the Housatonic Cairn Terrier Club, and followed this win with Best in Sweepstakes and Best of Winners for five points at the Trinity Valley Specialty show in an entry of ninety-six. Tessie bred to Halston produced Ch. Killarney's Image of Wildwood, now owned by Gary Hess, and Ch. Fashion Tag of Wildwood, owned by Norman and Anne Campbell. "Tags" was Winners Bitch at the 1984 CTCA national Specialty. Tessie also produced Ch. Wagaway of Wildwood by Ch. Cairnwoods Fiver.

The Wildwood Cairns were consistent in type and always gave a good account of themselves in the showring. The Williamses are less active in breeding at this point, since Mr. Williams has developed a very successful business in antique books, photographs and other collectibles.

CANADIAN KENNELS

Cairngorlynn

Both Alan and Margaret McClory are from Scotland, and Alan's aunt owned a Cairn in Scotland. The kennel name derives from the names of the three McClory children: Karen (Cairn), Gordon (gor) and Lynne (lynn). This kennel was registered with the Canadian Kennel Club in 1965. In 1969, the McClorys purchased Iona of Highhedges from Barbara Hollings. Iona was bred to Betty Hyslop's Ch. Vinovium Errol Flynn and this breeding produced Ch. Cairngorlynn Kirsty O' The Brae. The McClorys acquired Ch. Vinovium Wayne from Mrs. Margaret Jagger of Bishop Auckland in England. Wayne produced Cairngorlynn Bunty O' The Brae and Ch. Cairngorlynn Red Ruffie, both good winners for the Cairngorlynn prefix. The McClorys purchased Ch. Carron Rhu Gaelic Cairngorlynn (Ch. Foxgrove Jaunty ex Ch. Ugadale Amazing Grace), which brought Foxgrove breeding into their gene pool. "Rhu," when bred to Ch. Foxgrove Jeronimo, produced Ch. Cairngorlynn Joy Cairndania, owned by Betty Hyslop. Cairngorlynn Rebecca Jean, owned by Edith Skellet, was bred to Ch. Rogerlyn Seahawk's Salty Sam, and produced Ch.

Cairnmoors Salty Sam's Sadie, owned by Ann Manning, who was Best in Sweeps, CTCA, 1980. Edith Skellett's Cairngorlynn Ruffie's Radar was judged Best Puppy at the same show.

Cairnmoor

Edith Skellet became a Cairn Terrier fancier in 1974 when her husband brought home a "rescue" Cairn. Charlie's owners were moving and could no longer keep their pet. He was seven years old when he came to the Skelletts, and lived to be fourteen. The Skelletts were newlyweds at that time, and had ten acres. "Charlie" seemed to be lonely, so a search for a companion resulted in Edith's first purchase, Cairnmoor's Ginger Snap.

Edith next acquired Cairngorlynn Rebecca Jean, who lived to be sixteen, from Margaret McClory. "Becky" produced Cairnmoor Salty Sam's Sadie, winner of the CTCA Sweepstakes in 1980 in an entry of 140! Edith had another Sweepstakes victory in 1982 with Cairnmoor Hogan Cairndania, co-owned with Betty Hyslop.

Becky also produced Cairnmoor Douglas's Dana, the first homebred Canadian champion for Edith.

Edith met Betty Hyslop in 1976, and credits her success to Betty's encouragement and guidance. Several dogs were co-owned between Edith Skellet and Betty Hyslop, including Ch. Cairnmoor T's Tige Cairndania and litter sister Am. & Can. Ch. Cairnmoor T's Tammy Cairndania.

Edith has also been very active in Canadian Cairn rescue, and was instrumental in organizing and operating the Canadian rescue service. Edith is still active in rescue, currently the chairperson for the Cairn Terrier Club of Canada, Ontario, and Eastern Regions Rescue, and liaison with the CTCA Rescue organization.

Skerryvore

The Skerryvore Kennels of Dick and Gloria (Chickie) Mair were registered in Canada in 1977, although Gloria has owned Cairns for most of her life. The Mairs' foundation bitch was Ch. Cairnorth's Mac Nighean (Am. & Can. Ch. Tycan's Ready Or Not ex Ch. Cairnorth's Perky Miss, CD). When bred to Am. & Can., Bda. Ch. Braebrair's Brody, she produced Am. & Can. Ch. Skerryvore Ceilidh O' Kaird and Am. & Can. Ch. Laird of Skerryvore,

Am. Can. Ch. Skerryvore Pipes of Pan, owned by Dick and Gloria Mair. Alex Smith.

CG. These two have produced well for the Mairs, and have also done very well in the showring.

A half brother/half sister mating produced Am. & Can. Ch. Skerryvore Grey Vixen and Am. & Can. Ch. Skerryvore Greyling, CG. Greyling bred to Am. & Can. Ch. Woodmist Highland Falcon produced Ch. Skerryvore Pipes of Pan and Ch. Skerryvore Peerie Flea. In 1994, "Pan" was Best of Breed from the classes at both the Cairn Terrier Club of Greater Detroit under English breeder-judge Mr. A. Arrowsmith, and the Chicago Suburban Cairn Terrier Club, under Sandra Goose Allen.

Worrindale

Stella Newby began her Worrindale Kennels with Wire Fox Terriers, and was a professional handler in Canada. Shirley Canfield was the first to ask Stella to show a Cairn, Can. Ch. Folly of Highhedges. Folly was subsequently bred to Wendanny Fionn, an English import, and this litter included Cannycairns Finnigan. Finnigan gave a good account of himself in Group competition in both the United States and Canada. Finnigan bred to Blynman Tuppence of Sulinda sired Ch. Sulinda Samson of Worrindale, the sire of Ch. Bold Oaks Play It Again Sam.

The Newbys have returned home to England. Some of the Worrindale dogs have been exported to Hawaii, and several others remain in the Washington and Oregon area to carry on the bloodline.

There are many other important fanciers I would have wished to cover more fully, but could not. For example, we are fortunate to have Mr. David Wright, Ljekarna Kennels, England, now living in America. David married Gwynne LaMonte, Glenmont, and they have pooled their breed knowledge and expertise. David was approved to judge Cairns in England, and has also judged in the United States. Also included should be Ann Shuler Blair and her Blaircairns, Keith and Kris Armour's Kilkedden, with Kilkedden Solar Eclipse, Winners Bitch, CTCA, Montgomery County in 1986.

Nan Anderson, Lincairn Kennels, and Walter Buczkowski and his Mistiwyns must be included here. Carol Wubbell, with her Ch. Kyleakin Sir Bingley, comes to mind as does Clark Pennypacker, Fenwick, now a professional handler. Ann Kerr, Cairnbrae, and her recent English import, Ch. Penticharm Jack The Lad, Geraldine Sedora, Cairnluv, Nancy Cassel, with her Tosaig Kennels, and Nancy Hatton of Mac Nan Cairns are all staunch breed supporters. Dan and Marjorie Shoemaker, Waterford, are no longer breeding Cairns, but had some very fine ones. Dan is currently very active with the Montgomery County KC.

Other breeders who deserve notice include Marilyn Swearingen, Meriwynds; Pauline Hardy, Brigadoon; Roy and Laura Strong, Glencairn; Julia Hague, Kisncairn; Joy Ganyo, Mc Pooh; Ann Stevens, Blynman; F. J. McGregor, Kihone; Charles and Sandra LeClair, Chasands Kennels; Neal and Carol Kelly, O'Windy Pines; Bertha Rae Lain, Raelain Kennels; Norman and Anne Campbell, Bal Brae; Pat de Neui, Spring Valle; Kathleen Spelman, Ragtime; Deb and Randy Rogers, De Ran; Elfie Payne, Terratote; John and Dixie Orman, Daveleigh; and William Grourke, McKeeGue.

No written account of North American Cairn breeders would be complete without including Mary Andregg, Lochreggand Kennels. Mary is well known for the beautiful, sound Cairns she has produced for many years. She is also well known for her great knowledge of pedigrees, which she generously shares with all. However, I will always remember Mary for her knowledge of natural remedies, herbs and vitamins. Mary is a fascinating person, well worth knowing. She handles professionally, very successfully, and she has owned, imported and bred many, many good dogs under the Lochreggand prefix.

There is not enough space to mention every breeder or go into the detail that I would like, but the concern and dedication of all breeders mentioned, and those whom I could not include as well, are reflected in the general well-being of the Cairn Terrier of today—still a lovely dog, exuding an aura of antiquity, both in its heritage and in its reason for being. A dog that could run the moors and dig for a fox or otter if called upon to do so.

Chapter Eight

The Essence of the Cairn Terrier

There are many ways to describe a Cairn Terrier, not all of them complimentary! The Cairn is typically very independent, but to the breed's credit, bribery works very well. Most "independent" Cairns will do anything for a dog biscuit, even coming when called. Cairns fully understand the commands they have been taught, but they may not always want to obey them. On the other hand, they are very sensitive but also adaptable. When a Cairn shares your life, and you can marvel at the tremendous intelligence reflected in those beautiful eyes, you can better understand the bond between Cairns and their people. You can then see for yourself how every little moment you spend with your Cairn brings you both closer together. The communication level can become truly astounding. Dogs learn to respond, not only to words, but to body language and motion having nothing to do with formal obedience training, or any other formal training. I am talking about communication between a dog and its owner. That communication can be one of the most beautiful things in the world. I cannot imagine living life without a dog by my side, and for me it would always have to be a Cairn Terrier.

APPROACHES TO TRAINING

Short training sessions with generous rewards is the correct approach to training a Cairn Terrier. A severe scolding, using a harsh tone of voice, is correction enough for the sensitive Cairn. A loud noise such as a hand clap serves as a warning that the dog is doing something wrong.

Harsh correction, physical or not, is never justified, and is always detrimental.

Even such simple lessons as lead breaking should be taught in short sessions. Dogs learn to understand routines, words, tone of voice and body language. Be aware of this and make the most of effective communication in your training. The importance of training can never be overstressed.

Every dog, no matter what its destiny in life, should have enough training for people to enjoy its company. This may mean not jumping on guests, or it could mean not climbing on furniture. The spectrum of behavior is broad. You must decide what is acceptable behavior for your pet, and then be consistent about discouraging conduct to the contrary. Allowing your Cairn to play in its water bowl because you think it's cute is fine. However, when "Mac" then jumps on the new white couch with wet, dirty feet, he shouldn't be punished if you haven't taught him to stay off the furniture! Consider what actions you are going to allow that are acceptable for your lifestyle. Then be consistent. It is unfair to allow your dog on the furniture today, and then forbid him tomorrow when it's raining, for example, and expect him to understand and obey. Either get the dog his own chair, or keep cleaning materials handy, or teach him never to get on furniture. It works the same for any behavior pattern. For myself, I can't imagine life without Cairns draped on my furniture, and always pushing the throw pillows to the floor!

Another example of inconsistently applied training would be playing rough with your Cairn, and then being upset when he bites you. Remember, the puppy learns its manners from its dam and its littermates. It learns not to bite hard because when it gets bitten, it hurts! It learns respect from its dam, who makes her puppies leave her alone by pushing them away or warning them off with a growl when she doesn't want them near.

When the puppy enters its new home, it will learn from those around it. How your puppy behaves is strictly up to you. Patterns you set with a young puppy will continue for the rest of its life. Always remember that the Cairn wants to be in charge. Be sure he understands that you are in command at all times. You will both be much happier.

HERITAGE PLAYS A PART

Remember, the Cairn was bred to hunt. An important part of the Cairn Terrier's unique personality is derived from that heritage. The Cairn was not bred for the master's manor, but rather for the humble crofter's cottages. The thick, harsh coat was to keep the dog from harm, and the dense undercoat to keep him warm and dry. He wears this beautiful mantle with pride. Most Cairns know how nice they look after grooming and comport themselves quite proudly. This is a wonderful breed with an aura of antiquity, and to forget its history would be to lose some of this remarkable heritage.

Take your apartment-dwelling Cairn to the country for the first time, and chances are he will take to hunting and water immediately. The typical Cairn is much happier with responsibilities and will enjoy being a hunter and being lavishly praised when he brings in a catch.

Three Feldspar Cairns out for a walk.

The Cairn is a tough little shaggy dog that does not know it weighs only about fifteen pounds. Indeed, his heart alone weighs that much, to those of us who know and love him. I cannot say often enough how courageous this breed is. Nor can I overemphasize Cairn intelligence. This intelligence becomes more pronounced with every hour you spend with your dog, whether he is a champion, winning in every competition, or your beloved pet, sleeping on the sofa every chance he gets, or a titled obedience dog, which delights in playing a new trick on you each time he gets you into the ring. Some Cairns are more independent than others. Some want to be with you, moving from room to room with you, while others will check on you, to be sure you don't need their assistance with house cleaning or giant killing, and then go on about their own affairs, which can include keeping the neighborhood safe from aliens, squirrels and birds, and large and noisy vehicles, and of course, playing with the children. Males are often more affectionate than females. Females can be more independent.

Your Cairn will also enjoy being the official greeter of the residence, but you must be aware that the Cairn is sure that the visitors have come only to see him. Cairn Terriers relish being children's' companions, so in homes with children, an adult must take care that the children treat the family pet with great consideration and kindness at all times. Children who learn early to have compassion for animals carry the benefits of such lessons throughout their lives.

The Cairn has a keen intelligent eye. Often he will meet your gaze, and you wonder just how much he does understand. He will turn his head quizzically, and you know he wishes to comprehend more.

The Cairn is a very sturdy little dog. He loves the outdoors and to run and dig and do what he was bred to do: find his adversary, below or above ground. His vocal threats will easily quell an uprising of intruders. This is not a dog that should be left alone or ignored. This breed thrives on human attention. The fully mature Cairn can accompany you on the morning jog, as long as he has been conditioned gradually to the length of the run. Most Cairns also love to ride in the car.

Cairns easily learn many tricks—they can announce when the phone or doorbell rings, they can perform any number of charmingly naughty actions that you must be prepared to find amusing. This is one reason the Cairn is shown so naturally in the ring. It is not possible to pose a Cairn to make him look better than he can make himself look, just by being himself. He can be showing himself off by looking at another dog, or looking at an airplane flying over, or the Old English Sheepdog (all

Sixteen-week-old Cairn puppy, bred by Gina Dawkins, keenly trying to comprehend her world. Doris Vidigal.

Bramblewood's Hurry Sundown on his first water adventure. Photo courtesy Kathy and Jim Stabler.

that hair), a favorite adversary or barking at a tent flapping, or the hat on a visitor, or perish the thought, a judge!

If you are fortunate enough to have a Cairn Terrier in your life, treasure the companionship. You will never have a more devoted, faithful friend. I often return home after a trying day, tired, or depressed, and experience an immediate upswing of mood when the Cairns run to greet me, so overjoyed simply with my presence. My experience with this is by no means unique. A Cairn is a joy to have around because it is so cheerful. Almost anything you want to do will be joyfully undertaken as long as they are at your side.

Cairn Terriers also have an ongoing love affair with water. The accompanying photo is of a youngster and his first time in the water. His instincts are certainly intact! Cairns are as much at home in water as they are on dry ground. I have seen many Cairns totally submerge their entire heads underwater, hold them there and then shake!

The Cairn is an adaptable breed. I have always tried to retire my Cairns from the showring and my breeding program at fairly young ages (five to seven years) and place them as pets. They are in most cases very happy to hop in the car with their new family, and never give a backward look! This attribute is good in this type situation; however, the family pet can be overly friendly or trusting. Never take a Cairn outside off leash. They are bold and yet trusting, and that can create difficulties. Cairns just like people, and sometimes we must make the judgments for them.

Some Cairns are protective of their home and family, and some are not. This appears to be an individual characteristic. Many, however, possess territorial instincts about invasion of their property by another dog. It is best to be aware that your Cairn may not appreciate visits to his home from strange dogs brought by well-meaning friends or relatives.

THE INVALUABLE CRATE

This is a good place to discuss crates and crate training. Crates are *not cruel*. The dog is a den animal, and having his own crate equates to his

A lovely head study of a Holemill Cairn.

natural security blanket. This is a place of his own where he can feel secure. Also, a dog is safer riding in a crate in the car.

Crating a young puppy will help in housebreaking. No dog wants to soil his sleeping quarters, and will try to wait to relieve himself until he has been picked up and taken outside. Layers of newspaper and old towels are good bedding for puppies. Papers can be discarded, and towels can be washed, and chewing either is not generally harmful.

Do not use the crate as a means of punishment; rather, give a dog a treat or a toy when placing him in the crate. Don't let children annoy the pup in his crate. If he is tired and goes there to sleep, shut his door and let him rest. Let the crate always be his haven.

Always remember that the more time you devote to your Cairn Terrier, the better a companion he will be.

Chapter Nine

The Cairn Terrier Standard

The Cairn Terrier Standard is a diagram of the structure of the ideal specimen, set down in words. Therefore it can be subject to various interpretations, based upon the wording. The breed Standard that has been recognized and approved by the American Kennel Club was submitted by the Cairn Terrier Club of America. The Cairn Terrier Standard presently in use was approved by the American Kennel Club on May 10, 1938. It is a great source of pride to the members of the Cairn Terrier Club of America that a Standard written so long ago is still an effective tool, for both the breeder and the judge. Several years ago an attempt was made to standardize all breed Standards into one uniform format. The Cairn Terrier Club of America resisted this effort, and the 1938 Standard remains unchanged.

Of primary importance, when considering the value of a breed Standard, is whether the Standard states the purpose for which this dog was bred, and draws a "diagram in words," which makes it possible to see why the dog was constructed in this fashion, and for what purpose.

A Cairn Terrier was bred to go to ground, to force out vermin in all terrain and conditions. The expression "going to ground" means literally that the Cairn often ran with a pack of hounds that would run down weasels, foxes or other vermin, and force them into their holes. The valiant Cairn was then brought in to either force the prey out of the den, or if necessary to destroy it in the den without severe damage to the Cairn.

In order to perform the functions described herein, a Cairn must have *temperament*. Since the dogs often were used in packs, they could not be too quarrelsome; however, they had to be possessed of great courage, knowing no fear of man or beast. In order to defend himself, the Cairn must have a good, strong mouth, with large teeth and full dentition. Nothing could be more essential in a fight to the death with a badger or fox. To withstand the weather in the Highlands the Cairn had to have a thick, double coat. The undercoat must be very profuse, and the outer coat very harsh and thick. These double coats will protect from rain and snow, and also briars, attacking animals and, of course, the cold.

All Standards are open to interpretation, which can be influenced by many things. Amount of exposure to the breed, experience within the breed, personal likes and dislikes (which should be put aside) nevertheless enter into how one sees a breed. A written Standard will always have limitations and this encourages differences of opinion among serious fanciers. This is very healthy for the Cairn. Breeders are free to interpret the Standard based on their individual education and experience, their skills of interpretation, the type of animals they see most often and various other outside influences. Breeders are free to produce what they believe the Standard sets forth. Therefore there will always be variety within each breed based on the breeder's subjective opinions regarding what is called for in the Standard. This allows for constructive controversy about the entire gamut of Cairn characteristics and is most desirable for the breed.

Breeders can become "kennel blind" without an objective view. While we all hope that this is not the case, we should re-read the Standard often, with an eye toward refreshing our own direction in our breeding programs. We must never forget that the Cairn is first of all a working Terrier! All breeders should consider the Cairn Terrier's working ability an essential part of this breed. The American Kennel Club now recognizes both working Terrier trials and agility tests. Obedience training, which is already an option for the Cairn, does not require the same characteristics. Failing to recognize working Terrier qualifications would be similar to no longer breeding for Cairn type as opposed to Scottish Terrier or West Highland White Terrier type. The Cairn would lose its unique aura of antiquity in either instance.

It is interesting that the American fancy legislated the prohibition against interbreeding of the West Highland and the Cairn before their British counterparts did. In 1917, the English Standard did not mention a color disqualification, but rather listed the most desirable colors. The United States prohibited interbreeding of the Cairn and the West Highland some eight years before similar action was taken on the other side of the Atlantic.

The Cairn Terrier Club of America in 1985 published a clarification of its Standard. This work was done by a committee composed of chairperson Mrs. Mildred Bryant, Mark Alison, Betty Hyslop, Neal Kelly and myself.

The subsequent paragraphs present (1) The Official Standard of the Cairn Terrier, approved May 10, 1938; (2) the Interpretation, Clarification

HEAD shorter, wider than other terriers; well-furnished with hair on top, softer than body coat; foxy expression

EARS small, pointed, well-carried, erect, set wide apart; free from long hair, dark desirable

BODY well-muscled, strong, active; neither leggy nor too low to ground; proportions balanced

TAIL well-furnished with hair, not feathery; carriage gay, not over back; set-on at back level

HINDQUARTERS strong, well-muscled

LEGS medium length, not too heavily boned

SIZE males, 14 lbs.; 10" at withers; females, 13 lbs.; body length, 14½ to 15" from sternum to point of rump (for mature dogs of two years)

EYES wide apart, rather sunken, size medium; hazel or dark hazel; eyebrows shaggy

STOP distinct

NOSE black

BACK level, medium length, strong, not heavy

RIBS deep, well-sprung

MUZZLE strong; not too long or heavy; dark desirable; teeth large; neither over nor undershot

SHOULDERS sloping

FORELEGS straight; elbows turning neither in nor out

FOREFEET larger than hind feet, may turn out slightly; pads thick, strong; should stand well up on feet

COAT hard, weather-resistant; outer, profuse, close, harsh; inner, short, soft, furry; legs covered with hard hair

COLOR any except white; dark ears, muzzle, tail tip desirable

and Amplification of the Cairn Terrier Standard; and (3) my own additional comments. The Standard appears in boldface type, the clarification in regular-face type and the author's comments in *italics*.

The following is the first paragraph of the Interpretation, Clarification, and Amplification of the Cairn Terrier Standard:

The following analysis and clarification is not intended as a total restatement of the Official Standard, which appears in boldface type. As stated in the foreword to the Analysis of the Standard, the purpose is to clarify and amplify (to compensate for omissions) those areas of the Standard that particularly need more attention from judges, breeders, and exhibitors. PLEASE READ THE STANDARD BEFORE READING THE RESTATEMENTS.

General Appearance:

That of an active, game, hardy, small working terrier of the short-legged class; very free in its movements, strongly but not heavily built, standing well forward on its forelegs, deep in the ribs, well coupled with strong hindquarters and presenting a well-proportioned build with a medium length of back, having a hard, weather-resisting coat; head shorter and wider than any other terrier and well furnished with hair, giving a general foxy expression.

A well-proportioned Cairn Terrier in a normal standing position. A. Priddy.

Clarification:

This first sentence describes the essential picture of "a big dog in a small package." The Cairn is one of the short-legged terriers, but a working terrier, not so low to the ground as to have a "weasely" look, yet not too high on leg as to appear "up on stilts." The word "medium" is the key word throughout this Standard. Not a short-backed, square-looking terrier, but a terrier with enough length of back to be able to twist and turn in and out of the holes and among the rocks with quick movement is ideal.

Author's Comments:

The Cairn is neither a short nor a long backed dog. But there is much to be said in interpretation of the above statement. It is my contention that as stated in the Standard, "from the front of the chest to back of hindquarters," allows for some overhang—in both front and rear, which I believe does not indicate a dog that appears long backed to the observer. The Cairn can be too short-backed, but a medium length of back can appear deceptively short, based on amount of coat carried in front and behind, and density of coat, weight and trimming.

The Cairn should be able to turn in a den, but medium is the correct terminology here. Too long is just as abominable as too short. I suggest that most breeders do not take the tape measure and/or ruler to their dogs, but train themselves to evaluate dogs with the naked eye and defend their position accordingly. Balance is supremely important. Picture the dog of correct balance. All else will fall into place. Proper amount of bone must also enter into general appearance. If the dog does not have the proper amount of bone, it will affect his general appearance, which could cause the casual observer to fault the dog for lack of balance.

A well-proportioned Cairn Terrier head. K. Kauffman.

SKULL:

Broad in proportion to length with a decided stop and well furnished with hair on the top of the head, which may be somewhat softer than the body coat.

MUZZLE:

Strong but not too long or heavy.

Clarification:

The head is very broad and short. The muzzle shorter than the length of skull. The ideal proportion of muzzle to skull is four to five. The muzzle is full but not heavy, yet broad enough to hold a full set of large, strong teeth. Heads may go to extremes and be too heavily boned—appearing coarse or too fine—appearing "snippy." Please note the Standard does not call for a foxy head—only for a foxy *expression* (smart, alert, cunning), which is lost if the head is coarse or overdone.

Author's Comments:

Breadth of skull is not the only criterion whereby the Cairn head should be judged or evaluated. Dogs should be judged on proportion and balance, i.e., breadth of skull versus proportion of skull to body. The head should be the right size for the body and the breadth of skull must be in balance with the body. One cannot measure the top-skull of a twelve-inch dog against that of a ten-inch dog and consider the larger dog the better because his top skull is broader. A huge dog with a huge coarse head may be in balance, but is not what we require at all. A long muzzle and top skull are always unacceptable, no matter how big the dog.

TEETH:

Large, mouth neither overshot nor undershot.

NOSE:

Black.

EYES:

Set wide apart, rather sunken, with shaggy eyebrows, medium in size, hazel or dark hazel in color, depending on body color, with a keen terrier expression.

EARS:

Small, pointed, well carried erectly, set wide apart on the side of the head. Free from long hairs.

Clarification:

Large, strong teeth are important. There should be six incisors, upper and lower. The bite is either level or scissors—not overshot or undershot. The nose is black only. The preferred eye color should be dark hazel (not black), medium in size, oval in shape and wide set, giving the Cairn a decidedly "devilish" look. Ears are small, wide set, properly placed on the sides of the head but carried upright are correct.

Author's Comments:

With regard to teeth, I feel breeders should certainly breed for the correct number of both upper and lower incisors, but should pay attention to the pre-molars as well. Strong teeth cannot be emphasized enough. A level bite is acceptable according to the Standard, but as a breeder, I do think that you have to be very careful when breeding level bites. Take pains to try to breed animals with good scissors bites. Level bites cause teeth to wear excessively at an early age, leading to their loss, and also level mouths have a way of becoming crooked or even somewhat undershot in later years. In my opinion, breeding level bites without a great deal of caution often results in the production of wry or undershot mouths in the next generation.

Good, dark pigment on the nose and around the eyes is very important to proper expression. It is best to be aware of coat color when evaluating eye color. An acceptable hazel eye in a wheaten brindle will appear much lighter and less acceptable when the coat goes naturally darker with age.

The eyes must be set deeply, and there should be a decided stop in order to create proper expression.

The ears appear larger on a puppy without full head furnishings than they will appear when he is an adult and the development of those furnishings is complete.

Too large an ear can ruin the Cairn headpiece very easily. Ears set too high give a Scottish Terrier–type expression, and they are extremely unattractive.

TAIL:

Tail in proportion to head, well furnished with hair but not feathery. Carried gaily but must not curl over back. Set on at back level.

Tail Carriage

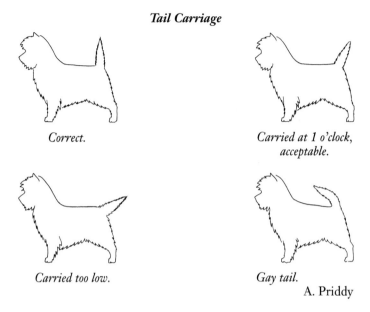

Correct.

Carried at 1 o'clock, acceptable.

Carried too low.

Gay tail.

A. Priddy

Clarification:

Length of tail should equal height of ears. A standing Cairn should be able to have a ruler parallel to the ground from the tail's tip to the ear's tip (Fig #14). The tail is set high, at back level, but the ideal tail carriage is not necessarily vertical and should never be curled over the back. A Cairn going around the ring and carrying its tail at one or two o'clock is fine.

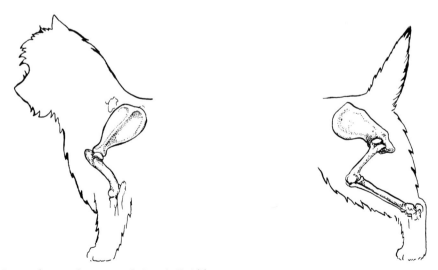

Proper front and rear angulation. A. Priddy

Author's Comments:

I much prefer to see the tail carried perfectly upright. To me if a Cairn's tail is not carried upright, the tail is either low set, or the dog is not sure of itself. The Cairn should love the showring, and its tail carriage indicates this. The Scottish Terrier Standard states "No judge should put to Winners or Best of Breed any Scottish Terrier not showing real terrier character in the ring." This could be said of most of the Terriers, and most certainly the Cairn.

BODY:

Well muscled, strong, active body with well-sprung, deep ribs, coupled to strong hindquarters, with a level back of medium length, giving an impression of strength and activity without heaviness.

Clarification:

A firmly put-together body with a heart- (or egg-) shaped rib cage, not barrel ribs, or slab sides is correct. A level back is desired. A good topline is a combination of proper placement of the bone structure combined with correct angulation.

Author's Comments:

When considering a Cairn's structure, one must always keep in mind that the dog was bred to hunt and to go to ground, and that the Cairn must have agility and endurance, as well as strength.

SHOULDERS, LEGS AND FEET:

A sloping shoulder, medium length of leg, good but not too heavy bone; forelegs should not be out at elbows, and be perfectly straight, but forefeet may be slightly turned out. Forefeet larger than hind feet. Legs must be covered with hard hair. Pads should be thick and strong and dog should stand well up on its feet.

Clarification:

There should be some body overhang in the front; the pro sternum should be fairly prominent with the front legs well back in under the withers. Front legs are straight and well muscled without a tendency of a fiddle-front, but front feet may turn out slightly for digging purposes. However, this does not mean "east-west" front feet. Front feet are larger than back feet (again for digging purposes) with good depth in the pad and strong pasterns, never down on the pasterns. Feet should be tight—with no indication toward a splayed foot. Nails must be kept short. Hindquarters: bend of stifle should be in proportion to shoulder layback to allow for a smooth, even gait. Hindquarters muscled with straight hocks. Cow hocks and open hocks should be severely penalized. Gait: should move freely and easily with reach in front and drive in rear on a loose lead. When viewed from the front, the legs should be straight and show reach. Any tendency toward winging or paddling should be penalized—as should crabbing. When viewed from the rear, the gait should show drive with the hocks parallel to each other and not too close together.

Author's Comments:

The Cairn should be very well angulated, both front and rear. As with most short-legged Terriers, fronts are not always as good as they should be, and breeders must give them constant attention. If the dog does not have the proper amount of bone, he will be "weedy," or if he has too much bone, he will appear "coarse."

MOVEMENT

Author's Comments:

The Cairn Standard only describes movement in the following terminology, "should move freely and easily on a loose lead."

I feel that it is important that what I consider to be proper Cairn movement should be described here.

When the Cairn Terrier moves, forefeet and hindfeet should travel in a direct line. The forefeet skim the ground, with long strides emerging straight from the point of the withers.

All four pads should be visible when watching the dog gait, going away.

In other words when the Cairn is moving at a trot, the front and rear feet strike the ground under the appropriate joint, moving very square and true. As dogs move faster, there may be some convergence, but this is a characteristic of normal movement and not to be faulted.

It is also important to understand parallel tracking. The footprints of a dog that parallel tracks fall wider apart on either side of the center line of travel than those of a dog that single tracks. Speed and structure influence the degree to which the legs incline inward.

We have all thrilled to the sight of an elegant animal moving well, whether in the showring or in rough or rocky terrain, doing what it was bred to do. We need not be technical experts on skeletal structure to appreciate proper movement. We do have to study animals moving and be able to ascertain true efficient movement, and to breed for that critically important virtue.

COAT:

Hard and weather-resistant. Must be double-coated with profuse harsh outer coat and short, soft, close furry undercoat.

Clarification:

This hard, double coat is most important in the Cairn Terrier, as it was designed to keep cold and water from penetrating to the skin. The profuse coat should be thick and a minimum of 2 inches in length. It should be the same length all over the body. Any appearance of the "jacketed" or "sculptured" look of the more stylized Terriers should be severely penalized.

Author's Comments:

I think it should be pointed out that the coat can be of varying lengths, but that a short jacket and long skirt are not correct or desirable. However, when rolling a coat, for example in order to keep a special in the ring for several years, the hair on the topline may be kept a little shorter. This will keep the outer coat from getting too long, and blowing or dying. The end result of the rolling process is to give the exhibitor many different lengths of coat, well blended, all over the body, particularly the head and legs. The coat should give the appearance of a "rough" Terrier.

COLOR:

May be of any color except white. Dark ears, muzzle and tail tip are desirable.

Clarification:

Any color except white is permissible, however, any markings resembling the old black and tan terrier (Doberman type markings), or parti-colored markings, are highly objectional and should not be allowed. Dark points—muzzle, ears, and tail—are desirable.

Author's Comments:

One of the most interesting things about this breed is the fact that the brindles will darken with each coat. The totally clear wheaten and red coats will usually remain the same color for life.

IDEAL SIZE:

Involves the weight, the height at the withers and the length of body. Weight for bitches, thirteen pounds; for dogs, fourteen pounds. Height at the withers, bitches nine and a half inches; dogs, ten inches. Length of body from fourteen and a quarter to fifteen inches from the front of the chest to back of hindquarters. The dog must be of balanced proportions and appear neither too short nor too long in body. Weight and measurements are for matured dogs at two years of age. Older dogs may weigh slightly in excess and growing dogs may be under these weights and measurements.

Clarification:

While the weight and height limits are important, it should be stressed that the overall balance of the dog is most important. A well boned, properly-coated dog may appear larger than a light boned, short-coated dog. A slightly under or oversized dog of obvious quality is preferable to a proper sized dog lacking the desired attributes. . . .

Author's Comments:

I have gleaned knowledge voraciously from all who would share with me. One of these is Mildred Bryant. She was fortunate to have had many good teachers, among

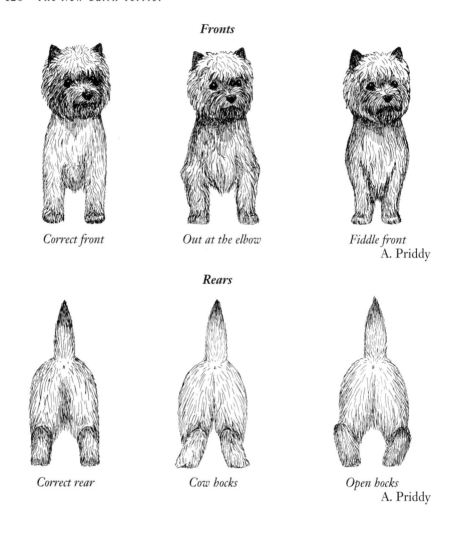

Fronts

Correct front   *Out at the elbow*   *Fiddle front*
A. Priddy

Rears

Correct rear   *Cow hocks*   *Open hocks*
A. Priddy

them, Lee E. Murray, who at the time of his death was an all-breed judge. When Mildred started her judging career, one of the bits of advice Mr. Murray offered her was "Leave the size to the breeders, unless there is a disqualification." Having applied this advice to my own breeding program, I have owned large and small dogs, and found the right place in my breeding program for all of them.

CONDITION:

Dogs should be shown in good hard flesh, well muscled and neither too fat or thin. Should be in full good coat with plenty of head furnishings, be clean, combed, brushed and tidied up on ears, tail, feet and general outline. Should move freely and easily on a loose lead,

A well-balanced Cairn moving in a proper trot. A. Priddy

Front Movement

Correct   *Out at the elbow*   *Fiddle front*
A. Priddy

Rear Movement

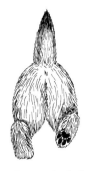

Proper rear movement   *A cow hocked*   *An open hocked*
with pads visible   *dog moving*   *dog moving*
A. Priddy

should not cringe on being handled, should stand up on their toes and show with marked terrier characteristics.

Clarification:

A Cairn should not be too heavy in body or in weight. They are not chunky little dogs and should have a little extra length of loin to be agile. In feeling behind the rib cage along the sides of the dog, a very slight depression is good in the loin area. Not that you want to feel the hip bones, but you do want to feel the ribs and you want some leanness through the body. Cairns are not as heavy boned as the Westie or the Scottie.

Full good coat means a two- or three-inch-long coat all over the body—unlike the Westie or Scottie, which have much longer coat on the legs and undercarriage. The Cairn is not stripped on the back leaving a flowing skirt. The entire body is stripped, not just the back. Nor should it be skinned down at the neck or carry an abundance of long, silky, dead furnishings. This style of grooming should be heavily penalized in the showring. A coat should be worked entirely with the thumb and forefinger. Scissor marks should never be seen on the Cairn body. Scissors may be used around the feet and just at the very top of the ears.

The fad of blow-drying the Cairn should be discouraged. This treatment only puffs out the coat and presents a very unnatural appearance for a rugged, sturdy animal. In order to preserve the Cairn Terrier in its best old-working type, fanciers must resist any temptations to succumb to "current fashion."

Proper trimming and grooming of the tail is important for adhering to correct Cairn type. The hair covering the tail should taper from the base to a point at the tip like a Christmas tree or an inverted ice cream cone. A skinned-down tail is both unsightly and incorrect.

In addition to the typical presentation of a good head study, I offer the reader an actual head study of a Cairn. This head represents typical grooming, and the proper wedge shape. Correct proportion of the head, eye and ear placement will allow you to draw an imaginary line from the center of the nose, through the center of the eye, to the tip of the ear. The wedge formed by this imaginary line will come close to equaling one-fourth of a circle, or a 90 degree portion of the 360 degree circle.

Judges are encouraged to examine Cairns on a table for eye-level viewing and assessing. The Standard calls for the dog to be shown on a loose lead. A loose lead is most important for the natural presentation of a Cairn. Also, those handling should be on their feet, not squatting and posing their dogs. Cairns are active, lively dogs, standing and facing the world proudly.

Author's Comments:

Muscle tone should be firm. The Cairn is an active dog and should maintain excellent quality muscle tone without any special exercise regimen. Normal outdoor activity should keep the Cairn perfectly fit.

It is very difficult to keep a Cairn in full coat when the coat is allowed to grow to three to four inches in length. There should be no suggestion of the overgrooming so prevalent in the showring today; however, a two inch minimum on the topline, blending down the body into longer hair will present the proper appearance.

The shorter coat gives the groomer a better opportunity to keep the coat rolling.

The only scissors that should be put on the Cairn coat, even on feet and ears, should be very fine thinning scissors.

Another description of the tail shape is that of an inverted carrot. The tip of the ears and the tip of the tail should be the same height.

FAULTS:

1. **Skull: Too narrow in skull.**
2. **Muzzle: Too long and heavy a foreface; mouth overshot or undershot.**
3. **Eyes: Too large, prominent, yellow and ringed are all objectionable.**
4. **Ears: Too large, round at points, set too close together, set too high on the head; heavily covered with hair.**
5. **Legs and Feet: Too light or too heavy bone. Crooked forelegs or out at elbow. Thin ferrety feet; feet let down on the heel or too open and spread. Too high or too low on the leg.**
6. **Body: Too short back and compact a body, hampering quickness of movement and turning ability. Too long, weedy and snaky a body, giving an impression of weakness. Tail set too low. Back not level.**
7. **Coat: Open coats, blousy coats, too short or dead coats, lack of sufficient undercoat, lack of head furnishings, lack of hard hair on the legs. Silkiness or curliness. A slight wave permissible.**
8. **Nose: Flesh or light-colored nose.**
9. **Color: White on chest, feet or other parts of body.**

Chapter Ten

Breeding Quality Cairns

Before beginning any discussion of breeding specifics for the novice breeder, it is first necessary to discuss some breeding theories.

There are basically three methods of breeding dogs. They are linebreeding, inbreeding and outcrossing.

OUTCROSSING

Outcrossing simply explained means breeding two dogs that have few or no common ancestors in a three- or four-generation pedigree.

Many breeders feel that outcrossing can bring about many benefits for their bloodlines. Outcrossing can be done to bring in a quality that is lacking in a particular family, such as good shoulder layback or dark eye color for example. Some breeders feel outcrossing can be a means of breeding away from genetic defects, particularly if the dogs within the kennel are tightly linebred, and that outcrossing will create more vigorous and active animals.

LINEBREEDING: THE SAFEST COURSE

Linebreeding means mating two animals that have several common ancestors, or show ancestors that appear at least twice in the same pedigree. This system uses breedings of near, but not close relatives. Typical linebred matings would be grandfather/granddaughter, uncle/niece, or first cousin/first cousin. Linebreeding is used to set type, or physical characteristics. Linebred dogs will tend to produce the qualities apparent in themselves and their ancestors. It is important to remember that when you linebreed, you will be setting the faults along with the good points. For example, if you were to breed two related Cairns, with excellent length of neck, topline and tail set, but that also had missing incisors and light eyes, you would set the bad traits along with the good ones.

INBREEDING: PROCEED WITH CAUTION

Inbreeding is mating to a close relative: mother to son, father to daughter, brother to sister. In my opinion, inbreeding should be undertaken only rarely. The narrowing of the gene pool in the animals produced makes it not worth the risks, except in very unusual cases.

It is important to mention at this point that financial gain by responsible dog breeding is impossible! Very few breeders break even on any one litter, considering only those expenses that relate immediately to the litter, such as stud fee and medical expenses for the bitch and shots for the puppies. And we must never forget the tremendous responsibility involved in the placing of the puppies.

You may want to eventually develop your own strain, which it is hoped will produce those characteristics you think are the most valuable and important in the Cairn. In order to set type, you will have to attempt to tighten the gene pool of the Cairns you are breeding from. This can be done by linebreeding or inbreeding.

Attempting to linebreed from mediocre stock is pointless. Linebreeding or inbreeding should only be done with outstanding animals. To do otherwise is to court failure.

GETTING STARTED

Buy the best bitch you can from a breeder with a good reputation. Show her to her championship and learn what you can along the way, by attending as many dog shows as possible. Study closely all the Cairns you see and other breeds as well, because you will learn by doing so.

I have not yet mentioned type, but I feel that in order to breed successfully, you must determine the type that you feel most accords with your understanding of the written Cairn Standard. By breeding for your chosen type, you will feel pride in producing and presenting your best in the showring. Learning type is a matter of exposure to different types. Visit any Cairn Terrier kennels that are accessible to you. Study pedigrees, and attempt to learn about the dogs in your dog's pedigree. One excellent manner to learn about dogs in pedigrees is the CTCA yearbook, published yearly, which includes a picture and three-generation pedigree of all Cairn Terriers finished that year that were owned by CTCA members. These books are available from the current club secretary for a nominal cost, and provide a worthwhile history for all serious breeders.

Other good learning grounds are the CTCA, regional Cairn Terrier clubs, parent clubs in other breeds and all-breed kennel clubs in your local area. Communication with other breeders can also be very enlightening.

Starting by going to a prepotent stud dog is very wise. If you see a dog that you like, consider breeding to his sire, as well as breeding to him. Many great dogs have been produced by using this breeding strategy.

You must learn to be objective about your animals. You cannot hope to breed superior Cairns without a realistic view of the stock you have to work with, which means being able to fault your dogs honestly. Once you have determined the areas that most need improvement, set out to locate a stud that (1) produces the qualities that you feel need improvement, (2) has the appearance (phenotype) you are looking for, and (3) is sufficiently prepotent so that you can be assured of the general look of the offspring, judging by the get you have already seen out of this dog. There is a lot of luck in breeding; all these suggestions may or may not work just right for every individual. But they are guidelines with which to build your own opinions and start you in the right direction in your search for a stud dog.

Probably the single most educational experience for the beginner is attending the national Specialty. I suggest that for your first one, you do not take a dog. Instead, take a notebook, a pencil and a camera. Set yourself up in a spot at ringside, and *study* the Cairn in action. During judging, study the dogs in depth, and perhaps engage experienced breeders in conversations about various questions that you have.

Once you have determined the potential stud dog and the time frame for the mating, contact the owner of the stud dog and make all arrangements for the breeding. At this time, discuss all items relating to the breeding including all costs and any extra fees or veterinary expenses incurred during the mating. Travel expenses are the responsibility of the owner of the bitch.

The bitch should be vaccinated before her season, and checked for internal parasites. Some testing will probably be required—Brucellosis and Mycoplasma, for example.

The owner of the stud should be advised of any special requirements or bad habits the bitch may have.

It can be noted here that breeder's opinions are, to a certain degree, subjective. If you want to know about certain qualities that the stud may or may not possess, it is always best to be very specific with your questions. "Does he have a good rear?" is not a detailed enough question. More effective would be, "My bitch is a little straight in shoulder, and I need a dog with a good layback of shoulder." There is nothing to be gained by not being honest about the faults in your bitch you would like to improve.

One concern that always appears within this breed is the question of size. Size is a very touchy issue with some breeders. Some prefer what they consider to be more like the old working Terrier from the Isle of Skye, longer in leg, and proportionately longer in back to balance the length of leg.

Still others prefer to attempt to work within the American Standard, which calls for the Cairn to stand nine and a half inches to ten inches at the shoulder. Since there is no disqualification, I feel that breeders have the option to use judiciously the size they feel comfortable with. I think a portion of the disparity in size in the Cairn is due to the fact that the dogs of Waternish ranged from eight pounds to about eighteen pounds, and indications are that the different sizes may have been bred for different game. It seems that the medium-sized dogs with the short, rough coats may have been better at going into dens of otters, and perhaps the larger ones were better with foxes.

Coat texture cannot be evaluated from ringside, nor from viewing photographs. Dogs should have dense, double coats, with properly harsh outer coats and correct undercoats.

A general inquiry into the overall health of the dogs in the bloodlines of the stud you are considering is appropriate. Ask about not only puppies he has produced, but about his littermates and his parents, and what they have produced. Inquire in such a manner as to assure the owner of the stud dog that you are only concerned with breeding a healthy litter, and you should receive appropriate response. You should also be prepared to specifically express any particular concerns you have about your own bloodlines. Open communication among breeders is the way to build a brighter future for Cairn Terriers and all who love them.

Temperament should certainly be a consideration in selecting a stud. Overaggression, hyperactivity and shyness seem to filter down from generation to generation and can become more pronounced. Do not ignore temperament. The Cairn should be a happy friendly individual, not reserved with people, but holding his own in all canine encounters.

GESTATION

Once you have accomplished a breeding, your concern is with the health and well-being of your bitch during gestation. Care should be taken to see that she is properly nourished. Some bitches go off their food during the first trimester of pregnancy. If this occurs, you might try offering food later in the day. Eventually her body will dictate to her that she needs to eat, and her normal appetite will return. Consult with your veterinarian regarding vitamin and calcium supplementation during pregnancy. Do not allow the bitch to become overweight during pregnancy, as this could increase the difficulty of labor.

Cairns normally get enough exercise to ensure proper muscle tone; however, if you have a Cairn bitch that is less active, you might take her for walks on a regular routine. Be sure not to overdo as the pregnancy advances, and be careful of heat.

WHELPING

The Cairn still maintains many of its earliest instincts. These instincts will dictate that the whelping area be quiet and secluded. Isolate the Cairn bitch from any canine friends about two weeks before the birth of the litter, and keep them away until after the puppies are weaned. A Cairn bitch that is whelping and rearing a litter needs peace and quiet. This is no time for stress of any kind.

Your whelping box should be of a material that can be sterilized after each litter. Some viral and bacterial contamination can persist to infect future litters unless you disinfect the whelping box after each litter. Thick layers of whole newspaper and shredded newspaper on top make ideal bedding for the whelping box. Let the bitch sleep in the box for two weeks before she is due, to accustom her to her new surroundings. Doing this could prevent whelping occurring where you don't want it, like on your bedspread, or in your lap!

Items Needed for Whelping

1. Sterile scissors
2. Forceps
3. Small box
4. Heating pad
5. Alcohol for sterilization
6. Iodine to dab on umbilical cords
7. Baby scale
8. Small, thin towels
9. Ear syringe for clearing fluid from nostrils and mouth

Nothing can take the place of a good working relationship with your veterinarian. Veterinarians who are willing to work with breeders and teach them essential skills are resources to be treasured. If your veterinarian is one such, you are blessed.

There are various indications that should signify when the actual delivery is approaching. All, some or none of the indications may be present in your bitch. Experience is the best teacher. A good person to contact about whelping is the breeder of your bitch. Ask the breeder if there are any idiosyncrasies that you should watch for, and what that breeder considers to be normal whelping behavior. Activities that indicate whelping is close are (1) tearing paper, (2) not eating and (3) a drop in temperature. As labor becomes more intense, many bitches will shiver. As contractions become harder, you will be able to see them in her body. Your bitch will key her mood to yours. You must remain calm. Either stay with her, or check on her frequently as labor progresses. After the puppies begin to arrive, stay with the bitch constantly.

A brisk walk will often speed up labor if your bitch seems to be tiring or pushing for a long time. Take a towel along on your walk! Never allow a whelping bitch to move around unattended. Your bitch may not be herself during whelping—she may be nervous or panicky, and difficult to work with. I once had a bitch that was determined that her newborns would be born on the couch in the whelping room. Every time I would open the door to her whelping box, she would dive for the couch with a puppy in her mouth. It is very difficult to "reason" with a Cairn bitch holding a newborn puppy in her mouth!

Cairns are very protective of their newborns. For that reason, I do not clean the whelping box until the entire litter has arrived, and the mother has accepted them, nursed them and has reached a calm state herself. *Then*, when she needs to relieve herself, I remove most of the soiled papers on her first trip out of the box, but leave some for the smell. I remove the last of them when she is outside next, each time replacing with fresh newspaper.

Some Cairn bitches are even more protective of their newborns than most. Your bitch may resent your touching them at all. However, you must check them over carefully. If she resents this, do it when she is away from the whelping box.

After the litter has arrived, check the bitch's temperature every day for the first week, to make sure no infection is present. Check the puppies for dehydration and make sure they are all active, not limp. Also make sure the bitch's milk is a good, clear white, not sticky or stringy, and make sure she does not have too much milk. If she has too much milk, her breasts will become hard, and this can lead to trouble, if the puppies do not nurse enough to drain the milk supply. Nature usually takes care of this situation in a few days, but it is best to be aware of the potential problem. It seems to be quite common in Cairns.

Some Cairns are better mothers than others. If the mother does not lick the puppies, which stimulates them to urinate and defecate, they will become restless and cry. Puppies only cry when they are hungry, uncomfortable, sick or too hot or cold. If you suspect constipation, pick up a puppy and gently rub its genitalia with a lukewarm cotton ball or paper towel, simulating the mother's tongue licking the pup. If you get large amounts of stool or urine, the mother may not be doing her cleanup job properly. A trick to stimulate her interest in this job is to rub butter or cooking oil on the pup in front of the tail, on the tail and on the genitals. This may also stimulate the bitch's all-important nurturing instincts.

If you have a puppy that has become chilled for whatever reason, warm it immediately, but gradually. Cover a heating pad on low with a towel, and place it in a small box, just large enough for the heating pad. Place the puppy on the towel and cover the box with a second towel. Warming the puppy in your hands and gentle rubbing are helpful as well. People make the mistake of trying to feed a chilled puppy immediately. The puppy's body temperature must be elevated before you give warm nourishment of any kind.

When supplementing a litter, I use a formula that consists of one can of evaporated milk and one can of bottled water. Refrigerate this mixture, and heat only small amounts. As a precaution, I suggest that you dispose of any unused mixture daily, and sterilize both the refrigerator container and the nursing bottle daily. This is a very cautious method for either supplementing or bottle feeding, but it is worth the small amount of extra effort to avoid having even one sick puppy.

If you continue to breed Cairn Terriers, it is possible that you will encounter a difficult whelping that will necessitate a Cesarean section. Try not to be overly alarmed, but do not let a bitch labor more than two and a half hours without contacting your veterinarian. It is a good idea to notify your veterinarian whenever you have a bitch whelping, in order for him or her to be aware of your possible need for his or her skills. A Cesarean section is a very common and successful veterinary procedure.

A Cairn Terrier is sensitive to anesthesia. Anesthesia must be given slowly, and you will need to make your veterinarian aware of this. After the surgery, both the bitch and her puppies will probably feel the effects of the anesthesia. The bitch should not be returned to her litter without supervision, until she is no longer groggy, which could be a few hours or longer. The puppies will probably cry feebly, which won't help your nerves at all, but is this is normal. When the puppies are fully alert, try to let them nurse the mother. You may want to bottle feed them also. If so, use the formula mentioned above. Keep a close watch on your new arrivals. After one week, if all appears normal, the puppies should be off to a good start in life.

A bitch that has undergone a Cesarean section must wait until the second season following surgery before another breeding is undertaken. Depending on the actual reason for the section, the breeder should think carefully before breeding her again.

IMPRINTING

Ethologists constantly study animal behavior. For example, newly hatched ducklings follow the first moving object they see that produces the duck exit call. The call acts as a trigger for the learning process. It is thought by ethologists that these principles can be applied to many mammals, such as horses and dogs. Experimental early stimulation of foals by human attendants is currently being conducted and appears to be succeeding. The sorts of stimuli include verbal communication, physical handling and even breathing into the newborn animal's nostrils. Horses reared in this manner are much easier to train and have less fear of humans.

Whelping puppies is normally stressful for the human attendant, and perhaps the newborns don't get the proper stimuli. I plan with my next litter to spend some time breathing on them while waiting for the balance of the litter to be born, and really stroking them, instead of simply performing midwife duties. This theory is called *imprinting*.

SOCIALIZATION

Most dogs' eyes open at ten to fourteen days, but it is common for Cairns' eyes to open as late as fifteen to seventeen days. Shortly afterward their ears will open, and they really start to experience life. At this time, puppies need appropriate outside stimulation. A radio playing in the whelping room and supervised time out of the whelping box with family members all contribute to the development of well-socialized animals. Gradually continue to widen the puppies' level of new experiences. Handle them daily, but not to excess. Each pup should get individual time for human contact, away from its littermates.

All puppies should be socialized extensively from three to twelve weeks. One excellent book on this subject, and a personal favorite of mine, is *The New Knowledge of Dog Behavior*, by Clarence J. Pfaffenberger.

Socialization of a Cairn Terrier means lots of time with the family, constantly supervised play with children (your own or borrowed ones if you have none), riding in the car, becoming used to loud noises, radio and television broadcasts and other routine commotion. Individual attention for each puppy away from his littermates is also essential.

It would take a heart of stone to pass up this Cairn baby's invitation to play.

The earlier a Cairn is lead broken, the less of a battle it will be. I begin lead breaking by first letting the puppy trail the lead on the ground. I then pick up the lead, and occasionally apply a little tension, so the puppy realizes there is a string around its neck. Then when they begin to run on lead, I run with them, and they really think they are walking me. Obviously, they really enjoy this. Occasionally I apply a little tension on the lead, calling the puppy's attention back to me. At this

Ch. Bramblewood's Stetson, owned by Chris Carter, contemplating a Stetson of another kind.

point I use treats to get the puppy to walk beside me—once it becomes accustomed to the lead.

PUPPY GROOMING

Trimming puppy nails weekly will prevent major struggles over this important routine later. The puppy should be placed in a grooming situation weekly. Quietly tolerating brushing of the coat and standing still on a table are both good training experiences for any youngster.

At about six weeks, remove the top third of the hair from the ears. Besides making the puppy look prettier, removing that hair will help the ears stand, if they haven't already done so. *Don't work on your puppy unless you are in a good frame of mind.* Puppies need reassurance and patience, and you can't transmit this if you are out of sorts.

Most breeders prefer to remove the black overlay from the puppy coats before placing their puppies. This allows the first adult coat to come in unhindered. It is not necessary to pull the long black hairs on the head and legs, but the body should be done. The coat becomes loose enough to pull at about eight to ten weeks.

When pulling a coat, always grasp the hair firmly between thumb and forefinger, and pull firmly and gently and always in the same direction as the coat grows. Never jerk. Try to make every grooming session fun. The best reward your puppy can have is praise from you, and treats, of course.

VETERINARY CARE

A stool sample should be evaluated at three weeks, and if any parasites are detected, the puppies should be wormed. Continue to check stool samples at two-week intervals, until the puppies are eight weeks of age, or two consecutive checks have been negative. The most common parasite for small puppies is the roundworm. Happily, roundworms are easy to get rid of.

Contact your veterinarian about vaccination schedules. Normally, immunization is started at six to eight weeks, and followed through consistently for at least a series of three shots. There is not sufficient information to indicate when puppies lose the maternal antibodies. This is the reason for giving shots at eight, ten and twelve weeks. A parvovirus booster is suggested at seventeen weeks. Any active kennel should boost all dogs for parvo semiannually. Other booster shots can be given yearly.

DAM/PUPPY MAINTENANCE

Cairn Terrier puppies start to interact early. They nuzzle one another and sleep in piles. Shortly after their eyes open, they begin to interact in earnest. By three and a half weeks, you can probably expect to hear little growls and squeals, as they try out their various functions, like batting one another around, teething on brother's ear or body wrestling. At about four weeks, puppies are beginning to get on their feet and stumble and play clumsily. At five to six weeks, the mother will begin to play with them, and will sometimes be a little rough. This is okay, within reason. After six weeks, she may be justified in an occasional firm correction when baby teeth pinch her ear or some other sensitive part of her anatomy. The puppies learn necessary life skills from playing with their mother, and this is very good. There is a school of thought that suggests removing the mother from her offspring at an early age—by five weeks—to ease the drain of nursing. I prefer to leave the puppies with the mother for six to eight weeks. If you feed your puppies well, and separate mother for periods of time, the milk supply will start to dry up gradually. Mother can still play with her puppies and they will learn much from her. I do not allow the bitch to try to produce enough milk for several six- to eight-week-old puppies. This is far too hard on her.

My procedure now is to allow the bitch to remain with the litter as long as the bitch enjoys the puppies, until eight weeks. Many Cairns are born mothers, and would stay with their litters forever if they were allowed to do so.

THOUGHTS ON BREEDING

You should be thinking at this time about which puppy you are keeping. With the increased awareness of the number of unwanted dogs today, it is my opinion that a conscientious breeder will only breed a litter when he or she feels the mating could improve on the sire and dam, and with the intent to keep something. Indeed, many breeders no longer breed a litter until they have deposits for puppies on what they consider an average-size litter. There are still breeders who breed without planning, care little for type and soundness, and seldom exhibit their dogs at shows, and perhaps sell puppies to dog dealers. It should be evident that these practices are detrimental to the Cairn Terrier, and to all purebred dogs in general.

We have now raised these puppies and given them all their vaccinations, and are preparing them to be good citizens in the world shared by dogs and people. We have socialized them. We have loved them. And remember this: We caused each puppy to be born, and we bear responsibility for this puppy each and every day of its life. It is our responsibility to find the best home for each of these puppies, and to maintain contact with the new owners. Cairns are wonderful pets, but their high spirits and intelligence can be a bit much for the unsuspecting new pet owner, who has not been properly educated. An excellent investment of your time is spending as much time as possible with the new owners of your puppies, teaching them all the intricacies of Cairn behavior as we know and love it. This should help prepare them for the little problems, and ensure that those little problems do not develop into overwhelming ones through lack of knowledge.

Some breeders breed their bitches two seasons in a row and then skip a season. I am not sure that with the current animal rights legislation movements, and attempts to ban breeding in counties and even states, and the number of dogs being euthanized today, that this is a good idea. At least two hundred Cairns are rescued—either from shelters or accepted by owner surrender—by the CTCA rescue network yearly, and there is no way of telling how many more are placed and/or euthanized. I think responsible breeding should be one of our top priorities. My opinion is based on the state of the dog fancy today.

Chapter Eleven

Grooming the Cairn Terrier
for the Showring

In 1990, the Cairn Terrier Club of America published an excellent booklet on grooming the Cairn Terrier. I chaired the committee for this project, which included Mildred Bryant, Kenneth Kauffman and Lynne Nabors. It is available at a nominal cost from the CTCA secretary (see bibliography).

The booklet, a CTCA publication, goes into greater depth than space allows here, but I will cover the most important points as well as some different material in this chapter.

The Cairn Terrier Standard refers to the Cairn Terrier as "having a hard, weather resisting coat"; "tidied up on ears, tail, feet and general outline," i.e., shown in a natural state.

As with most Terrier breeds, the Cairn Terrier coat must be hand stripped for the showring. Hand stripping is very much an art. It literally means pulling the harsh outer coat from the dog's body. This is not necessarily a painful process. Gentle firm grasp of the individual hairs and gradually easing them out is the entire process. When the hair is pulled, the growth will show the same vibrant color variations as the previous coat, although it may come in darker. Examination of the individual brindled hairs reveals several colors along the length of each hair. If the hair is cut or clipped, it becomes softer in texture because it is really the old dead coat left in. For the same reason, the color becomes pale and looks washed out.

Your thumb and forefinger are the best tools for stripping, but a good stripping knife can also do the job. It is much easier to break the coat when using a knife instead of correctly pulling it out. Very fine thinning scissors, with teeth on one blade only, may be used to finish the ears and feet *only*.

"Are those for us?" Carol Kelly.

Necessary grooming equipment:

1. Greyhound comb
2. Pin brush
3. Nail clippers
4. Pocket comb or palm brush, for the ring
5. Mars coarse undercoat rake
6. Coarse stripping knife

The long teeth of the Greyhound comb allows one to comb through the coat with the greatest ease. A pin brush is the only brush that should be used on a show coat. The slicker brush is for working through tangles and general maintenance at home, on dogs not being shown. The slicker brush pulls out too much hair to risk using it on dogs that will be shown. Use the pin brush instead.

The best way to get a Cairn into a full coat for the showring is to strip the dog's coat. A puppy's coat will generally open and appear blousy at about ten months. When this happens, the entire body coat needs to be pulled out, and once started, the pulling must be finished within a few days, or there will be different coat lengths. The reason for pulling all the coat is to bring in a good tight jacket all of one length. When stripping is finished, the dog should be clothed only in his undercoat, *with the exception of the legs and head.*

I recommend only partial plucking of leg hair. Growth of leg hair is extremely slow; building these furnishings is a long-term, ongoing part of grooming. You may pull long straggly hairs on legs at any time, but remember to do so judiciously.

I prefer a dog to have three to five different lengths of hair on both legs and head. Many different lengths of hair will allow both legs and head to appear much fuller, and the head hair will stand up better on its own, without further enhancement.

Coralrocks Class Act, as a puppy, after most of her long, black puppy coat has been removed.

Take out about a third of the hair on legs and head, making this a clean, even trim. Do not leave holes or open spots on either legs or head. Shape the head in the proper rounded shape even though it may appear sparse. *Do this thirty days before you strip the body.*

In many locations, the shows diminish in number during both the summer and the winter months. In order to make the most of a new coat, the timing of the shows must be considered. A properly competitive coat needs from ten to sixteen weeks to develop from the time the old body coat was stripped out. Other factors that affect the timing of coat growth include the local climate and the amount of time a Cairn spends in the house. A dog that is not exposed to natural elements except for brief exercise periods has no need for the thick, dense coat the Cairn of the Highlands was bred to carry, and therefore will not develop one.

Every exhibitor has his or her own tricks of the trade. You would be well advised to seek advice from the breeder of your Cairn regarding grooming, particularly if you live nearby. Learn what you can from your first teacher. Learn the fine points of grooming as you know it. Then branch out, purchase grooming tapes, study books on other breeds and develop your own style. The most common mistake novices make is asking everyone for advice. This leaves them confused, and both their grooming and handling are a hodgepodge, because they do not have enough frame of reference to determine which advice best suits their own Cairns.

When the body jacket starts coming in, pick at it as soon as you can get your fingers on the hairs, at about one inch in length. By continuous plucking at the coat you can keep it presentable for long periods. This process is called "rolling the coat." Effective rolling means grooming sessions at least twice a week in order to maintain an even, showable coat.

GROOMING TIPS

Grooming a Cairn Terrier is relatively simple compared to the same routine for some of the other Terriers. The Scottish Terrier and the West Highland, for example, have more extreme trims, emphasizing shorter body coat and longer hair—known as a "skirt" on the lower portion of the dog. *There should be no appearance of a "skirt" on a Cairn.*

To trim a Cairn head for the showring, picture in your mind's eye a chrysanthemum. Try to shape the head into a roundish shape leaving plenty of hair to form a fall over the eyes. The purpose of trimming or "finish" work is to enhance the dog, emphasize its good points and minimize weaknesses as much as possible. For example, if a dog has a little larger ear, leave the hair on the top skull a little longer, which will de-emphasize the size of the ear. Shortening the hair slightly all around the muzzle will give the appearance of a shorter foreface. Many people let head hair grow when trying to cover up a longer muzzle and top skull, when the opposite is often more effective. These tips should be carried out in moderation, and experimented with at home. The way to learn is on a dog that you are not showing, so the mistakes won't matter. I once trimmed the head of one of my early Cairns like a Westie's, and then a Scottie's. Then, I really knew how to trim a Cairn. I have also owned a Wire Fox and a Welsh Terrier, and I believe much is learned about trimming when you must work with a really short jacket and attempt to cover faults working with such short hair.

Neaten up the hair on your dog's neck. I urge novices to hang a picture of a well-trimmed Cairn in their grooming room, along with a picture of a Westie. Many Cairn people seem to be afraid to clean up the neck for fear the dog will look like a Westie. On the contrary, neatening will give the appearance of better length of neck, and smoothly sloping shoulders. Having the Westie and Cairn pictures to refer to will keep your grooming from becoming too extreme.

"Neatening" will help the general appearance of the shoulders and forelegs. Pluck the excess hair to present a smooth outline to the judge. Your dog should present a picture of a rough, hardy Terrier, but that picture can be greatly enhanced with a little judicious plucking!

The legs should not have any long, straggly hairs hanging from them, as they will fly when the dog moves, detracting from its action. Have someone move the dog for you, so you can evaluate its gait. Then determine what trimming will make it look better. Remove some of the hair at the elbows, for if you do not the dog will look out at the elbow whether it is or not. This happens because when the dog is moving, the elbows touch the body, pushing extra hairs away. These protrude through the coat, detracting from the dog's movement. Removing this hair is done from underneath, not taking the top layer, but the softer hair at the elbow. Remember to continue to keep this hair short. Comb through the front legs gently, so as not to pull excess hair, then shake the leg by the foot, and gently comb upward. Then shake again, and comb down the outer hair on the leg. This will show you all the long hairs that should be removed.

Moving on to the topline, have someone again move the dog for you. Make sure the topline appears level. If it does not, remove excess hair where possible to give this impression. Often hair seems to grow faster over the loin and in front of the tail. Pull a few hairs at a time, being sure to pull the entire area that needs correction. Beware of pulling a hole in front of the tail, which will cause the tailset to appear low. Take this very slowly, stop often, brush, observe and continue as needed.

Also study the appearance of your dog's underline. If this hair is never trimmed, it can affect the entire outline. If the hair is too long in the center, it will create an optical illusion of a soft topline. If the underline is too short it may cause the dog to appear too high on leg. The underline should at least reach the elbow and taper gradually toward the hindquarters.

When your dog is being moved for you, look at it going away from you, coming back and, *very important*, from the side. Remember the judge in the ring has little more than two minutes to evaluate your dog in its class. Your exhibit must look its best while it is being shown.

For the hindquarters, simply neaten up the area to match the front. Leave the same amount of hair on all four corners of the dog.

If a dog does not have a proper bend of stifle, you can trim the leg to give the appearance of a better one by leaving hair at the bend of the stifle and trimming in angulation on the front side of the leg, at the front of the joint. If the dog is cow-hocked, you can clean off inside the leg at the top of the hock, and leave hair on the outside. If a dog moves too close either front or rear, cleaning off some of the hair on the inside of the legs will create an optical illusion of better movement.

The tail should have thick, short hair covering it. A tail with feathers or long hair dangling is very distracting to the judge. If the tail is carried too far over the back, this can be de-emphasized by allowing more hair to grow on the front of the tail.

A floor mirror is an excellent tool for those times when you are trimming and there is no one to walk dogs for you.

Now it is time to address a very tricky subject—the actual preparation of the Cairn for showing. I have already quoted the Standard. The Cairn is to be "tidied." There are still purists in the fancy who only pluck some hairs, tidy the ears and tail, and bring exhibits into the ring with minimal presentation. To make the really full-coated dog look its best, this trimmer must be a true master at grooming, and unfortunately, this is almost a lost art. Exhibiting a mature Cairn in a longer fuller coat is quite a task. It makes it much more difficult to effectively emphasize the reach of neck, level topline and good movement. Not allowing excess hair to detract from movement is quite a task by itself. It can be done, and presents a beautiful picture when done properly.

A Cairn Terrier in serious need of grooming. Ann Priddy.

A properly groomed Cairn Terrier. Ann Priddy.

A Cairn Terrier should never be trimmed to resemble a Westie. A comparison of this and the previous illustration leaves no doubt that there is a world of difference between the two. Ann Priddy.

A MATTER OF STYLE

At this juncture, I do want to discuss grooming that is a little more stylized. Most people do it, and I feel that guidelines should be delineated. I find nothing at all offensive about a clean dog. I do bathe *the legs and belly* of all exhibits that I bring into the showring. There is the option of blowing this hair dry, or letting the dog stand in a clean exercise pen and dry naturally. This takes some time, and if the show site is cold, this practice could be detrimental to the dog's health.

Many people add styling gel and powder to the legs and belly, which will give a fuller look. The same thing can be accomplished with the rolling process described previously, and much less enhancement will be required. This manner of presentation has the additional advantage of not being in opposition to the American Kennel Club ruling that prohibits foreign substances in dogs' coats in the showring.

I do not recommend bathing the head. This will soften the head furnishings, which means they will droop and it will be more difficult to get

the chrysanthemum effect. I do not think this natural Terrier of the Highlands lends itself to teasing and back combing of the head hair.

To clean the jacket or body coat of the Cairn, a little alcohol on a clean
towel can be used. Simply put a small amount of alcohol on a clean hand
towel, and rub over the coat in the direction in which the coat grows.
Overuse of alcohol will dry the coat, so use this only as a show preparation. Remember also that bathing is detrimental to the Cairn coat, and
will cause it to open up and become blousy.

SOME CLOSING THOUGHTS

This chapter discusses only the highlights of grooming. If you are planning to show your Cairn, there is no substitute for experience. Go ahead
and pull a few hairs. They will grow back, even if you do pull a hole in the
coat! Again, ask advice from fellow fanciers. But my best advice is to select
a mentor, and listen to this one person, until you have become good at
what that person can teach you, and you have begun to develop your own
style. Nothing is more confusing than taking conflicting advice and trying
to adapt it accordingly. Become good at what you are doing, and then try
to improve your skills gradually. Watching what others do at dog shows is
always an educational experience, but it must be remembered that every
dog in the hands of an expert is groomed to make the most of its individual assets. What is right for one dog could be disastrous for another.
Remember also, although many people pride themselves on their own
personal little grooming tricks, they may not share every tip with the
novice, but much can still be learned from simple observation.

Chapter Twelve

Handling

Showing dogs is a great form of recreation for many people. If you are fortunate enough to have a show quality puppy, you may be considering trying your hand at some dog shows with him or her. For the novice, there can be no more rewarding approach than handling your own dog. Happily, there are many ways to learn the art of ringcraft.

All-breed shows are regularly conducted by kennel clubs throughout the United States. These clubs have been licensed by the American Kennel Club and approved to hold shows under AKC rules. The AKC also recognizes clubs that hold Specialty shows and matches exclusively for their breeds.

A dog show is an elimination contest. All recognized breeds are divided into seven variety Groups based on original function—Sporting, Hound, Working, Terrier, Toy, Non-Sporting and Herding. The first phase of competition is by sex, by breed. A championship is awarded by the AKC after a total of fifteen points—including two major wins of at least three points, awarded under two different judges, and the balance under at least one more judge—have been earned. The AKC publishes a rule book available at no charge for single copies, detailing eligibility for the various classes; it is a wealth of information for any exhibitor.

The Best of Breed dog or bitch is the only dog allowed to go further in the elimination contest, and it is eligible to compete in Group competition later in the day. The balance of competitors within the breed are not eligible for further competition at that particular show.

During Group competition, one exhibit from each breed competes, the Best of Breed dog or bitch. Each dog is evaluated by the judge based on how well the dog compares to its individual breed Standard. Placings are awarded, one through four.

After Group judging is completed, there will be only seven dogs competing for Best in Show, the first place winners in each of the seven

Ch. Caledonian Berry of Wolfpit makes a beautiful picture as he "free baits" into a natural position, just as the Cairn Terrier Standard describes. No manual intervention by the handler can improve on this.

Groups. This is a very dramatic episode, and the dogs seem to know it! Here is a chance for handler and dog alike to prove how much they really belong in the Best in Show ring. Any one of them could walk away with this coveted honor.

Our newcomer to this fascinating world should now be eager to join the ranks of his or her successful peers, and learn to win at dog shows. The following information will get you started. Remember, nothing is a quick fix, and there is no substitute for hard work.

CONFORMATION CLASSES

Classes are beneficial in many respects. The noise and confusion of the classes and the presence of other dogs will be good experience for your puppy. However, the Cairn is easily bored, so extensive training could be a mistake. As soon as the Cairn will go willingly on lead with tail and ears up, and strange noises and several other people and dogs are not intimidating, then classes are optional. The classes may be necessary for the novice handler, however.

Conformation classes are only as good as the instructor. Your instructor should be able to help you with strategies that will make your puppy look its best, such as the speed at which you gait the dog, where to place the lead and how to encourage the puppy without getting it too excited. Make every effort to absorb what your instructor is trying to teach you.

READING

Read everything available to you. Books, magazines and videos on dog handling are not always applicable to Cairns, but much can be learned from their study.

ATTENDING DOG SHOWS

While you are learning, attend as many shows as possible. The best advice I was given was to take a notebook, and make notes of everything that I saw. That was more than twenty-five years ago, and some of those notes really exposed my ignorance as a novice. I had entirely different opinions of judges that my dog was shown to, about six weeks apart. Unfortunately, those opinions are based on how my first dog placed! We all love that first dog. You are not alone. And the hurt you feel when that dog does not win is universal.

If you are fortunate to have a "good" Terrier handler in your area, go to the ring where he or she will be showing dogs all day long and study the actions of that handler. If this person allows a dog to forge or lag behind, for instance, you can be sure that the handler is doing this for a reason. I repeat, go and watch the *great ones*. Consider the way the dog is trimmed. Do you see excesses of hair in certain areas? If you do, there is probably a reason. Perhaps we are camouflaging a poor bend of stifle, etc. Along with your other dog show equipment, take a notebook and a pen. Take notes. Observe.

If there is more hair in front of the dog than there should be, watch the dog move. You can evaluate front movement from the rear of the dog, and rear movement from the front of the dog.

Training yourself requires hours of study. Something that will be of great value to you in evaluating movement is slow-motion videos. However, Cairn fanciers are fortunate enough to have access to a video produced by Dana Cairns Associates, for the Cairn Terrier Club of America, entitled *Movement in the Cairn Terrier*. The photography and critique for this video was done by Rachel Page Elliott, author of *Dogsteps*. Copies are available from the Secretary of the CTCA.

Study the ring procedures used by the professionals. Do they show all the dogs in their care differently? Do they gait them slower or faster? Do they show some dogs on tighter leads than others? Are some allowed to appear out of control, either going away or returning to the judge? If so, there is a reason. You *can* form reasonably accurate opinions regarding a dog's structure from ringside. Watch where the dog's feet touch the ground when moving. If they are not in the correct position, the dog is not constructed properly, no matter how well it is made to appear, either by trimming or handling.

A floor mirror is excellent for studying your dog's gait. If your dog appears to converge or move wide, the speed at which he is gaited can minimize these faults. Always remember that the short-legged Terriers, and particularly Cairns, move *true*. At a trot the front feet should touch the ground in stride, immediately under the elbow. The same holds true for the hindquarters. The driving motion should push back from a point directly in line with the front feet. There is enough drive in the Cairn gait that when viewing from the rear, the pads should be clearly visible.

PRACTICING AT HOME

Putting the Dog on the Table

Pick the dog up under the ribs with your left hand, and support head and neck from underneath with your right hand. When you place the dog on the table elevate the rear slightly, while gently dropping the front in the exact position you want the judge to see; then set the rear. You will need a lot of practice in front of a mirror making sure your dog looks its best. This procedure allows you more time to set the dog to its fullest advantage from any angle. If the judge is approaching rapidly, this little trick gets your Cairn ready much faster.

At home, you will need a mirror facing your grooming table. This allows you to determine how best to pose your dog in the ring to its best advantage.

While learning to pose a dog on the table, a photograph of a dog that you think is well posed can be used. Study why that dog looks proper and try to pose your dog to look the same. Pay particular attention to where you have positioned the feet. Are they immediately under the shoulder? Have a look at the topline. If the dog appears high in the rear, for example, placing the rear feet wider apart will help to level out the topline.

Place the lead immediately under the jaw, and right behind the ears, not halfway down on the neck. Positioning the lead high on the neck will emphasize the dog's reach of neck.

A Cairn should show happily in the ring, with ears and tail up, looking like it was born to be there. The Cairn has a mischievous nature, often obvious in the ring, as the dog cleverly makes a fool of the handler by coming up with some new behavior to momentarily shake him or her up. The Cairn should not be propped up in the ring. Rather it should stand on its own with its tail up, showing interest in its surroundings and its handler. The Cairn should be happy to stand on its own, showing itself off with assurance! The sight of a ring full of Cairns with handlers kneeling behind them propping them up sends a message that misses the entire character of the breed. Judges should recognize a Cairn standing on its own as proper, in essence showing itself, and reward that.

Courteous behavior in the ring is an absolute! So is prompt arrival in the ring. Say a courteous thank you to the judge, no matter what color the ribbon you receive, and exit the ring in a professional manner with a smile on your face, and above all show consideration for the dog. Its safety and emotional security should be your first priority. Displays of temper or poor sportsmanship are always unacceptable.

The Cairn should be *sparred* in the show ring. There is no sight more glorious than two Cairns looking alertly at each other, with all four feet on the ground. They should be allowed to show their Terrier characteristics and "up on their toes" attitude. The key here is the definition of sparring. Sparring cannot be described better than in an article written by Dora Lee Wilson and Judi Hartell, first published in Dick Beauchamp's magazine *Kennel Review*.

SPARRING THE TERRIER

In today's computerized world, have our "tough" Terriers become robots? Have we bred the correct temperament out of our Terriers, or have we over-trained them to become liver-seeking statues waiting quietly and patiently for that little bit of reward? The sparkle and excitement present in the Terrier Group of years past is largely missing from today's competition. Some of the great Terriers of the past are remembered as super showmen, exhibiting the correct Terrier attitude toward other dogs. How many of our top Terriers of today show the same steady gleam of challenge as they size up the competition?

Sparring should be an integral part of judging the correct Terrier temperament, as well as proper expression, ear placement, arch of neck, length of back, tailset and topline. Most Terriers were developed as pack dogs, bred to control vermin and rodents. Within the pack, one dog would rise to the ranks of dominant dog, by his aggressive nature and ability to meet each challenge presented him. He would bow down to no foe and pursue his quarry with relentless determination. The intelligence of the Terrier is evident as he assesses the challenge before him. He stands with an alert attitude, staring nose to nose, and eye to eye, ready for battle. Thus the term *sparring* came into our dog world vocabulary as a one-word definition of true Terrier temperament. Some Terrier Standards include as part of temperament section, a hard-bitten or intent, piercing expression, which can only be properly judged when a dog is sparred.

The rapid growth of dog shows has brought waves of new exhibitors and judges, with increasing interest in our Terrier breeds. Unfortunately the novice exhibitor and newly licensed Terrier judge often misinterpret the term *sparring*. In the breed and Group ring today, we find Terriers are often not sparred or are improperly sparred. It is the responsibility of the experienced exhibitor and Terrier judge to instruct the novice in the proper manner in which to spar the Terrier.

In the ring, a Terrier should be allowed to show on its own, expressing interest in the dogs and activities around him. Exhibitors should allow enough room between themselves so that their dogs can spar without getting too close or causing a fight. It should be understood that sparring does not license viciousness or an uncontrolled dog. While the dog should be ready to accept all challenges, he should be under control at all times. "Control" is demonstrated by all four feet on the ground. The dog *should not* leap and snarl. Not more than three or four dogs should be brought out to spar at one time. By limiting the number of dogs sparred, the exhibitor is better able to control his charge, and the judge may better evaluate the dogs.

Handling a Terrier properly is an art to be developed through the experience of living with, conditioning and showing these breeds. From birth a Terrier puppy begins the process of temperament development. Observe the aggressive puppy that pushes others in the litter away from the breast he chooses to nurse. As the puppies grow older, the more dominant in temperament will instigate wrestling matches among themselves and compete more strongly for food and attention. This type of competition is healthy and should be encouraged. Any displays of viciousness, of course, should be discouraged.

For an older dog that seems to lack spirit, there are several training methods that have been proven successful. In a kennel situation, walk the dog up and down the aisle on a lead and let him look at the dogs that are in runs. By nature the dogs in runs will challenge the newcomer. Allow the dog to face his challenger, and praise him for his interest. Always be sure he keeps four feet on the ground and avoid direct contact with the other dogs. Should a kennel not be available, you may follow the above guidelines using a dog in an exercise pen. Walk the new dog around the pen in the manner described above.

Many times an experienced dog can be used to encourage the youngster. Put a lead on each dog. Have someone walk the experienced dog up to face the beginner. You may need to turn the youngster around several times to let him know he should look his competition in the eye. Again, be sure both dogs stand with all four feet on the ground and avoid direct contact. The procedure should then be reversed, allowing the beginner to be the challenger.

We are the caretakers of our Terriers and are responsible for their temperaments. As breeders we must select temperamentally sound stock and provide an environment that will develop correct Terrier temperament. As exhibitors, we must allow our Terriers to maintain their individuality, showing gameness and interest in their surroundings. Ultimately, we must see that the Terrier is properly presented. Controlled sparring should be part of the judging procedure to accomplish this goal.

Dora Lee Wilson
Judi Hartell

The wonderful, intelligent character of the Cairn is never more evident than when he recognizes those dogs against whom he regularly campaigns. Often these dogs will develop real dislikes for one another, and can recognize each other across the dog show venue. An occasion comes to mind when two campaigners saw each other again after several years when both had been entered in the Veterans' Class. It was as though they had seen each other yesterday. The animosity was still there!

Handling can be a truly rewarding experience, giving you a chance to step outside of yourself. The competition centers around the dog you are showing, not yourself. Good handling gives you an opportunity to help the dog show itself to its best advantage. There is no substitute for skillful presentation in the showring, and no substitute for the pleasure and thrill of winning with a well-presented, well-trained dog.

"How far to the Emerald City?" Used by permission of Turner Entertainment Co.

Chapter Thirteen

The Cairn at Work and Play

Given the opportunity, most Cairn Terriers enjoy keeping busy and prefer an active life to that of a "couch potato." In this chapter we will look at the breed's many achievements in the entertainment world, advertising, obedience, agility, tracking, going to ground, earth dog trials, pet therapy, hearing dogs, mushing in Alaska and Team Pedigree Flyball.

THE WIZARD OF OZ

There have been many movies in which dogs have appeared—*101 Dalmatians*; *Benji*; *Lady and the Tramp*; *Lassie Come Home*; and *The Ghost and Mrs. Muir*, featuring a Cairn, are some examples. Few, however, have had more significance than the MGM screen classic *The Wizard of Oz*, from the book by L. Frank Baum, starring among others, a Cairn Terrier. The premiere of *The Wizard of Oz*, starring Judy Garland, Ray Bolger, Bert Lahr, Frank Morgan, Billie Burke, and Margaret Hamilton, took place at the famous Grauman's Chinese Theatre on Tuesday, August 15, 1939. The innovative production was an immediate success and still ranks among the top movies of all time. Its fiftieth anniversary in 1989 was celebrated with all sorts of memorabilia.

Just by coincidence, 1989 also saw the emergence of Ch. Cairmar Cowardly Lion, a Cairn Terrier owned by me, Anna Lee Rucker and B. N. Carroll, as a leading campaigner. "Leo" was campaigned extensively in 1989 and 1990, ending with a career record of eight Bests in Show, fifty-one Group Firsts and the rank of No. 1 Cairn all systems in 1990. In 1991, Ch. Foxairn Tinman, owned by Betty Hyslop and handled by Peggy Beisel, emerged as No. 1 Cairn in two systems, and No. 1 all systems in 1992. Tinman's record to date is sixty Group Firsts and six Bests in Show.

It is interesting that *The Wizard of Oz* would inspire two different breeders to name such promising dogs for characters from the movie, and

Drawing by Carol Kelly

that their careers would coincide with the fiftieth anniversary of a movie that brought many changes to the world of cinematography.

Stage performances of *The Wizard of Oz* have starred Cairns bred by many fanciers. And the adaptable Cairn continues to charm audiences from coast to coast in the memorable part.

Cairn enthusiasts join the fun by appearing in costumes, such as those pictured on page 159. Jane Attaman and Carol Warden use the dogs seen here in costume in pet therapy as well as obedience.

The 1989 CTCA national Specialty annual dinner and fund raiser saw some of its most prominent figures dressed in *Wizard of Oz* costumes— Mary Desloge was the Wizard, Kris Armour was the Scarecrow, Karen Smith was Dorothy, Ken Kauffman was the Tin Man, Penny Prior was Glinda the Good Witch, and Bob Abhalter appeared as the Cowardly Lion.

Collectibles still fascinate the American public. The North American Bear Company recently introduced "Judy Bearland and Toto," pictured on page 159. Judy is complete with her ruby slippers.

CAREER CAIRNS

Cairn Terriers have also taken part in other kinds of business-related activities such as advertising. The Cairn model in both the Kibbles 'N Bits and the Old Maine Trotters advertisements is Happicairn Cinnamon.

Lakewood's Katie O'Gracious, owned by Michelle Petit, has been featured in a Wolf Camera commercial. Although at work in the advertising world, Katie was able to earn her CD, score in the top-ten Delaney system (which tabulates obedience scores) for 1992, and earn her CGC and TDI degrees.

A Cairn Terrier frequents the offices of the American Kennel Club in New York. "Lexi" is owned by Jim Dearinger, vice president of obedience for the club, and his wife, Janet Ford Dearinger, administrative assistant for dog events. Lexi has her own chair in Janet's office, and is the self-appointed office mooch.

Nell Stumpff has provided to the U.S. Air Force more than twenty drug-sniffing Cairns, including Ch. Lakewood's General Sherman. "Tank" served three years on an Air Force submarine, and was still going strong when last heard from. The Air Force selected the Cairn as one of six breeds used in this fashion, because of its size and abilities in this field.

I have a magazine article about a Swedish policemen who walks his beat with two Cairn Terriers,

Jane Attaman dressed as Dorothy with her Cairn, In Memory O' Mittens, Can. CD. Am. CDX, CGC, TDI, as the Tin Man, and Carol Warden as the Wicked Witch of the West with her Cairn, Carol's Carrie MacWarden, CD, CGC, TDI, costumed as the Cowardly Lion. Booth Photography.

Judy Bearland and Toto, posing with the "real thing." Bear Courtesy North American Bear Co., Chicago, Illinois.

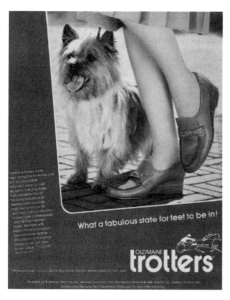

Happicairn Cinnamon posed in this Old Maine Trotters advertisement.

Happicairn Cinnamon in a Kibbles 'N Bits advertisement.

preferring them to larger dogs for their keen sense of smell and excellent eyesight. The article tells of his Cairns Trulsa and Primula being instrumental in capturing a fleeing burglar scenting and locating him hiding in a building.

OBEDIENCE

I strongly recommend some form of obedience training for the Cairn Terrier. In view of what the Cairn was bred to do—hunt and perhaps kill vermin, working independently of humans—it is clear that this is a headstrong fellow. Praise and reward are the best training methods. Cairns are very trainable, but require great patience. The results, however, are well worth the effort.

The reason most of us have dogs is because we really like them and enjoy their company. We like doing things with them, and the more we do with our dogs, the stronger the bond we build with them, and the more we enjoy each other. Obedience training is an important way of strengthening and maintaining this bond.

The Obedience sport is a very important aspect of the American Kennel Club's responsibilities. There were 2,030 Obedience Trials held in 1993, with more than 124,000 dogs competing.

Obedience classes follow a set format, with exercises increasing in difficulty as dogs advance. Included are various heeling exercises, while on leash, a stand for examination, off-lead heeling, and long sits and downs. More advanced work includes retrieving at various levels of difficulty, and eventually working with hand signals, and in challenging scent discrimination exercises.

One of the early outstanding Cairns in Obedience was Can. & Am. Ch. Alexander McRuff O'Southfield, CD, CDX, TD, CG (1972–82), bred by Martha Baechle and owned by Jess Nixon. Alec earned his TD in 1975, his CD in 1976 and his CDX in 1979. He earned his Certificate of Gameness in 1976 through the working terrier trials organized in California by Jane King. He continued to work until his death in 1982, when he was working on his TD. This remarkably versatile Cairn also sired nine champions, and was a top producer in 1977 and 1979.

Another outstanding Cairn in both the show ring and obedience was Am. & Can. Ch. Tradorohg's Dunstan Claymore, Am. & Can.

"Lexi" with Jim Dearinger, AKC vice president of obedience.

CDX. Dunstan Claymore won the CTCA national Specialty in 1975, and sired fourteen champions. "Dusty" remains the only CDX Cairn to win the national Specialty to date.

Dorothy Higgins, "Tradorohgs," owned the first Cairn with a Utility degree, Ch. Red Rock Candy Tomboy, UD. The Cairn Terrier column in the September 1965 issue of *Popular Dogs* reported that Mrs. Higgins's "Pinky" was the first American-bred Cairn and the first Cairn champion to win a UD. The writer was Mary S. Allen, Craigdhu Kennels. From Mrs. Higgins's letters, Pinky's history-making score of 192 was made on May 22, 1965, at the Greater St. Louis Training Club, and the judge was Mr. M. E. Hollister. Mr. Hollister gave Pinky her first Obedience degree, and the last leg on her Utility degree. Pinky had already earned her CD when she completed her championship at fifteen and a half months. Obviously, Dorothy Higgins was gifted at getting the most out of these feisty little Terriers, who like doing it their way.

It is interesting that one of our contemporary breeder-judges, Ken Kauffman, began with an Obedience Cairn, Lord Duffer McBriar Rose, and went on to five Highs in Trial. "Duffer" was the No. 2 Cairn in Obedience in 1976 and No. 1 in 1977 as tabulated by the Delaney system.

More recently, Tom and Kathy Anderson and their two Cairns have been doing very well in Obedience competition. On Saturday, October 9, 1993, Bonnie Marie On Crocker, UD, at six years, scored a 198 in Open B. This earned her High in Trial, and completed all her first place requirements for an OTCH. On the same day, Thane Theodore of Thornhill, CD, at two and a half years, scored 197½ in Novice B. The following day, "Teddy" scored a 198½ in Novice B, earning him a High in Trial. Bonnie was No. 1 Cairn in Obedience in 1989 (Delaney), 1990 (Delaney), 1991 (*Front & Finish*), 1992 (*Front & Finish*) and 1993 (*Front & Finish*). In 1993, in the *Front & Finish* system, two Cairns were in the top-ten Terriers, Bonnie, who ranked fifth, and Dunvegan's RiteAway UD, who ranked tenth, owned by J. and G. Herz.

Bonnie is the Andersons' first pet and first Cairn, which makes these achievements truly remarkable. Tom feels that his Cairns really enjoy pleasing him in the Obedience ring, and that their intelligence, inherent curiosity and perky attitude make them very well suited for Obedience.

Betty Luttier acquired Ch. Ragamuffin's Pojo at eight years of age. Betty is an Obedience enthusiast, but put off training Pojo until he was thirteen. Pojo earned his CD in five trials, shortly before his fourteenth birthday, a remarkable achievement.

AGILITY

The sport of Agility began in England in 1978. It was even featured as extra entertainment between events at the world-famous Cruft's. The sport has become very popular and variations on the original form have been developed. The sport now thrives not only in England, but in Europe and the United States as well. Emphasis in this sport is on the athletic ability and conditioning, flexibility and responsiveness of the dog, and a lot of pure fun and teamwork between handler and dog. Agility is one of the most exciting events I have seen in showring. The *joy* these dogs show in performing for their handlers is nothing short of extraordinary.

In Agility, a dog negotiates an obstacle course composed of open and closed tunnels, weave poles, dog walks, seesaws and tire jumps, A-frame, pause box and a variety of different jumps. Dogs' performances are scored on freedom from mistakes, and the amount of time taken to run the course.

Courses vary from event to event, and handlers are advised on the particulars of the course during the judges' briefing, immediately before the event. This is one sport that almost defies description—it simply must be seen to be appreciated fully. Happily, Cairns seem to love competing in Agility.

Agility is an off-lead event, so some obedience work is necessary beforehand. Again, positive reinforcement and encouragement through food seems to be the best manner in which to proceed.

Agility is less stressful and structured than Obedience. The handler may talk to, encourage and direct the dog during the "run." This is a fast-paced, upbeat activity. Cairns seem to regard these unusual obstacles as an adventure, adding yet another dimension to their already busy lives. Agility is great exercise, and develops great self confidence in the dogs and their handlers!

Allison Huck with Redwood's Too Hot To Handle, CD, TDX, CGC, Ag1 and TDI, and Mr. Bilbo Baggins, CD, TDI.

In doing research, I have located a few Cairn Terriers doing Agility work. One, Am. & Can. Ch. Merry Georas MacFerniegair, CDX, TD, CG, Ag1, Ag11, is owned by Merry Berglund. "George" is currently training for his UD. Allison Huck, and her Redwood's Too Hot To Handle, CD, TDX, CGC, TDI, have completed the Ag1 title as well. Betty Luttier is doing Agility with Cairns as well. Karengary's Tucquan Sprite, owned by Sue Haney, is another noteworthy Agility Cairn at the time of this writing.

TRACKING

Tracking is a sport for those who love the outdoors, their Cairns and a true challenge. In Obedi-

Too Hot To Handle coming out of the Agility tunnel.

ence and in conformation the handler and the dog are a team working together for a goal. In tracking, *only the dog knows where the track is,* and that leaves him in charge, which is exactly what the Cairn craves. A

Bedrock's Barney R., CD, TD, CGC, TDI, owned by Sheilla Gheesling, working in the tracking harness.

Terrier working in artificial earth.

properly trained tracking Cairn can track without the handler, which is not possible in either Obedience or conformation.

As yet only a handful of Cairns have the Tracking Dog Excellent title (TDX). Allison Huck's Redwood's Too Hot To Handle is among the few. "Maggie" earned her TDX on February 23, 1992. This was only her second test, and she was the only dog out of twelve to pass. Hellen Rutledge owns Ch. Scotch Mist's Gingersnap, TDX, who earned the title in 1987.* JC's Masked Bandit Hollytoo, UD, TDX, also earned the TDX degree sometime before 1988. The TDX degree is extremely difficult to achieve. According to *Pure-Bred Dogs— American Kennel Gazette*, only twenty-five Terriers earned that title between 1980 and 1990, and the only Cairn Terriers were the three mentioned above. The TDX program was begun in 1979.

The AKC provides free of charge a brochure on tracking, which details all applicable rules and procedures.

WORKING TERRIERS

Patricia Adams Lent founded the American Working Terrier Association in 1971. AWTA trials offer dogs bred to go to ground the opportunity to perform their breed's work. The artificial "earths" used are of different lengths and degrees of difficulty. Rats are caged at the end of the earths, and dogs must go to the ends of these earths and bark and scratch at the rats for a set time in order to qualify.

---

*Many of the obedience statistics quoted above were obtained from *Front & Finish, The Dog Trainer's News*, Galesburg, Illinois, with the help of Phyllis.

The AWTA also offers Hunting Certificates for larger Terriers that do not ordinarily go to ground. Mrs. Lent owns and hunts Cairns herself. The first Certificate of Gameness (CG) was earned by her Canonach Tatty of Foxrun.

Earthdog Tests

On September 17, 1993, the AKC held a Terrier Hunting Advisory Committee meeting. This meeting was called to make progress toward a new AKC performance event, Earthdog Tests. The event is so named because it is designed for dogs originally bred to go to ground for badger, fox and otter. Obviously, Cairn Terriers are among the eligible breeds. Specialty clubs and other groups will be allowed to conduct this event. Clubs may hold both sanctioned matches and licensed tests.

PET THERAPY

Pet Therapy is relatively new on the scene of "doggie" activities. It probably came as an extension of Hearing Ear Dogs, where dogs are trained to signal household sounds for their hearing-impaired owners.

Pet Therapy takes helping the less fortunate many steps further. Now active certification courses are available, which train therapy dogs for as much as a five-month period.

For years people have been taking dogs into nursing homes to visit a family member who misses their pet, but the new breed of Pet Therapy Dogs are trained workers. Cairns enter training as their usual, fun-loving selves, and quickly adapt to the training for the work. They develop a special personality for the workplace, becoming the more familiar bundle of energy once they leave the hospital or nursing home.

Cairns make exceptional Pet Therapy Dogs because they are so intelligent and so sensitive to their owner-handlers, their surroundings and what is expected of them. The sights and sounds of all the strange medical equipment are just another adjustment to the Cairn, which is prepared to accompany his trainer and perform his tasks without further ado.

Another aspect that makes the Cairn ideal for therapy work is its love for doing tricks. Patients are often thrilled with the opportunity to be part of any activity. Ball playing or even brushing the Cairn's coat is excellent for the patients, particularly those in rehabilitation. Regaining motor skills while holding a dog and brushing it is much less tedious than the usual physical therapy routines.

Betty Luttier is a participant in Pinellas County, Florida's, Project PUP (Pets Uplifting People) program. She mentions among other things that the elderly like to engage in conversation, and the very nature of the Cairn encourages talk. Questions as to what breed and are they *Wizard of Oz*

Betty Luttier with Tammara of Twisted Oaks, CDX, on a therapy visit to an appreciative patient.

dogs often encourage residents to participate in conversation. The Cairn is a good size for a lap and a bed. A few commands are essential. "Stay" for one, and "Come" for another. Each well-behaved therapy dog paves the way for another.

One marvelous story was sent to me by Patricia R. Broyles, and it was related by Beverly Josephson, R.N. Beverly related that Joyce, a "forty-ish" patient in her care, with a mental age of eight, had been admitted for surgery and was not doing well at all. She had suffered several bouts of pneumonia, and it was feared she would die. Upon learning that Joyce had a dog of her own, Beverly, one of her nurses, made all the necessary moves to get Pat Broyles's Pet Therapy Dog involved. The doctors agreed and Pat brought in her Cairn, Maggie. Joyce, who had been very lethargic up to then, became aware of Maggie on her bed, and Maggie is credited by many as the turnaround point in Joyce's recovery. Joyce eventually did go home to her Poodle.

Training your Cairn to be a therapy dog is wonderfully rewarding for both you and your Cairn. Any owner can do this. It matters not whether your dog is a conformation champion or a highly trained obedience dog, or simply a much loved pet. You and your Cairn could enrich the lives of others who are less fortunate.

If you would like to become involved in Pet Therapy, contact your local Pet Therapy group. If there is no group near you, contact a local nursing home and ask to speak with the activities director. Explain that you are interested in bringing a well-mannered dog to visit. Most facilities will be delighted. Explain that the dog will be clean and under control. Putting a dog on a bed, and keeping your hand there for reassurance, is a good practice. It is a privilege to have our dogs with us, and for a few minutes out of our busy lives, we can give that pleasure to someone who could benefit from sharing that happiness.

HEARING DOGS

Most hearing dogs trained by agencies such as Texas Hearing and Service Dogs (THSD)—where I got my information with the kind cooperation of its president, Sheri Soltes Henderson—are adopted from local animal shelters. The Hearing Dog organizations do not, as a rule, accept animals as donations, preferring to save lives via the animal shelter route.

Hearing dogs are trained to alert the hearing-impaired person to all manner of noises, such as the doorbell, smoke alarms, telephone and often a person calling their name. These animals are becoming accepted in today's workplace, thus providing the hearing-impaired with more occupational options. Training is always by the reward method. This is a likely occupation for Cairn Terriers, since they are so keenly aware of everything going on around them at all times.

Heathcairn Charlie.

Martha Brewer's Ch. Heathcairn Charlie was given to Martha McReynolds after she finished her championship. "Charlie" trained herself to be a hearing dog, and would alert Martha to both the telephone and the doorbell almost by instinct.

CAIRNS AS SLED DOGS

Yes, really! As a delightful ending to this chapter, which offers many ideas for other activities you and your Cairn can share, I am fortunate to be able to share with you quite an unusual activity being pursued in the state of Washington.

Eva Wright, Alaskairn Kennels, has trained a team of seven Cairn Terriers to pull a sled. This activity is referred to as "mushing," and is normally associated with the Siberian Husky or the Alaskan Malamute. Top racing teams often include other breeds and mixed breeds. It has been reported that when mail was hauled by dog sled in Alaska, there actually was a team of Airedale Terriers used for this work. It is believed that Eva Wright is the only person running Cairn Terrier teams.

This seems a natural progression for dog lovers breeding the hardy, active Cairn and living in a land of ice and snow. In such cold climates, it is often difficult for the active Cairn to get enough exercise in winter, so after careful evaluation of the breed, in terms of structure, coat and vigor, the Wrights set out to train their Cairns to work in teams.

The Wrights are extremely careful in working only the very healthiest of dogs. All Cairns are trained to walk in harness, but not allowed to pull a sled until over twelve months of age. New trainees are harnessed with an

Maud Earl (English, 1986–43), Come Play With Me, *1900, oil on canvas, private collection.* Photo courtesy William Secord Gallery, New York.

Brightridge Angel's Chloe "taking her friend to the barn."

Ch. Lakewood's Wareagle with a rabbit friend.

older, experienced teammate and taught commands such as "Easy" (slow down), "Gee" (turn right), "Haw" (turn left), "Whoa" (stop) and "Wait." The Cairns seem to do better when harnessed with a familiar dog, and matching gaits is a consideration as well.

CAIRNS AT PLAY

I will close this chapter with a vignette on Bed-rock's Barney R, owned by Sheilla and J.Barry Gheesling. Barney has his CD degree, his TD and his CGC award. But Barney will be remembered most for his participation in Team Pedigree Flyball.

Bedrock's Barney R., CD, TD, CGC, TDI, a member of Team Pedigree Flyball, owner Sheilla Gheesling.

I would have to classify Barney as being "at play," in spite of his many accomplishments. Team Pedigree Flyball travels throughout the Southeast performing in a wide variety of venues. Team Pedigree Flyball is strictly an exhibition team, the competition is all in fun and the participants are not paid, but the team is supported by Pedigree Food for Dogs.

Included here is a pictorial summary of Cairns at play. These Cairns are doing many of the things this wonderful breed can be taught to do or do on their own.

Ch. Goosedown's Tailor Made taking a well deserved dip—after his retirement from a successful career in the showring.

Chapter Fourteen

The Cairn Terrier Club of America

The Cairn Terrier Club of America (CTCA) was founded in 1916. We must assume that the first officers, Mrs. Henry Price, Mrs. Byron Rogers, Mrs. Payne Whitney and William R. Wannamaker, were among the six founders. The CTCA became an American Kennel Club (AKC) member club in 1917, being the ninth Terrier breed club to do so. In that year, thirty-two Cairns were registered in the United States. This was an upsurge from 1913, when the first Cairn, Sandy Peter Out Of The West, was registered in the United States. In 1993, eighty years later, 5,386 Cairn Terriers were registered in the United States.

Current information indicates the first Specialty was held at the Morris County Golf Club in 1921. The first CTCA yearbook was published in 1921, and included advertising for nine studs, with fees ranging from $35 to $40, and a champion stud listed for $50. One stud was advertised as being "Particularly good for weak-faced bitches."

From its inception in 1916 to 1926, the club grew to 123 members, with 87 percent of the membership being from the northeastern part of the country, and sixty-one members from New York State. Only sixteen of the forty-eight states were represented. Today, all but six of our fifty states are represented. States currently without a CTCA member are Hawaii, Idaho, Montana, North Dakota, Utah and Vermont. There is no reason to think this will not change in the future. There are currently ten affiliated regional clubs as well.

Cairn fanciers have seen numerous dramatic changes take place in the field over the years. Ethel Obenauer recalls shipping a bitch for breeding by rail. The cost of the rail fare was about $15, and the length of the trip was between six and ten hours. Dogs that traveled in this fashion were transported in handmade wooden crates with food and water attached in the baggage car, and usually placed beside the baggage car attendant.

Many breeders have made valuable contributions to the breed since the early days. Some are still active, and all have served the breed well, attempting to keep the Cairn safe from the fads of dog shows and still fit to do what it was bred to do. Some of these breeders are Frank and Dorothy Blackwood (Cairnhoe); Susan and John Farrow (Croydon); and Hettie Page Garwood (Het's). Mrs. Garwood is also renowned as a breeder and judge

Ch. Dees Birdwatcher at Robine, CD.

of Basset Hounds. Mr. and Mrs. George Gilbert also stand out as do Carmen Harkins (Kim-E-Cairns); Irv and Suzette Heider (Heiland), publishers of *Cairn Courier*, and their daughter Helen Zanzarak; Marilyn and Herb Joachim (Cairncrest); Carol and Neal Kelly (O'Windy Pines); Mr. Gerry Klein (Bagpipes); Bea and Max Krasno (Killiecrankie); Lynne Nabors (Twigbent); Mrs. Barbara Natarus and Mrs. Ethel Obenauer (Kildrummy); and Mr. Don Ritter and Rosemary Zagorsky (Kamidon).

The club is fortunate to have a number of breeder-judges among its members, some since the 1970s and others having joined more recently. Two noteworthy examples are Mrs. Mildred Bryant, now approved to judge four Groups, and Mrs. Lydia Coleman Hutchinson, approved to judge all Terriers and a number of the Toy breeds. John Honig is a well-known Collie breeder and multiple Group judge who bred Cairns and Collies under the Accalia prefix. Mr. and Mrs. Honig owned and campaigned the lovely Cairn Ch. Cairnwoods Golden Boy. Kenneth Kauffman is approved to judge sixteen terrier breeds, Dennis Barnes is approved for all Terriers and Dan Shoemaker (Waterford) does ten breeds. Mrs. Gail Kusack (Barberi Hedge) does six breeds, Mr. Palmer Glenn (Quixote) does four breeds and Nicholas Furillo is approved to judge Cairns. There are also several relative newcomers to judging, including Mrs. Molly Wilder, Jack Smith, Mrs. Karen Wilson, Mrs. Marilyn Swearingen, Raymond Tyra and most recently, Jon Kimes and Christine Carter. Betty Hyslop was approved for a number of years to judge both Cairns and Great Danes, but has always preferred to be in the ring exhibiting.

The CTCA has continued to be a driving force in Cairn history and leaps today to the forefront in many activities that encompass the future of all dog breeds.

Upon the direction of the CTCA, Mildred Bryant, delegate to the American Kennel Club, proposed the historic change in show rules that allows neutered dogs and bitches to be shown in the Veterans class at independent Specialties only. This rule change took effect in December 1991.

The following information on the progress of the CTCA's effort in the field of education was compiled and prepared by Lydia Coleman Hutchinson, the club's director of education.

The CTCA has sponsored educational programs beginning in the 1960s, when the president, Mrs. Ralph E. Stone, asked Lydia Hutchinson to present a grooming demonstration in conjunction with the national Specialty in Chicago. Grooming programs by Lydia, Martha Brewer and others continued, and in 1988, a grooming seminar in which four breeders participated (Ken Kauffman, Lydia, Bill MacFadden and me) was on the schedule during the Atlanta Specialty weekend.

Lydia Hutchinson has always been the backbone of the CTCA's educational process. In 1974, she organized a very successful lecture program conducted by Dr. Wayne Riser of the University of Pennsylvannia concerning "Orthopedic Problems of Short-legged Terriers." In addition to the many CTCA members present, a sizeable contingent of West Highland White and Scottie fanciers responded to an opportunity to hear this worthwhile program.

On the national Specialty weekend, in 1982, Cairn breeders were privileged to hear Miss C. H. Dixon (Rossarden) speak on the newly enacted British Standard for the Cairn Terrier.

During the presidency of Mark W. Alison, an Education Committee of the CTCA was formed, with Lydia serving as chairperson, a position she continues to hold to the present. The original committee members were Mary Andregg, Ann Kerr, Betty Marcum and Dan Shoemaker. Programs have been presented without exception since that time, during the national Specialty weekend, and have included such personalities as Dr. W. Jean Dodds, Mr. and Mrs. J. E. Clark and Dr. Helen Hislop. Most recently, the 1993 program was an all-day affair and included Dr. G. W. Padgett of Michigan State University, School of Veterinary Medicine; Dr. Sharon Center, School of Veterinary Medicine, Cornell University; and Dr. Paul Poulos, executive director of the Institute for Genetic Disease Control in Animals.

All Terrier breed clubs were invited to participate. It is hoped that the CTCA's forward progress can be shared through the Terrier Breeders Network, which held its initial meeting that day in the same location. The network also hopes to involve all parent clubs, and bring about the sharing of research information on many health-related concerns, thereby saving time and money for all.

The CTCA sponsored the video *Movement in the Cairn Terrier* (see page 151). Additionally, the CTCA supports an extensive rescue movement, placing about two hundred Cairns yearly, and publishes a very well-done quarterly newsletter. In recent years, the CTCA has established a genetic study group, then a "troika" to implement their findings and finally a foundation to gather funds and implement genetic research. Jack Smith, Redcoat, was very instrumental during this developmental period. This research will study Cairn Terriers in particular, but not exclusively. The foundation is charged to support all activities that will enhance the welfare of Cairn Terriers and other dogs.

Surveys and educational programs have furthered breeder awareness of changes in dog breeding, and the most professional manner in which to approach the subject. A manual offering up-to-date information on genetic problems was provided in 1993, under the guidance of Jennie Willis, director of the Health Related Concerns Committee.

The Cairn Terrier Club of America implemented an advanced code of ethics in 1990, which addresses such points as the minimum age at which a bitch should be bred, members' conduct and breeding animals that have produced genetic defects.

The CTCA produced a clarification of the Cairn Terrier Standard in 1985, a grooming booklet in 1990 and a general information brochure in 1991. All are available at a nominal cost from the club secretary, as a part of its public education service. The name and address of the current CTCA secretary is available from the American Kennel Club, 51 Madison Avenue, New York, NY 10010.

The CTCA has been a leader among parent breed clubs in educating its membership about genetic problems, offering grooming seminars and providing other education material.

In fact, thanks to Dr. Helen J. Hislop, professor and chairperson of the Department of Biokinesiology and Physical Therapy at the University of Southern California, the CTCA is well on the road to researching the problems within the Cairn breed. Dr. Hislop recognized as early as 1985 that there were genetic problems within the breed that should be documented. Dr. Hislop developed the first Cairn Terrier breeder survey, which has given the CTCA much good information from which to begin to develop a database. Tests are available for certain disorders, and concerned breeders should be availing themselves of this knowledge.

The Foundation of the CTCA has paved the way to allow registration of Cairn Terriers with the Institute for Genetic Disease Control in Animals. GDC is the first open registry in the United States, and is patterned after the open registry in Sweden, established by the Swedish Kennel Club. An open registry is a data bank of genetic history for any dog breed. The database is established by breeders registering with the GDC, with veterinary documentation, the absence or presence of certain diseases that are easily diagnosed and documented by radiographs. Data are currently being collected at GDC on many breeds. Registration is available to the Cairn Terrier in the following diseases: hereditary dysplasia, Legg-

Perthes, craniomandibular osteopathy and medial patellar luxation. Data are available to people attempting to reduce genetic disease in a kennel or in the breed as a whole. An open registry delivers information on specific animals to breeders in order for the breeder to make knowledgeable selection of mates whose bloodlines indicate a reduced risk of producing genetic disease.

George A. Padgett, D.V.M., professor of pathology at the College of Veterinary Medicine at Michigan State University, is the veterinary advisor to the CTCA. His input over the years has been invaluable.

The following paragraphs are drawn from an article contributed by Jennie Willis of the Department of Molecular Biology at Vanderbilt University. Jennie is the chairperson for the Health Related Concerns Committee for the CTCA. This information deals with the fascinating future of dog breeding.

Over the years, conscientious breeders have strived to produce a better Cairn. In the past, the major emphasis of breeding programs has been dedicated to enhancing the appearance and attitude of the dog. Breeders have concentrated on such traits as harsh coats, good temperament, proper expression, strong quarters, etc., while breeding away from crooked fronts or bad mouths, etc. Whenever a dog possesses traits of excellence, our desire is to concentrate and solidify those traits in our genetic line, and we begin to inbreed and linebreed. Now, we realize that when we inbreed or linebreed, we also inadvertently concentrate the defective genes, as well as the good ones, which expose genetic problems.

A mutation of a gene is caused by a mistake during DNA replication. (DNA, formally Deoxyribonucleic acid, a long, chainlike molecule that consists of two complimentary strands. The subunits are the four bases, a pentose sugar [deoxyribose] and phosphate. The arrangement of the subunits is used to store all the information necessary for life.) A change in the product may alter the body function and, if serious, leads to a genetic disorder. Mutations will continue from generation to generation. If the expression of the gene mutation is visible (phenotype), we of course would not breed two animals with this mutation. Today's breeders have to realize that they also have to deal with the consequence of the "carrier state." Carriers may not exhibit the gene mutation phenotypically, but carry a copy of the mutated sequence in the genome (the entire gene complement possessed by a cell or individual). The breeder will not be aware that the dogs are carriers until a breeding produces the disorder. Statistically the expression of the fault may be rare, but the mutated sequence is still passed on and on, and eventually will be expressed. By then we have implanted that mutated sequence in siblings of several generations, and we are faced with a "contaminated" gene pool, along with a greatly increased probability of producing the problem.

Suddenly concerned breeders' goals have changed! The only way to eliminate carriers today is through test matings, a procedure that is relatively slow. A method of identifying the genetic makeup of an animal would clearly be better. We could eliminate carriers from our breeding stock, and also predict whether a puppy might develop a late onset genetic disease.

This thought brings us to the human Genome Project. This research effort endeavors to identify all of the genes in the human being, with special emphasis on those genes responsible for genetic disorders in the human body. Many human genes have already been successfully identified, and the pace of this research effort is rapidly increasing. This technology could be applied to the canine genome, and presently there are multiple veterinary research groups working in this area.

This technology is referred to as genetic mapping, which can be used to identify individuals likely to develop particular traits or to identify carriers of genetic disease. If this technology for dogs becomes successful, it will be possible to detect both affected animals and carriers of diseased genes at a very early age, just by taking blood samples from a puppy.

Diagnostic DNA markers will allow us to realistically envision the day when many genetic disorders can be totally obliterated from our gene pool.

Many breeders attempt to breed out persistent gay tails, missing teeth or other minor problems, which are probably polygenetic in origin. Often a pedigree shows no immediate ancestors affected with these faults, yet a puppy or two will possess the defect. This does not mean one should give up breeding. It means more study is needed, and in my opinion, the affected puppies should be removed from your breeding program. I am not a geneticist, but I have been breeding Cairns since 1969, and I have learned a lot through experience. A problem will not disappear because you wish it would. It will only be corrected because you have learned about it and its mode of inheritance, if known, and you have tried to breed away from it, or block the genes you wish to discard, by breeding to an animal not carrying the same gene pattern—you hope!

There is no doubt that solutions such as DNA diagnosis are feasible in the future, and the possibilities are endless and wonderfully exciting to contemplate.

In recent years, the CTCA has developed a position of leadership among parent breed clubs. This has been given in this chapter by mentioning the accomplishments in education, research and rescue, and even changes in the manner in which dog shows are conducted, with reference to the CTCA's suggested motion, proposed by former CTCA delegate, Mildred Bryant, that spayed or neutered animals be eligible to compete in specialties where there is no further competition. Surely the CTCA will maintain its leadership status in the dog fancy due largely to the efforts of club members who continue to work for the good of the Cairn.

Chapter Fifteen

Cairn Terrier Rescue in the United States and Great Britain

There are many unwanted dogs in today's world. Many thousands, including purebreds, are euthanized in shelters and humane societies every year. And, yes, many of those purebred animals did come from puppy mills. However, concerned breeders have very strong responsibilities when placing their puppies into new homes. These include educating the prospective pet owner in great detail about the idiosyncrasies of Cairn Terrier temperament. Fewer puppies will wind up in distress if prospective owners are told exactly what to expect from their new pet. Ultimately, the breeder bears the responsibility for the entire life of every new puppy he or she brings into the world. The Cairn Terrier puppy and its prospective owner both have the right to expect a happy, mutually fulfilling relationship. This occurs when puppies are placed in wonderful, loving, well-suited homes, where lifestyles will suit the maintenance of a pet. It is the responsibility of the breeder to put the right puppy in the right home, and make sure the puppy and the new owners are as happy as they have every right to be.

I was very involved in organizing the rescue program for the Cairn Terrier Club of America. The idea came in 1987 from a liaison committee meeting between the regional clubs and the vice president of the CTCA. Initial information was gathered by contacting other parent clubs, particularly those within the Terrier Group. Christi McDonald (Gamac) did all the legwork for this part of the project. We also derived a lot of good advice from Lynne Nabors, who was already involved in Purebred Dog Rescue in St. Louis. Once we got responses from the other parent clubs, we set up our rescue network on a geographical basis, with thirteen regional chairs and three national co-chairs: Lynne Nabors, Sue DeWitt

"Toby" rescued by his owner, Cindy Eli, shown here when he completed his Companion Dog degree at the Texas Kennel Club, 1991. His ILP (Indefinite Listing Privilege) number enabled him to compete in obedience without being registered. The trophy presenter, Hellen Rutledge, is also a Cairn fancier and proud to share this special occasion. Don Petrulis.

and me. The reason for three chairs was to have someone that could be contacted with a problem at any time. This began in 1988, and the efficiency of the program increased considerably with the appointment of Rebecca Stamps as secretary.

Our rescue organization provides handouts at the annual meeting detailing success stories, information available from AKC, breed pamphlets at no charge and telephone contacts, and provides a schedule of reimbursable items.

It's hard to believe that a cute guy like "Trubbie," photographed in his holiday finery, ever needed a home!

CTCA rescue also benefits from the CTCA annual fund-raiser, held in conjunction with the annual club dinner. Events include a flea market and auction, enjoyable for all. In the early days, money was tight, and some funds were solicited from donors who wish to remain anonymous. Cairn rescue remains profoundly grateful to these generous benefactors to this day. To the credit of our volunteers, our rescue program is now basically self-supporting. Donations made when an animal is adopted often meet expenses. Volunteers have asked caring veterinarians for reduced rates on veterinary fees and other costs for the rescue animals, and many have helped. The CTCA stands willing to help financially, however, in the event of need.

"Toto" and his family.

The CTCA rescue group offers merchandise for sale bearing the rescue logo. Many regional Specialties support CTCA rescue efforts. There is also a scrapbook with pictures of our success stories, including one from a woman who made me promise not to use her name. She is afraid someone is going to want her beloved male Cairn back!

CTCA rescue did engage in two small puppy mill buyouts, involving only a few dogs, and I mention this because they were not a great success. Perhaps another rescue organization can learn from our experience. The first one was handled by Allison Huck and Nita Haas, and the second by Lynne Nabors and Clark Pennypacker. In both cases the adult dogs were very difficult to place, due to their lack of socialization. Some were placed successfully, and continue to do well. Some, however, never lost their fear of humans and would cower in the far end of their runs or crates no matter how much attention they were given. After placement, others were unable to adjust to the normal confusion of family life and were returned.

Puppies from a litter included in the group sale were very placeable. Some of the dedicated volunteers provided in-home time, and they all worked hard to make this effort a success. Cairn Terrier Rescue has since adopted the position that we will no longer engage in buyouts of animals in puppy mill situations, nor will we purchase puppy mill animals at auctions.

The CTCA rescue effort is alive and well today under the capable hands of Sue DeWitt (Connecticut) and Karen Smith (California).

Special recognition should be given here to Shirley Weber for her efforts, including compiling and publishing at her own expense comprehensive books on all rescue workers in all breeds. The books are entitled *Project Breed Directory (Breed Rescue Efforts & Education Directory)*, and consist of *The Yellow Book* (first edition) and *The Red Book* (second edition), which includes Cairns. The books include a listing of all rescue volunteers whom she could locate, working with parent club rescue organizations and anybody else she could find.

UNITED KINGDOM

Sybil Berrecloth kindly furnished information on rescue in the United Kingdom at my request, and she advised that the British service, the Cairn Terrier Relief Fund (CTRF), marked its twenty-fifth year of operation in 1993. The CTRF has eighteen trustees, each of the six breed clubs having three representatives. This group rescues upwards of one hundred Cairns a year. Mrs. Berrecloth is extremely articulate about rescue, as I find most volunteers are. I quote excerpts from her writings here:

> Every member of a breed club should consider rescue as their collective responsibility. Rescue is the same wherever you are—often the only difference is in numbers. Anyone involved in rescue is only too familiar with the heartrending stories—some completely genuine, some total fabrications, the majority, I suspect somewhere between the two extremes.

It is unfortunate to note from Mrs. Berrecloth's article that "puppy farmers" abound in Britain, as they do in the United States. Those puppies suffer the same disadvantages as do the output of puppy mills in the United States: transportation at too early an age; no socialization; lack of responsibility for the puppy; and inadequate information given to the new owner about Cairn temperament, proper diet, care and training.

Considering the amount of rescue animals that are seen, breeders should stop and think before they breed litters, and be very careful about placement. Making sure that the puppy suits the home, and that the new owners understand Cairn temperament and their need for exercise and attention, can make the difference between a successful placement and one that is not. I always tell prospective puppy purchasers that the amount of attention they are willing to devote to their new puppy will be given back many times over, as a Cairn really blossoms with quality attention. Sadly, the reverse is equally true.

The Cairn Terrier is a wonderful, happy, healthy little animal that benefits greatly from his heritage. He was prized for qualities such as gameness, hardiness, loyalty and courage. He still possesses all those qualities today, and we as guardians of the Cairn Terrier must maintain that prized, ancient breed that originated so long ago on the Isle of Skye.

1985 Cairn Terrier
Champions of Record

Alessandro of Ugadale
Audrey's Misty Heather
Avenelhouse Firebird
Barberi Hedge Sam's Roark
Barich Bajan's Canny Vixen
Barich Extra Edition
Barich Ginger Snap
Barrett's Bonnie McNiff
Barrett's Touch of Honey
Benway's State Occasion
Bias Sir Michael Cairn
Bold Oaks Apache Sunrise
Bon-A-Star's Piper McCrimmon
Bonfyre's Bounty
Bonfyre's Serendipity
Bonnie Glen's Abby O'Misty Moor
Brandy Berry of Wolfpit
Brehannon's Barefoot Boy
Brehannon's Bronco Billy
Brehannon's Codbank Pizazz
Brehannon's Demon Drum
Brehannon's Drum Majorett
Brigadoon's Marvelous Marty
Brigadoon's Twigs Twinkle
Brightfields Rob Roy
Brightridge Charlie Brown
Brocair Applejack
Brocair Weekend Warrior
Buccaneers Iris at Terratote
Cairjac's Goldie Howd
Cairjac's Red Dawg Saloon
Cairjac's T J Finnigan
Cairland Cornerstone
Cairland Mighty Contender
Cairland Mighty Showman
Cairland Mr Fillkatom
Cairmar Catch Me a Cat
Cairmar Color Guard
Cairmar Coppertone
Cairmar Private Collection
Cairn Glen's Pixie

Cairndania Jeronimo's Joker
Cairndania Keal's Kelsey
Cairndania Sam's Starbelle
Cairnoaks Rainmaker
Cairnwolde's Woodsprite
Cairnwoods Crackerjack
Cairnwoods Off Key
Cairnwoods Shortbread
Cairnwoods Sour Note
Cairnwynds Show Star
Camarest Mother Schucker
Canorwoll Barb Wire
Canorwoll Bostonian
Caries Fast Layne
Chasands Knight Rider
Chasands Willie In the Ruff
Chriscay's Absolutely
Clan Makaws Maid Marion
Clayridge Priddy McBryce
Concannon Jenner
Copperglen Fame N Fortune
Coralrocks Yankee Andy Dandy
Craigly Jamie McNeill
Craigly-S Glencairn Maggie
Craigly-S Pennroyal
Crofter's Gate Diabol
Dees Just Call Me Angel
Fashion Tag of Wildwood
Feldspar's Scarlet Doublet
Feldspar's Scarlet Ribbons
Flickwynds Golden Amber
Flickwynds Golden Rose
Flickwynds Red River Buffy
Gayla Cairn's Edith
Gayla Cairn's Flame South Down
Gayla Cairn's Killdear
Gayla Cairn's McKim
Gayla Cairn's Mouse
Gayla Cairn's Zeus
Gingerbred's Juju Beads
Glencairn Jenni McNeill

Happicairn Here Comes Benji
Heathcairn Jennifer
Heilands Pride N Joy
Hillrim's Haymaker
Howdy's Serendipity Lucy
Howdy's Serendipity Sophi
Jamie Selkie of Amelita
Jet Star Ship of Shoops Isle
Joywood's Molly McGee
K-Star Aries Cty Cromaty
Kandl's Rockaboy
Karendale Coriander
Karengary's Spirits Image
Karengary's Wind Spirit
Kiku's King James
Kiku's Lovelands Bentley
Kilkeddan's Hear Ye Hear Ye
Killiegrahams Boney's Brat
Kim-E-Cairn's Faerie Queen
Kim-E-Cairn's Touch of Class
Kutisark's Fool's Gold Quixote
Lachdale Magnum
Laddie Tarridon
Lakewood's Bit Of Bourbon
Lakewood's Cameo
Lakewood's Contessa
Lakewood's Darby Dickens
Lakewood's Golden Charm
Lakewood's Keeper
Lakewood's Nurse Goodbody
Lakewood's Silver Snapper
Lakewood's Spring Mist
Lakewood's Winchester
Loch Katrine Joy's Dhrambuie
Lochreggand Piper
London Choirmaster O'Wolfpit
London House Pandemonium
MacJess' Heather
Marblehill's Ice Crystal
Marblehill's Summer Breeze
Maricairn Sea Ransom
Mary Wilf Held Ransom
Mary Wilf Radiant Ray
Mayberry of Wolfpit
McDuff's Where Thou Goest
McLin's Hello Dolly O Cairmar
Meriwynds Mohawk
Meriwynds Rolling Stone

Meybriar's Aaron Burr
Misty Meadow's Miss Pert
Misty Moor's Wee Nessie
Morihas Midnight Brigand
Morihas Midnight Special
Morning Mist of Meybriar
Nightfalls Good-N-Plenty
Ohioville Farrah
Old Orchards Topper
Patter's Jenny Lind O'Cairmar
Pilli's PR of Image
Pinetop Penelope
Quixote's Glenperi
Ragamuffins Margot
Ragamuffins Simon O'Charbe
Razzberry of Wolfpit
Recless Kelly Joe
Recless Toddie Flambeau
Redwood's Bramble Brer
Robin Macruff O' The Brae
Rose Croft Dearglean Abh
Royola Rose of Alamawa
Royalscott's Dynamite Dude
Sandcrest Coralrocks Keeley
Scotch Mist's Ginger Snap
Sharolaine's Abigail
Sharolaine's Kalypso
Shin Pond Broctini
Spring Valle Benson Bru Jo
Spring Valle Tif-Aron Banner
Sundune Sadie's Sophie
Sunshine Sal
T'Is Herself Indeed
Terratote Brushpoper
Terrorific Black Marble
Tigh Terrie's Chelsea Chimes
Tigh Terrie's Currie Clown
Tigh Terrie's Honey Happicairn
Tigh Terrie's Sugar 'N Spice
Tigh Terrie's Two Timin' Ted
Tillietudlem's Isbister
Tillietudlem's Murchie
Twobees's Willie McGee
Ugadale Princess
Uniquecottage Georgie Girl
Uniquecottage Storm Bird
Wagaway of Wildwood
Warlyn's Amber Glow

Waterford Quick Fix
Weeknowe Walsing Gold Slew
Whipshe Wench
Woodmist Polly Flinders
Woodmist Tiger Lily

1985 Companion Dogs
Beauregard of Braemar
Bruce McDuff
Cathleen's Candy Kiss
Dunvegans Kiloran O Wiget
Furguson's Anne B
Heilands Red Peper
Jc's Masked Bandit of Hollytoo
Kaird-Cairn's Lord Duach
Kaird-Cairn's Lord Rufus
Kathcairns Twinkle Starr
Mister Magoo
Movie Star of Shoop's Isle
Moyers Little Princess Zelda

Ms Tafy MacTavish
Ch. Pennylane Kim-E-Cairn's
   Oliver
Ragatams Mighty Mite Misty
Ridgley Aphrodite
Smidgen's Molly
Spring Valle Qui-Tif's Mikey
Teddy Berry Bear
Tobi Berrie Bear
Tramp-A-Bit of Wolfpit

1985 Companion Dogs Excellent
Bit O Scotch II, CDX
Rocky Mountain Sunshine, CD
Tammara of Twisted Oaks, CD

1985 Tracking Dogs
Jc's Masked Bandit of Hollytoo
Bonnie Bess

1986 Cairn Terrier
Champions of Record

ASA McNaughtie of Kishorn
Annwood Privateer
Annwood Quicksilver
Annwood Renaissance Rose
Ariel's Mr Beaux Jangles
Arn-Mar's Andy Boy
Avenelhouse Royal Glint
Barberi Hedge Bonny of Belle
Barberi Hedge Henry Higgins
Barich Enticer's Holly Berry
Blaircairns Coralrocks Rory
Blaircairns Coralrocks Tory
Blynman Caite Did
Bonfyre's Early Delivery
Bonfyre's Masquarade
Bonnie Hobo of Wolfpit
Bonnie Hocus Pocus of Wolfpit
Brehannon on a Rampage
Brehannon's Marywilf Tuff Guy
Brightridge Barney's Tiger
Brightridge Benson

Brightridge's Texas Talker
Brown's Rockie Road of Kishorn
Burr Wilep Tyler of Foxtail
Cairjac's Brass Band
Cairland Blaze of Glory
Cairland Highland's Delight
Cairland Money Market
Cairmar Golden Light
Cairmar Rhikkie of Glenmore
Cairmar Sunshine Mist
Cairmar Sunshine Time
Cairmar's Tawny Troubadour
Cairn Glen's Little Vixen
Cairndania MacBasher's Michael
Cairndania Sam's Samton
Cairnhill Dominic
Cairnhowse Wild Star
Cairnoaks Maguffin
Cairnwolde's Razzle Dazzle
Cairnwoods Aggravation
Cairnwoods Benajay

Cairnwoods Sadie O'Haverford
Caithbea's Spicy Cubby-Beara
Car O Mik's Wizards Gasto
Chasands This Bud's For You
Cheyenne Arrow's Jaimi
Cheyenne's Burger
Chriscay's British Sterling
Cloudberry of Wolfpit
Concannon Glasgow
Crackerjack O'Kisncairn
Craigly Crystal Ducky
Craigly Frasier McFling
Craigly-S Glenbuckie
Creag-Mhor Chips Ahoy
Critterkins's Calif Crackers
Crossroads Smart Alec
Croydon's Coventry Garbo
Daveleigh's Kapricious Kate
Dees Bundle of Joy
Dees Different Drummer
DeRan Heat of the Moment
Dolly's Merry Magdaline
Donwin Brack's Fancy Face
Donwin Chief of Staff
Fancy Dress of the Highlands
Feldspar's Bit O' Butterscotch
Flame of Wolsingham
Flickwynds A Little Chivas
Flickwynds Pippin of Andyboy
Flickwynds Somenew Sir Jocko
Gairlock's Battle Prince
Gairlock's Highland Lady Troy
Gairlock's True Love O'Ragtime
Gamac Sorcerer
Gay Tayls Tobias Brigadoon
Gimmick's Widget of Wolfpit
Glenmores Heaven Sent
Glenmores Michael Angel O
Happicairn Rowdy
Heatherhaven's Amelita G C
Heatherhaven's O'Shawnessy
Holemill Applejack
Jodian's Raider
Jolly Robber of Ourglas
Karen's Forever Michael
Kiku's Bouncing Bonnie
Kim-E-Cairn's Hurricane Annie
Lakewood's Gold Spike

Lakewood's Grand Prix
Lakewood's Jonathan
Lakewood's Moon Shine
Lakewood's Silver Smoke
Lakewood's Sirius
Lakewood's Wildmoor Rufus
Lincairn Bobby Boulton
Littleclan Alexis
Loch Katrine Kim Gregarach
Loch Katrine Kim's Piper Dan
Loch Katrine Ruadh MacDuff
Lochreggand Apple Cider
Mac Nan's Coeur De Lion
Mac Nan's Hot Toddie
Mac Nan's Scotch Heather
MacJess Ghilly
Maryann III
McKeegue's Mark of Blynman
McLins's Vinegarroon
Meriwynd's Simon Sez
Milbryan Misty Dawn O'Cairmar
Morihas Classy Copper Penny
Morihas Rocky Bo Rocket
Nightfalls Shine On
Nightfalls Tulsa Time
O'Grady's Calluna
O'Grady's Jonelle Dickens
Patter's Dear Abby O'Cairmar
Piccairn's Paisley
Pinetop Melissa
Ragtime's Brash Brannigan
Rain-A-Shine Moon Doggie
Redmaples Bonnie Brigit
Redmaples Scotch Brandy
Rheny's Rick E Redfern
Roylaine's Misty Meadow Magic
Rutherglen Charter Oak
Rutherglen Heart of Oak
Rutherglen's Cairmar Edition
Sharolaine's Regina
Shin Pond Schepseleh
Solo of Raelain
Stebru's Wee Lochness Monster
Sunnyland's Sweeney McTodd
Terratote Lil Lulu MacFee
Terratote Place Your Bet
Terrorific The Griz
Three Falls Rosie

Tidewater Gold Coast
Tigh Terrie's Mickey McFinn
Tigh Terrie's Precious Peanut
Topnote Annie Piper
Topnote Tuppence Insouciant
Twigbent Iarann
Wally's Wizard of Mac Nan
Waterford Quintessent
Wee Winks of Wildwood
Whetstone Sportin' Life
Wiscairn Francesca
Wiscairn Thomas O'Toole
Zigfelds Amadeus

1986 Companion Dogs
Alichar's Sea Tea Bear
Ch. Barich Tc's Black Raspberry
Cairnhaven's Morning Star
Cairnhaven's Movie Star Boby
Cairnhaven's Trader Vic
Ch. Chriscay's Absolutely
Ch. Coralrocks Yankee Andy Dandy
Debonair Gent of Shoops Isle
Dunvegans Kiloran O Widget
Dustin Frederick
Ch. Gayla Cairn's Flame South
    Down
K-Z's Sea Sprite Samantha
Mac-Ken-Char's Sea Sarah

Meriwynds Shayna Colleen
Mister Macgregor XX
Mono Mike
O'Conners Passport to Wexford
Roca's Feather Bear
Tosaig Pipeband Baxter
Tuff Fulla Pep Pattie

1986 Companion Dogs Excellent
Jc's Masked Bandit Hollytoo, CD
Meriwynd Finnigans Fling, CD
Movie Star of Shoop's Isle, CD
Ms Tafy MacTavish, CD
Tamra of Alamawa, CD
Teddy Berry Bear, CD
The Red Knight of Misty Moor,
    CD
Tobi Berrie Bear, CD
Tuff Enuf Tina, CD
Vegacairn Mary's Toto, CD

1986 Tracking Dogs
Philray's April Fool of Gatsby,
    CDX, TD

1986 Tracking Dogs Excellent
Jc's Masked Bandit Hollytoo, TD
Ch. Scotch Mist's Gingersnap, TD

1987 Cairn Terrier
Champions of Record

Aislinge's Cally O Meybriar's
Annwood Venus De Milford
Ariel Amadan O'Cairmar
Ariel's Dream Weaver
Barich Ripple's Rip Tide
Barrett's Honey For Sale
Black Bart's Calamity Jane
Blaircairns Jenny Gilchrist
Bold Oak's Shady Lady
Bold Oak's Wee Tess
Bonfyre's Hobgoblin
Bonnie Whirligig of Wolfpit

Bonniecairns Ayr Abby
Braemar's Andrew MacAdam
Braemar's Bonnie O'Lincairn
Brehannon's Ransom Paid
Brigadoon's Sadie's Sammy
Brightfields Sara Lee
Brightridge Macintosh II
Brightridge Rebel Rouser
Brycairn's Bachelor Party
Buccaneer's Mac-An-Leigh Misty
Cairjac's Pixie Howd
Cairland Airtight Alibi

Cairland Brycairn Legacy
Cairmar Coquette
Cairmar Meg of Cairn Glen
Cairmar Sargent At Arms
Cairmar Tanya Tucker
Cairmar Winston O'Lincairn
Cairmar's DeRan Serandipity
Cairnbawn Hug-Some-Bunny
Cairncroft Bree-Zee
Cairncroft Brigand
Cairnjoy's Brightridge Gail
Cairnwolde's P G T Beauregard
Cairnwoods Match Maker
Capricairn Bold Promise
Cheyenne's Bits
Chriscay's Falcon Crest
Clan Makaw By Golly Miss Molly
Clandara's MacDuff
Clanranald Tam O'Shanter
Concannon's Cairland Classic
Coralrocks Class Act
Cragcastle Lady Margaret
Cragcastle Mac Duff
Craigdhu Sugarplum
Craigly Amy McFearsom
Craigly-S Missconduct
Croydon's SugarDanny Darla
Dees Littlest Drummer
Dees Mister Murphy
Dees Touch of Class
Dees Trace of MacGregor
DeRan Spy's Like Us
DeRan the Bess of All
DeRan the Bess of Times
Dein Ylsa Michelle
Donegal Ms Macgillacuddy
Donwin Rablin Rambo
Dundee of Drum Manor
Fenwick T McBain
Fillkatom's Little Dickens
Flickwynds Alan A Dale
Flickwynds Chun Sa Renada
Flickwynds Mighty McDuff
Foxborough's Char
Friar Tuck of Staten
Gamac A Better Mousetrap
Gay Tayl Bridgets Barnabas
Gayla Cairn's Una McKim

Gayla Cairn's Wilkinson
Gingerbred's Fudge
Glen-Ayr's Skyler
Glenmore Rusty Angel
Glenmores Betsy McCall
Gottulas Royal Rusty
Halo's K C of Worth-Mor
Happicairn Muffles B Cogut
Hearn Man O'War
Heilands Royal Blend
Janeways Sir Andrew of Tibbie
Jo-El's Beau Best of Kirkwall
Jodian's Little Man
Karen's Lacy J Dalton
Karendale Oh Calcutta
Karmas Weemack Kiss Me Kate
Kerryberry of Wolfpit
Kilkeddan's Key Witness
Kilkeddan's Solar Eclipse
Kim-E-Cairn's Battle Cry
Kim-E-Cairn's Sass With Class
King Duncan of Gwynedo
Kirkwall's Far Traveler
Laird of Skerryvore
Lakewood's Buckeye
Lakewood's Fancy Woman
Lincairn Delta Force
London Berry of Wolfpit
London Chutney of Glenmore
London House Towne Crier
Lynwil Cavalier
Mac Nan Jody's Jollification
Mactam's Shiver Me Timbers
Madam Razz of Wolfpit
Meri-Leigh's Scottish Bramble
Meriwynd McFee Fi Fo Fum
Meriwynds Donegal Dilly
Meriwynds Murphy
Meybriars' Ami O' Pinetop
Meybriars' Brea O' Lindy
Misty Meadow Spice
Nightfalls Finale
Noble Bentley of Arn-Mar
Oventop Macintyre
Pelletier's Pudgy
Penticharm Tartan Rocket
Razzbo of Wolfpit
Razzle Dazzle of Wolfpit

Recless Rosie O'Gaelic
Redcoat's Rufmuffin O'Ragtime
Redmaples Blythe Brianna
Redmaples Shin Pond Bobby
Renart's Little Rascal
Rose Croft Eagalach Abh
Rose Croft Falcon's Jester Beo
Sharolaine's Shaina
Shin Pond Cedric Devlin
Shin Pond Dreyfus
South-Down's Ozzie Osbourne
Spring Valle RC of Kirkwall
Stonebriar's Bold Keeper
T D of Farus Farm
Terratote Harris Tweed
Terratote Lotta Crabtree
The Goose's Gus
Thistledown's Wee Bairn
Tidewater Cloth of Gold
Tidewater Gold Dust
Tigh Terrie's Callme Casey
Tigh Terrie's Devon Delight
Tigh Terrie's Rusty Rogue
Topnote Special Edition
Tramp-A-Bit of Wolfpit
Ugadale Sunkist of Mac Nan
Uniquecottage Gold Coin
Uniquecottage Gold Lapwing
Wee Mack's Ginger Pie
Weeknowe Walsing Gold Asset
Westrose Mad Max of Joywood
Whetstone Jack Tar
Woodmist Dover
Woodmist Legacy
Woodmist Scarlet Hawthorne

1987 Companion Dogs
Alandale's Bonnie Lady
Ch. Annwood Venus de Milford
Avocairn Captivating Cool
Barich Bajan's Yogi Bear
Ch. Barich Enticer's Holly Berry

Barrington Brandi Brice
Ch. Binnie O'The Brae
Ch. Cairmar Caramel Candy
Carla's Crystal
Clandara's MacDuff
Enzee Ito O'Shea
Flecher Ramsey McMinn
Forbes Gay Buffy of Millbury
Imp Print's Caper of Wolfpit
Ch. Kim-E-Cairn's Gerolf
Marblehill's April Showers
Mister MacGregor XX
Mister Murdoch of Nessiteras
My Bairn MacGregor
Mr Bilbo Baggins
O'Connor's Lancer of Donegal
Ch. Piccairn's Muffett O'Brocair
Pj's Bonny Elven Bairn
Prince Toto Chelsie Blue
Ch. Ragamuffins Pojo
Rusty of Tasmania
Sir Tuffle Argyle
Ch. Scotch Mist's Gingersnap, TDX
Sparks of Kingussie
Spring Valle Mandi O'Tiff

1987 Companion Dogs Excellent
Ch. Barich Tc's Black Raspberry,
CD
Ch. Coralrocks Yanky Andy Dandy,
CD
Ch. Christycay's Absolutly, CD
Dunvegans Kiloran O Wiget, CD
Mac-Ken-Char's Sea Sarah, CD

1987 Utility Dog
Ms Tafy MacTavish, UD

1987 Tracking Dogs
Gayla Cairn's Will O the Wisp, TD
Tuff Enuf Tina, CDX, TD

1988 Cairn Terrier
Champions of Record

Annwood Xanthippe Sweets
Bagpipe's Jubilation
BalBrae's Fashion Blaze
Bann Hit Parade
Barberi Hedge Cinnabar
Barberi Hedge Prudence
Barberi Hedge Will B Tufters
Bold Oak's Cairngorm Fey Rey
Bonfyre's Blackmaler
Bonnie Cricket of Wolfpit
Braemar's Yankee Clipper
Brehannon's Hi Stakes Gambler
Brehannon's Marywilf Mac
Brigadoon's Full of Blarney
Brightridge Black Bart
Brightridge Boomerang
Brocair Gizmo Gabriel
Brycairn's Fancy Talker
Cairbrook's Little Heather
Cairland Fast Talker
Cairland in the Knick of Time
Cairmar Cameo
Cairmar Cat In The Hat
Cairmar Courtier
Cairmar Cowardly Lion
Cairmar's Caitlinn O'Feldspar
Cairmar's Firebrand, CD
Cairncroft Bronwyn Autumn
Cairncroft Chantilly Lace
Cairndania Samton's Sulmar
Cairngold Carmen of
   Uniquecottage
Cairnisma's Sweet William
Cairnmoor Samtom's Sonny
Cairnwoods Fun Flyer
Canacairn's Ode to Loch-Lomand
Canorwoll Garden Party
Clayrag's Litzie
Col Ollie By Golly
Coletowne Olivia
Collin Hites Luke of Cessnoc
Cook's Hard Day's Night
Cook's Rocky
Cook's Twist And Shout

Coralrocks Miss Tiffany
Craigly Charlie McFling
Craigly Darren McDuff
Dees Miss Kilbride
Denbryl's Jerome K Jerome
DeRan A Call to Excellence
DeRan Feel the Heat
DeRan Hot N' Spicy
DeRan Laddie McTavish
DeRan Penny Lover
DeRan Popular Choice
Donwin's Major General
Fillkatom's Henry Higgins
Fillkatoms Molli Brown
Firecracker O Kisncairn
Flickwynds Shelly Pearls
Fouraces Yankee Patriot
Foxairn Geez O'Pete
Foxairn Just Because
Foxairn Phoebe's Choice
Foxairn's Pixie of Zomerhof
Gaeli Brock's Rufus the Red
Gaelic's Jagger Cairndania
Gaelic's Jennifer Cairndania
Gamac Somewhere in Time
Gay Tayl Bridgets Bonnyellen
Gay Tayl Bridgets Rose Bud
Gimmick's Gambit of Macada
Heatherhaven O'Casey
Heatherhaven's Tara
Honey Bears Gentle Ben
Imp Print's Caper of Wolfpit
Jean's Bleu Belfre
Joywood's Donovan
Joywood's Elegant Elsie
Joywood's High Hope
Joywood's Remington Steel
Karen's Cash and Carry
Karen's Cookie Monster
Karengary's Catch the Spirit
Kilkeddan's Something Wicked
Kiloren Dust Buster
Kim-E-Cairn's LD Ruadhan Ridire
Kim-E-Cairn's Regal Lady

Kishorn's By Popular Demand
Kishorn's Educating Rita
Knightshire's Rhody Red
Lakewood's Bristol Cream
Laraland's Rufus Redneck
Lincairn Fire 'N' Ice
Loch Tay's Cocoa Bear
London Sonnet of Wolfpit
Loveland's Katie of Meridoon
Lydia's Britt Harmony
Lynwil Buccaneer
Mac Nan's Bundle of Joy
Mac-Ken-Char's Red Jamie
Mahas Apache War Paint
Marblehill's Winter Wonder
Marikov's Graylord
McGilligan of Raelain
McJay Katie Skye
Meri-Leigh's Bracken Brae
Meri-Leigh's Jubilee
Meri-Leigh's Scottish Thistle
Meybriar's Carbon Copy O'Asta
Meybriar's Darby Blue
Meybriar's Delightful Suprise
Meybriar's Highland Fling
Meybriar's Macho Nick O'McKin
Misty Isles Sargeant Pepper
Misty Meadow Amy's Comet
Morihas Ms Taurus of K-Stars
Muf-N-Den Sweet Nantucket
Muf-N-Den Top Gun
Nightfalls Encore
Nightfalls Merrily
Nightfalls Party Time
Ollie North of the Highlands
Patter's Mzzz Magnolia
Pennylane Crocodile Dundee
Pinetop Paperchase
Pipers Aunt Eloise
Pistol Pete's Son of A Gun
Prescott Great Expectations
Ragtime's Gypsy Rose
Ramblebriar's Tuff N' Stuff
Recless Foto Copy
Recless Jaunty Joe
Redcoat's Harvest Moon
Redmaples Bright Rose
Redmaples Great Guy

Redwoods Marshall
Redwoods Pasco Rascal
Redwoods Tilly Tango
Rose Croft Jester's Jazz Beo
Rose Croft Kestrel Abh
Rutherglen's Cairmar Triumph
Sandcrest Nickum Raukle
Sharolaine's Just Jamie
Sharolaine's Kamelot
Sheffield's Tom Terrific
Shin Pond Rosebud
Sir Beaux Scott
Skerryvore Greyling
Spicy Glen Torridon of Demar
Spring Valle Mi-Kel Marco
T'ls Oakalley's Thunderstorm
Taliesyns Korr Faylan
Terratote My Barbarian
Tharr Barr's Just For Pete
Tidewater Fairway Gold
Tigh Terrie's Sadie Sadie
Tigh Terrie's Sunny Sideup
Tosaig Meriwynd Signature
Uniquecottage Gold Grouse
Uniquecottage Kilmalaig
Uniquecottage Red Robin
Waterford Winken
Whetstone Sailor's Delight
Whipshe Wingtips of Cairland
Zigfelds Sweeny Todd

1988 Companion Dogs
Barberi Hedge Michael S
Bonny's Miss Molly
C J's Boomerang McScruff
Cairnbawn Catfish Hunter
Cairn Haven Scotch on the Rocks
Dazey May of Westpark
Ch. Dein Ylsa Michelle
Ch. Fillkatoms Henri Higgins
Formal Affair
Hazeldeen's Bertha Baby
Isethebyes's Wee Cindy
Jonathan Corky McTavish
Kisncairn's Prince Sparky
Marblehill's Summer Breeze
Marta Melody of Clan McKaw
McDuff of Fife

Our Katie
Pearson's Calico Girl
Sasanataba Ginny's Gift
Sheena Sparkles-Plenty
Taco Dandy
Victoria's Silver Shadow

1988 Companion Dogs Excellent
Avocairns Captivating Cool, CD
Prince Toto Chelsie Blue, CD

Ch. Scotch Mist's Gingersnap, CD,
    TD

1988 Utility Dog
Jc's Masked Bandit Hollytoo, CDX,
    TDX

1988 Tracking Dog
Denbryl Wee Bonny Patrick

1989 Cairn Terrier
Champions of Record

Avocairns Captivating Cool
Baleshare's Meghan of Wolfpit
Bann Begourah Ben
Barrett's Firestarter
Berry Special of Wolfpit
Blair Hill Hurricane Emily
Blaircairns Toddies Charity
Blaircairns Toddies Faith
Bonfyre's Constant Comment
Bonfyre's Sultan Pepper
Bonfyre's Tokamar Gold Fanci
Bramblewood's BMW
Bramblewood's Bob Kat
Bramblewood's Real American
Bramblewood's Reebock
Brigadoon's Mactavish
Brightridge Tartan's Toby
Burr Sheanboadicea Russett
Cairdeil Ferlies Bit of Erin
Cairland Jesmics Jessica
Cairmar Bobby's Girl
Cairmar Cat's Out of the Bag
Cairmar Crimson Tide O Ariel
Cairmar Free as the Wind
Cairmar Great Scot
Cairmar The Cat's Meow
Cairmar The Cat's Pajamas
Cairmar Top Cat
Cairmar's Cool Cat
Cairn Gorm's Master Blend
Cairndania Todd's Hot Toddie

Cairndania Molly McCairn
Cairnmoor T's Tammy Cairndania
Castle Cairns A Veri Meri Keri
Chesapeake Mary Wilf Rand
Clan Makaw Sunstreak Sampler
Coletowne Firecracker
Cook's Strawberry Fields
Copperglen Claim to Fame
Copperglen Great Attraction
Coralrocks Capt Abernathy
Critterkin's Aberdeen of Bo
Critterkin's Chief Hiawatha
Critterkin's Gitchee Gumee
Darpens Foxy Lady O'Meybriars
Dees Molly Malone
Dees Solo Bee
Diehl's Kaysie Sue
Drumm Manor Lilli Piccairn
Fenwick T Walton
Fillkatom's Pride 'N' Joy
Finnigans Blitzen Fox
Flickwynd's Tiffany O' Gunn
Flickwynds Black Knight
Flickwynds Dorothy Roy
Flickwynds Flashing Firefly
Foxairn For Heaven's Sake
Foxairn La Bamba
Foxairn Miss Moneypenny
Gaelic's Smartie Cairndania
Gay Tayl Aonghas Macmhaolain
Gayla Cairn's Supercharge

Glen-Ayr's Carbon Copy
Glenbrae Final Pippin
Goosedown's Tailor Made
Greenstone's Buffalo Bill
Greenstone's Doc Holliday
Happicairn Black Magic
Happicairn Pinetopper
Hearn Typhoon
Heatherhaven Lady Effington
Imp Print Just-A-Bit of Wolfpit
Jesmic Duncan of Laurielee
Jones Casey Shadow
Joywood's Labor of Love
Joywood's Laird Duff
K-Z's Sam's Bright Willy
Karengary's Dirkson By Design
Karengary's Pioneer Spirit
Kiku's Prince Theodore
Killiegraham Andy Magroo
Kim-E-Cairn's Spit Fire
Kirkshire's Spice O'Life
Kirkwall's Tough Turf
Lakewood's Church Lady
Lakewood's Jennifer
Lakewood's Reflection
Lakewood's Silver Ann
Loch Katrine Sno Kris Lossie
Loch Katrine Snokris Millie
Loch Katrine Snokris Mindie
Maha's Clay Pot
McJay Sheila Skye
McPooh's Dazzling Phoenix
Melrose Gypsy Road
Mentmore Caraway of Wolfpit
Mistybrigs Bogie Man
Mistywyns Molly MaGee
Mostly Merrie O'Glencoe
Muf-N-Den Ace in the Hole
Nanrich's Fergus
Nightfalls Saint Nick
Ohioville Hooper
Pennylane Top Gun
Queensline McGuf Cairndania
Ramblebriar's Two Bob Bit
Redcoat's Moonlight Bandit
Redwoods Mucho Maloney
Rheny's Asta Charles
Rose Croft Aon Cuilean Abh

Rosecairn D-Fer
Rossarden Tannisker
Royalscott's Sassy Princess
Rutherglen Mill of Kintyre
Savangelina's Touch of Sable
Shadey Glen's Wild Fire
Shadybrook Sam Houston
Sharolaine Markson's Marquee
Shaula of Blair Hill
Skerryvore Grey Vixen
Skerryvore Kiera
Spirecairn Simply Special for
    Monary
Spring Valle Jo Rhik Wendie
Sunshine Tiger Rag
T'Is Tornado Stormy Weather
TangleVine's Doug Flutie
Terratote Glen Plaid
Terratote Jersey Lily
The McDuff Laird O'Clancairns
Thistledown Coralrocks Jami
Thistledown Robert Bruce
Thorncroft Northern Lights
Tigh Terrie's Buttons 'N Bows
Tigh Terrie's Gypsy Girl
Tokamar's Amber Jewel Qui-Fan
Tokamar's Aztec Gold Qui-Fan
Uniquecottage Platypus
Uniquecottage Red Swift
Whitlow's Lord Bentley
Woodmist Brocade
Xroad Ms Liberty of Glenmoor
Xroads Quick Like a Bunny
Zigfeld's Markson Survivor

1989 Companion Dogs
Ardog Alexander
Avocairn's Tenacious Courage
Bonnie Lea Macgyver
Bonnie Marie on Crocker
Brightgride Macye's Casey
Bruff's Merry Muffin
Cairn Haven's Butterscotch
CairnAcres' Image of Islay
Cairnhoe McMartin
Carolyn Frederick's Skeezer
Cessnoch's Cricket on Lake
Ch. Brocair Applejack

Ch. Cairmar's Firebrand
Ch. Coralrocks Stoney Maloney
Ch. Glenmore Rusty Angel
Ch. Thorncroft Northern Lights
Georgie Washington
Hetzel's Sir Zoomer of Oz
Kelly's Shamrock O'Windy Pine
Kim-E-Cairn's Lady Criostal
Lindy's Rocket
My Bailey Mailey
O'Connors Passport to Wexford
Piccairn's Croch Brighinn
Rachael's Masquerade
Ranna of Emerald Acres
Sasanataba Typhonic Triffid
Sherman's Peppercorn
Taffy-Candies Delight
Terratote Glen Plaid

1989 Companion Dogs Excellent
Ch. Clandara's Mauff, CD
Ch. Clayride Priddy McBryce, CD
Mister Macgregor XX, CD
Mister Murdoch of Nessiteras, CD
O'Connors Passport to
    Wexford, CD
Pj's Bonny Elven Bairn, CD
Roca's Feather Bear, CD
Sasanataba Ginny's Gift, CD
Victoria's Silver Shadow, CD

1989 Tracking Dog
Redwoods Too Hot To Handle

1989 Utility Dog
Prince Toto Chelsie Blue, UD

1990 Cairn Terrier Champions of Record

Aislinge's Grey Knight
Aislinge's Red Baron
Aldryn Sprightly Sal At Monary
Ariel's Summer Storm
Avocairn's Marcasite Magic
Avocairn's Red Ruffian
Avocairn's Sparkling Gem
Barberi Hedge Dee Cee Dee
Barberi Hedge Ms C O'K-Star
Barich Bajan's Rumpole Bar
Barich Freddy Fox
Barrett's Lady Gwenivere
Belmonts Butter Scotch
Blackbeard of Wolfpit
Blaircairn Anna O'Coralrock
Blaircairns Toddies Hope
Bonletod's Bark Gable
Bonnie Ferelith of Wolfpit
Bravo's Rotten To the Core
Brehannon's Little Thatcher
Brehannon's Marywilf A Hellin'
Brigadoon's Binnie McBean
Brigadoon's Calliope

Brigadoon's Chatter Box
Brightridge Bright Spark
Buccaneer's Jasmine
Burr Sheanboadicea Devon
Cair West Henry O'The Blaze
Cairjac's Debonair Ring King
Cairmar Avant Garde
Cairmar Care Free
Cairmar Cat Dancer
Cairmar Coercion
Cairmar Stop N Smell the Roses
Cairncroft Carillon
Cairncroft Highland Badger
Cairndania Shean's Shammon
Cairndania T's Tige Cairnmoor
Cairnisma's Ridge Runner
Cairnkeep Kim-E-Cairn Geordi
Cairnkeep Rainstorm
Cairnluv Lincairn Appleseed
Cairnshaus Random Harvest
Cairnshaus The Ultimate
Cairnshaus Thrill of Victory
Cairnwolde's Robert E Lee

Cairnwolde's Tam O'Shanter
Cairnwoods Wrinkle In Time
Castlecairns Duncan
Chivari Swizzlestick
Clan Makaw Won for the Gipper
Coalacre Milliner
Cook's Misty Meadow Safari
Copperglen All That Jazz
Copperglen Foxtrot
Copperglen I'm It
Coralrocks Macivey
Cragcastle Great Scot
Cragcastle Royal Scot
Cragcastle Thalia of Cairmar
Critterkin's Happy Hooligan
Dees Belisama
Dees Betty Prior
Dees Birdwatcher at Robine
Dees Comanche
Dees Cotton Candi
Dees Dust Devil
Dees Lady in Red
Dees Touch of Gold
DeRan No No Notorious
DeRan The Lion Sleeps Tonight
Donwin's Ginger Snap
Feldspar's Charity
Flickwynds Butch Cassidy
Flickwynds Candy Cane
Flickwynds Oliver Twist
Flickwynds Paul Muad Dib
Flickwynds Teddy Bear
Foxairn Double Trouble
Foxairn Kiss N Tell
Foxairn Scarecrow
Foxairn Tinman
Gaelibrock's QT's Sassy Brat
Gamac Hokus Pokus
Gamac Oberon
Gayla Cairn's Elvira
Gimmick's Gabble of Wolfpit
Glen-Ayr's Play it Again Sam
Glenmont Briarpatch
Glenmores Esquire
Goosedown's Carbon Copy
Goosedown's First Edition
Greyfriar's Amazing Grace
Greyfriar's Bold Stroke

Happicairn Bangles N Beads
Heathcairn Barbarossa
Heilands Lil Mischef Maker
Imp Print's Wiz Bang of Wolfpit
Jesmic Jack O'Hearts
Joywood's Merry Noel
Joywood's Michelle Diane
Joywood's Tiger Lily
Karen's Mister Hush N Shush
Karengary's Follow the Spirit II
Kim-E-Cairn's Raz Ama Tazz
Kirkshire's Secret Agent
Lakewood's Britton Run
Lakewood's Foxy Beau
Lakewood's Laurel
Lakewood's Little Colonel
Lakewood's Pride O'Tara
Lakewood's Tiger
Lakewood's Tiger Toy
Larchlea's Obsession
Lincairn Night 'N' Day
Littleclan Lady Piper
Lizdig Cairnhoe Cricketer
Loch Katrine Cody of Snokris
Loch Katrine Snokris Rag Doll
Loch Katrine Stormin Snokris
Loch Katrine Willie Doll
Mac Nan's Copper Glow
Mac Nan's Mischief Maker
Mac-Ken-Char's Sea Samantha
Maple Leaf Farm's Burn'N Bush
Mapleleaf Farm Sir Gallahad
Marblehill's Wild as the Wind
Mary Wilf's Bubba
Mary Wilf's Jessica
Mary Wilf's Kristin
Melrose Chip Off the Old Block
Melrose Go For The Gold
Mentmore's Token Cairndania
Meybriar Skyedane Ventureout
Meybriar's Colorado Cody
Misselwaithe Windsong Tiffany
Mistywyns Cooper of Highnoon
Mistywyns Nan Tucket
Mistywyns Salty Grand Samson
Mistywyns Toto Wizard of Oz
Moriahs Jazzy Rufus Dufus
Murphy's Skye McSparks

Nanmaurs Show Star
Nightfalls Tattle Tale
Northwood Alexandria
Pennylane Daydreamer
Ragtime Sir Duncan Fitzhugh
Reanda's Britta at Redcoat
Redcarr Pockets of Plenty
Redcoat's Lord Peter Wimsey
Redwood's Lotta Hope
Redwoods Tierra of Kyleakin
Rose Croft Kiss-N-Tell
Sharolaine's Kingdom Kome
Spring Valle Bea-Jo Rachall
Spring Valle Bea-Jo Sean
Stebru's Rebel With a Cause
TangleVine's Donnybrook
TangleVine's PTO
Teddy Bear XXI
Terratote Dear Daphne
Terratote Tuolumne
Terriwood's Artful Dresser
Terriwood's Best Dressed
Terriwood's Twist Again
Thorncroft Gold Star
Tigh Terrie's Front 'N Center
Topnote Molly Flinger
Topnote Toffee Truffle
Tosaig Dawn's Delight
Tosaig Karengary Dexter
Turnberry's Tuff Talker
Whippersnapper of Wolfpit

1990 Companion Dogs
Aberdeen's Wee Enchantment
Bedrock's Barney R
Brightridge Angel Cloe'

Dunvagens Riteaway
Finnigans Oleander
Flickwynds Kate
Glenmont Briarpatch
Goldnessy of Windy Meadows
Hetzel's Sir Zoomer of Oz
In Memory of Mittens
Ch. K-Z's Sam's Bright Willy
Ch. McGilligan of Raelain
Our Rob Roy
Our Ruff N Ready
Rascal Todo Munchkin
Rutherglen Morag MacIver
Sasanataba Hobbes
Sharon's Karin
Shez Krista from Coletown
Sir Andrew Du Ritz
Sir Ripley of Kearney
Sir Rupert
Sir Studley Winstanley
Sweetie Girl Scruffina
Westwind Alliside
Where There's Fire

1990 Companion Dogs Excellent
Bonnie Marie on Crocker, CD
C J's Boomerang McScruff, CD
Ch. Fillkatoms Henri Higgins, CD
Forbes Gay Buffy of Millbury, CD
Ch. Glenmore Rusty Angel, CD
Our Katie, CD

1990 Utility Dog
Ch. Chriscay's Absolutely, CDX

1991 Cairn Terrier
Champions of Record

Annwood Zhivago
Armada's Anna Berri
Bagamore's Hell Fire
Baleshare's Royal Scotsman
Bann-RedHill's Bridie

Barberi Hedge Angus McLeod
Barberi Hedge Bronwyn
Barich Bearly Fox
Barrett's Darth Vader
Blaircairn Brats Valor

Bonnie Carousel of Wolfpit
Braemar Lincairn Catch A Star
Bramblewood's Kit-N-Kaboodle
Bravo's Apple of Our Eye
Bravo's Grin 'N Bear It
Brehannon's Miss Scarlett
Brehannon's Mista Rhett
Brightridge Big Mac
Brightridge Dee Dee's Abby
Brockcairn Casey's Flicker
Bryant's Lucky Lucinda
Cairland Borrowed Money
Cairland Highland Contraband
Cairland Whatsinaname
Cairmar Baileys-N-Cream
Cairmar Don't Mess With Texas
Cairmar Little Big Shot
Cairmar Pecan Brittle
Cairmar Risky Business
Cairmar's Rising Rocketsonde
Cairmar's Sparkling Star
Cairn Brae's Hint of Gold
Cairn Haven Scotch on the Rocks
CairnAcre's Scottish Melody
CairnAcre's Scottish Nosegay
Cairnisma Cairnhill Riffkin
Cairnkeep Call Me Camron
Cairnluv's Mt View Samson
Cairnshaus Vagabond Lover
Cairnwolde's Fraser Macduff
Cairnwolde's Maclarty
Cairnwoods Potscrubber
Caledonian Berry of Wolfpit
Chesapeake Bit O'Scot
Chivari Raider of Echocreek
Chivari Stone Sour
Clan Makaw's Moonlight Magic
Coach's Watch Those Sparks
Coletowne Crop Duster II
Copperglen Lindy
Copperglen Simply Sinful
Coralrocks MacHugh Alascairn
Coralrocks Rorys Laddie
Coventry Hannibal
Cragcastle Dixie Dark Star
Critterkin's Happy Bella
Daveleigh's Dixie Darlin'
Dees Calvin Calhoun

Dees Chipper
Dees Paddy
Dees Pattie
Dees Saratoga
Dees Toughnut
DeRan the Lioness
Donwin's Kathrina Of Kathmandu
Donwin's Red Streak
Falcroft's Madison Avenue
Falcroft's Pure Honey
Feldspar's Noble
Fenwick M McBain Wil-Har
Fenwick's Lilly McBain
Fillkatom's Back Talker
Fillkatom's Mischief Maker
Flickwynds Sara
Foxairn Heaven Forbid
Foxairn Heaven's To Betsy
Foxairn Kissmet
Foxairn Wizard
Glen Coe Tay O'Ballathie
Glencoe Busy Being Bad
Glenmont My Wee Yin
Glenmore Good As Gold
Goosedown French Kiss
Gremlins Me And Mrs Jones
Greyfriar's Patent Pending
Heilands Special Edition
Holemill Cairnluv Pie'd Piper
Jason McJasper of Wolfpit
Kilkeddan Sonata Witchy W'man
Kim-E-Cairn's Murry Blair
Kirkwall Linze O Spring Valle
Kirkwall's Dirt Devil
Kyleakin Cherry MacKendrick
Kyleakin Sir Bingley
Lakewood's Blithe Spirit
Lakewood's May Day
Lakewood's Mr. Wiskers
Lakewood's Samson
Lakewood's Splinter
Larchlea From Me to You
Lohk-Snokris Copper Cricket
Lomala Winston of Cairnluv
London Mace of Glenmoor
Mac Nan Hot Rod
Mac Nan She's Got Moxie
Macada's Burning Bright

Mactam's Rainy Day
Marblehill's Whirlwind
Maricairn Curtain Call
Maricairn Rave Review
Mary Wilf Apache Fancy Dancer
McCairn's Sir Henry Hudson
McErin's Bugle Boy Bif
McJames Giles O'Coralrocks
Melrose Knight of Cinderella
Meriwynds Ruby Slippers
Merry Georas MacFerniegair
Meybriar's Ruffy MacGregor
Misty Meadow Cook's Korina
Misty Meadow I'm Incredible
Misty Meadow's Willoughby
Mistybrigs Mister Mackintosh
Mistywyns Merriment
Monary Trudie
Nightfalls Sweet Talk
Nightfalls Tar Baby
Nightfalls the Grinch
Ohioville Rooster
Pennylane Wizard of Oz
Penticharm Private Eye
Rag A Bash Mr Macgyver
Ramblebriar's Tea For Two
Recless Ruff N Rowdy O Foxtail
Redcoat's California Girl
Redcoat's Golden Splash
Rosewood's Hawkeye Glen
Roughneck's No Holds Barred
Shady Glens Ms Ritz Bitz
Shiptoshore Braeman
Snorkis Gailaurie Wonder-Jon
Spring Valle Bann-Wen Darby
Stebru's Toowootsle Rool
Sunnyland Standing Room Only
TangleVine's Sydmonton
Terriwood's Dressed in Style
Terriwood's Lasting Legacy
Terriwood's Mighty Legacy
Terriwood's Texas Legacy
Tharr Barr's Golden Light
Tigh Terrie's Guinnes Stout
Tigh Terrie's Hello Dolly
Topnote Temerity
Topnote Theophilus
Totoket Windsong Mrs O'Leary

Tweedsmuir's John Macnab
Tweedsmuir's Piper's Tattoo
Valdawn's Tribute To Coventry
Whetstone Loose Change
Windsong's Honeybear
Windsongs Honeysuckle Rose
Woodmist Highland Falcon
Zigfeld's Gone With the Wind

1991 Companion Dogs
Blynman Carryon
Bravo's Rotten to the Core
Brigadoon's Grand MacDaniel
Brigadoon's Killer McTwink
Buff's Champagne Miss
Carol's Carrie MacWarden
Ch. Clan Makaw Sunstreak Sampler
Dunvegan's FireAway
Flickwynd Devoted Dr Watson
Karendon Jamie
McIntosh MacDuff of Afton
Merry Georas MacFerniegair
Mindy's Mister Biggs
Ragatams Pixie Too
Rose Croft Mirrie Magee Beo
Scooter Simpson
Toby
Tota of Cairn Den

1991 Companion Dogs Excellent
Brightridge Angel Cloe, CD
Cessnoch's Cricket on Lake, CD
Dunvegan's RiteAway, CD
In Memory of Mittens, CD
Karendon Jamie, CD
My Bailey Bailey, CD
My Brian MacGregor, CD
Sir Ripley of Kearney, CD
Sweetie Girl Scruffina, CD

1991 Utility Dogs
Bonnie Marie on Crocker, CDX
Vegacairn Mary's Toto O', CDX

1991 Tracking Dog
Ch. Thorncroft Gold Star

1992 Cairn Terrier
Champions of Record

Aislinge's Callahan
Avesfield Campbell My Man
Avocairns Bold Glory
Bagamore's Starbuck
Bann-Red Hill's Ryley
Barberi Hedge Tommy Toon
Barrett's Apple Dumpling
Barrett's Fire Fly II
Blackthorn of Wolfpit
Bonnie Thingamagig O'Wolfpit
Bramblewood's Cat Dancing
Bramblewood's Stetson
Bravo's Good News Bear
Brehannon Fire Over England
Brehannon's Marywilf Hellion
Brigadoon's Firestorm
Brigadoon's Lincairn Tallyho
Brightridge Butch Cassidy
Brocsbain Dark Victory
Cairmar Rooster Cogburn
Cairmar Wildfire of Raelain
Cairmar's In the Lion's Image
Cairmar's Talk of the Town
Cairmar's Tera O'WildeOaks
Cairndania Smartie's Sandell
Cairndania Todd's Sparkler
Cairndowns Bonnie Miss Thistle
Cairnkeep Brook of Fire
Cairnluv Misty Rose
Cairnluv Tangerine of Laird
Cairnluv's Best Yet
Cairnwolde's Macrufus
Canorwoll One Man Band
Car O'Mik Tata Ghillie Dhu
Castlecairn Glen Corrie
Cherokee's First Papoose A.T.
Chesapeake Rendition In Red
Chesapeake Rising Son O'Scot
Cimmarron Apache
Clanranald Highland Fling
Coach's Disastrous Dickens
Coalacre McDougal
Coletowne Brittany
Coletowne Eyecatcher

Cook's Misty Meadow I Love Lucy
Cook's Red Red Red
Copperglen Silhouette
Cragcastle Court Jester
Cragcastle Durango Drifter
Cragcastle Hershey
Cragden's I'm McKenzie Too
Critterkin's Frolic 'N' Fandango
Critterkin's Key Largo
Critterkin's Key Lime
Critterkin's Lord E J O'Kilmarnock
Dees It's Me Babe
Donwin's Sugar Baby
Falcroft Crazy Mazie
Falcrofts Nick of Time
Fenwick's K D McBain-O'Clardon
Flickwynds Ginger Snap
Foxairn Karousel
Gayla Cairn's Extrafat
Gayla Cairn's Like a Goat
Gimmick's Trooper of Wolfpit
Glen-Ayr's Mlle. Joie
Glenarden Debut Attraction
Glencairn Brynde McNeill
Glencairn Minx McNeill
Glencoe's Margaret
Gleneagles Red Robin
Glenmore's Essence
Goosedown Jessica Joywood
Greetavale Royal Orchids at
    Monary
Greyfriar's Games of Chance
Greyfriar's Instant Replay
Happicairn Brigadoon
Happicairn Pandemonium
Hearthside Wood Cairndania
Jesmic Mister Cory of Badon
Joywood's Jamie of Goosedown
Joywood's Lady Clare Kerri
Joywood's Liberty Bell
Joywood's Rob Roy
Karedon Jamie,CDX
Karen's Wired For Sound
Kim-E-Cairn's Dynamite

Kirkwall's Dandy-Lion O'McErin
Kyleakin Classic Mercedes
Lakewood's Gamekeeper
Lakewood's Katie O'Cricklade
Lakewood's Patriot
Lakewood's Silverstreak
LaMarc Free Spirit
Lincairn Brigadoon Hot Shot
Little Miss Muffin O'T
Loch Katrine Lady Meghan
Lochreggand Lyrae
Lomala Kudos Romany Rye
Maha's Tweedle Dee
McCairn's Margret Laurence
Misty Meadow I've Got a Secret
Misty Meadow's Petulla
Mistywyns Gaelic Firefly
Mr. Lincoln of Bann-Red Hill
O'Connor's Passport to Wexford,
   Am./Can. CDX
Pennylane Velveteen Rabbit
Pennyroyal's Desert Tempest
Pennyroyal's Mountaineer Jack
Rag A Bash MacBernie
Ragtime Ain'T Miss Behavin'
Ramblebriar's Will Scarlet
Raskelf Talisman
Razzle Berry of Wolfpit
Redwoods Wonderful Wizard
Rpm's Buffy the Cookie Krum
Rutherglen Ring of Fire
Seajay Brownian Motion
Shajas Rosebud
Sienna Golds Blossom of Dees
Silverbells Sweet Delight
Somerset Devon's Shaw O'Burr
South-Down's Speed Bump
Spawyche Elizabethan April
Spring Valle Bann Ra Shannon
Tanglevine's Johnny Rotten
Tanglevine's Song and Dance
Tanglevine's Twisted Sister
Terriwood's Man About Town
Th'Wiz of Glencoe
Tidewater Royal Gold
Tigh Terrie's Artful Dodger
Tigh Terrie's Cairnton Star
Tigh Terrie's Lady is a Tramp

Tigh Terrie's Leading Lady
Tigh Terrie's S'Wonderful
Tokamar Tin Pan Alley
Tokamar Tin Peddler of McBeth
Tokamar Wizard of Melrose
Traveler in the Ruff
Tweedsmuir's Dear Gabby
Wee Acre Kar-Mike-L
Whistle Lake's Spunk Star
Whistle Lake's Star Man
Wild moor's Silver Cloud Rr
Wiscairn Timothy O'Toole
Zigfelds Wind Jammer O'Cherbo

1992 Companion Dogs
Cairn Haven's Scotch Legacy
Cara Pederson
Carosel's Lady H of Raelain
Fillkatoms Barbie Doll
Fillkatoms Chui Praline
Gamekeeper's Carefree Lass
Gentle Sku Tar of Chathan
Green Mountains Wee Truffle
Heather O Dell
K-Z's Sam's Bright Fudge
Lakewood's Katie O'Garacious
Lincairn Carissa Katie
Mab G Frolicking Amity
Ch. Mac Nan's Mischief Maker
Margaret's Merry Mischief
Meadoway's Mandy O'Meybriars
Missy McClarke of Highpoint
Oliver's Precious Contessa
Princess Kathrine Macmartin
Quince's Foxgrove Bruff
Redwoods Too Hot To Handle
Rockford Benton Wheaten
Sasanataba Jazzboa
Shaffer's Charles P
Sir Winston Barnstormer
Spraggins Katenaround
Terran Alyska

1992 Companion Dogs Excellent
Dunvegan's FireAway, CD
Ch. Imp Print's Caper
   of Wolfpit, CD
Ch. K-Z's Sam's Bright Willy, CD

Ch. Merry Georas Mac Ferniegair,
   CD
Rose Croft Mirrie Magee Beo, CD
Sheena Sparkles-Pleanty, CD
Taffy-Candies Delight, CD
Ch. Terratote Glen Plaid, CD

1992 Utility Dog
Brightridge Angel Chloe', CDX, TDI

1992 Tracking Dogs
Ghillie O' Scotsmist
Bedrock Barney R, CD
Kirkwall's Keeping the Faith

1992 Tracking Dog Excellent
Redwoods Too Hot To Handle, CD,
   TD

1993 Cairn Terrier
Champions of Record

Aislinge's Prairie Spirit
Avocairns Miss Firecracker
BalBrae Katy Did
Barberi Hedge Bandit O'Brien
Barberi Hedge Bangaway
Barberi Hedge Jake O'Malley
Barberi Hedge Merry Moireach,CG
Barra Gwynn's Macintosh
Barrett's Honey Bunch
Barrett's Silhoette
Blair Hill Hurricane Edie
Braemar's Georgiana De Brus
Bramblewood's Murphy Brown
Bravo's Hope Springs Eternal
Bravo's St Beccas Amazing Grace
Braw Clan's Lonesome Dove
Brigadoon's A Feather In My Cap
Brigadoon's Gum Drop
Brigadoon's Rambunctious
Brightridge Chocolate Chip
Brightridge Cracker Jack
Brightridge Shadow Knows
Brinkhaven Maybe Magic
Cairdeil Rantin Rovin Robin
Cairmar Catch Me if You Can II
Cairn Gorm's McGuyver
CairnAcre's Primrose
Cairncroft Iron Horse
Cairncroft Iron Lady
Cairndania Todd's Rebell
Cairndowns Peppermint Patty
Cairnkeep Ball of Fire

Cairnluv Christopher of Lomala
Cairnluv's Mile High
Cairnwolde's Contrary Mary
Capscot's Brasce Macduff
Castle Cairn Glencairn Kilty
Chivari English Ivy
Coletowne Oliver
Cook's Misty Meadow Thistle
Cook's Northern Exposure
Copperglen Windwalker
Cragcastle Denver Golden Girl
Criffell Diamond in the Ruff
Criffell Waltzing Matilda
Dandor Jupiters Kallisto
Dandor Spinning Galaxy
Davoeg Sir Angus Mackenzie
Dees Bandito
Dees Bee My Valentine
Dees Just Plain Bill
Dees Thundering Applause
Dunvegan's All Dressed Up
Dunvegans Image at Greyfriar
Feldspar's Destiny
Foxairn Casey McCairn
Foxairn Maid Marion
Foxairn Pete's Rose
Galehaven Easy Does It
Galehaven Play It Again Sam
Galehaven's Puttin' On the Ritz
Galehaven's Showpan
Gamac Wind Dancer
Gay Tayls Knick Knack

Gb's Yosemite Sam
Gimmick's Copper of Wolfpit
Goosedown's Almond Joy
Goosedown's Lucas Joywood
Greenstone's Wild Bill Hickok
Greyfriar's Hallmark
Gunnlock's A. M. McGyver
Eng. Ch. Harlight Hooray Henry
Havenshire Burberry O'Wolfpit
Hearn Helmsman
Hearn Prima Donna
Hearthside Tinker Cairndania
Helen Howdy McCairn
Holemill Silver Sentry
Hollywoulds Chuck Full O'Fun
Imp Print Maccabee O Wolfpit
Ironwood Don't Worry Be Happy
Ironwood Pop Gun
Joywood's Agatha C of Kintra
Kaitlen Tt Ten Cents a Dance
Kyleakin Cottingley Belle
Kyleakin Rally of Redwood
Lachdale Little Debbie
Lakewood's Ima Bloke Too
Lakewood's Justin Time
Lakewood's Sugar Bear
LaMarc Presents the Emmys
Lennoxx Wee Tempest
Lesmars Duncan Stairs
Lincairn Melody of Love
Lincairn Music Man
Lochreggand Disco Dancer
Lomala Kudos Life of Riley
Lomala's Brindle Lacey Daze
Lowa's Holiday From Asgard
Mac Nan Gold Glitter
Mac Nan Rooster's Rogie
Maha's Scouts Honor
Mapleleaf Farm Lady Gallahad
Mary Wilf Kristin's Kathy
Mc'Erins Theo the Lionhearted
McKeegue's Barleycorn
Misty Meadow's Rosebud
Mistywyns Polly Anna
Ohioville Kennedy
Ohioville Polk
Pennylane Pretty Woman
Penticharm Jack the Lad

Pretty Girl Amber
Ramblebriar's Sweet Baby James
Reanda's Black Gold at Redcoat
Redcoat's Summer Harvest
Redmaples Buddy Ramblewood
Redwood Geena Davis
Redwoods Glimpse of Gold
Redwoods Ninja
Redwoods T-Bone
Riverbend Razzmatazz
Sandaig Spinner
Sandpiper
Scarlet Tananger
Shajas Brigand
Sharolaines Rett Butlor
Shin Pond Tradition Reflexion
Spring Valle Bann Ra Mollee B
Spring Valle Bann-Lin Hillary
Starcairn Tornado
Suncrest Lion Up Behind Me
Suncrest Sweet Caro-Lion
TangleVine's Skyeclad
Tartan Tailgunner McLeod
Terriwood's Abby of Homeport
Terriwood's Dressed in Lace
Tharr Barr Cheers for McBeth
Tharr Barr Dances on Roofs
Tharr Barr Leader of the Pack
Tigh Terrie's Ain't Misbehavin'
Tintop Alter Ego
Tosaig Emilie O'Karengary
Tweedsmuir's Miss Daisy
Whistle Lake's Phoenix Star
Woodberry of Wolfpit
Zigfelds Rok Moninof
Zomerhof's Friendly Lil Ghost

1993 Companion Dogs
Appleson Gillian of Brocair
Ch. Brocair Weekend Warrior
CairnAcre's Bold Scotsman
Cairns Sir Keegan of Lovett
Ch. Coralrocks Capt Abernathy
Coralrocks Tristan
Dandor MacBashers Ursa Major
Ch. Dees Birdwatcher at Robine
Goosedown's Raisin' Cain
Gremlins Bob Barker

Haley's Challenge
Ch. Imp Print's Wiz Bang of
   Wolfpit
Kirkwall's Keeping the Faith, TD
Kish-Hill's Buster McDonald
Lindy's Sonic Boom of KJ
Millie's Magic Murphy
P and B's Phoebe
Piper's Bonnie Brittas
Reba's Little Kelpie
Sasanataba Lil' Orphan Annie
Sassy Sara Leigh

Skye King Charles
Thane Theodore of Thornhill
Ch. Thorncroft Gold Star, TD

1993 Companion Dogs Excellent
Goosedown's Raisin' Cain, CD
Mab G Frolicking Amity, CD
Scooter Simpson, CD

1993 Utility Dogs
Barich Tc's Black Raspberry, CDX
Dunvegans RiteAway, CDX

Appendix
Top Producers

The information made available to the reader in the following appendices has been compiled by Clarence F. Vaughn.

He spent many hours verifying the accuracy of all the information included here. All the research is based on the AKC records, and I am very grateful to him for all his efforts. All statistics were compiled through the end of 1993, with the exception of the fifty-first champion for Ch. Cairmar Fancy Dresser. This event seemed important for the reader, and so I have changed that one statistic to include 1994 information.

Listed here for the reader are the ten Cairn Terrier dog and bitch top producers of all time. In the case of the dogs, included as well is a picture, and a four generation pedigree for easy reference.

Enough can never be said about pedigree study to the serious breeder/fancier/exhibitor, for our dogs today would not be what they are except for those who have gone before.

Of the top ten dogs, eight of the top producers are Line DGS. Other than those eight, Ch. Sharolaine Kalypso is Line I, and Ch. Persimmon of Wolfpit is Line DR.

A tail male line of descendancy is listed here down from Splinters of Twobees, through Ch. Redletter McJoe, sire of Eng. Ch. Redletter McRuffie, and Eng. Ch. Redletter McMurran And Eng. Ch. Redletter Fincairn Frolic, sire of Sir Frolic, from whom the eight all trace their origins. A tail male line of descendancy on Kalypso and Persimmon is also listed here.

LINE DGS
Am. Eng. Ch. Redletter McBrigand, (sired by)
  Eng. Ch. Redletter McMurran, (sired by)
    Eng. Ch. Redletter McJoe, (sired by)
      Eng. Ch. Bonfire of Twobees, (sired by)
        Eng. Ch. Splinters of Twobees

LINE DGS
Ch. Caithness Rufus, (sired by)
  Ch. Cairndania McRuffie's Raider, (sired by)
    Ch. Redletter McRuffie, (sired by)
      Eng. Ch. Redletter McJoe, (sired by)
        Eng. Ch. Bonfire of Twobees, (sired by)
          Eng. Ch. Splinters of Twobees

LINE DGS
Ch. Cairnwoods Quince, (sired by)
    Ch. Cairnwoods Golden Boy, (sired by)
        Ch. Caithness Rufus, (sired by)
            Ch. Cairndania McRuffie's Raider, (sired by)
                Ch. Redletter McRuffie

LINE DGS
Ch. Cairmar Fancy Dresser, (sired by)
    Ch. Dapper Dan of Wildwood, (sired by)
        Ch. MacMurrich of Wolfpit, (sired by)
            Ch. Cairnwoods Quince, (sired by)
                Ch. Cairnwoods Golden Boy, (sired by)
                    Ch. Caithness Rufus

Ch. Cairmar Fancy Dresser sired another top producer, Ch. Whetstone Halston. Halston sired the top producer Ch. Cairmar Scot Free.

LINE DGS
Ch. Caithness Barnabas, (sired by)
    Kamidons Country Squire, (sired by)
        Ch. Caithness Fay's Falcon, (sired by)
            Ch. Cairnwoods Golden Boy, (sired by)
                Ch. Caithness Rufus

Ch. Gayla Cairn's Davey comes down again from Eng. Ch. Redletter McJoe, through a different path as seen below.

LINE DGS
Ch. Gayla Cairn's Davey, (sired by)
    Ch. Pledwick Lord Frolic, (sired by)
        Eng. Ch. Uniquecottage Sir Frolic, (sired by)
            Eng. Ch. Redletter Fincairn Frolic, (sired by)
                Eng. Ch. Redletter McJoe

LINE DR
Ch. Persimmon of Wolfpit, (sired by)
    Ch. Vinovium Caius, (sired by)
        Vinovium Irwin, (sired by)
            Eng. Ch. Vinovium Graham, (sired by)
                Vinovium Dominic, (sired by)
                    Vinovium Demitrius, (sired by)
                        Hillston Ghillie, (sired by)
                          Hillston Gilly Grey

LINE I
Ch. Sharolaine's Kalypso, (sired by)
    Am. Can. Ch. Cairndania Targon's Thomas, (sired by)
        Am. Can. Ch. Cairndania Tammy's Targon, (sired by)
            Am. Can. Ch. Tammy of Mistyfell, (sired by)
                Glenmacdhui Tammy, (sired by)
                    Eng. Ch. Dorseydale Tammy, (sired by)
                        Eng. Ch. Lofthouse Geryon of Mistyfell, (sired by)
                            Eng. Ch. Blencathra Redstart, (sired by)
                                Eng. Ch. Blencathra Clivegreen Timothy

I have only listed the pedigree of the top producing bitch, Ch. Gayla Cairns Nora. It is interesting that Nora is Line I, and her line of descendancy is listed below.

Ch. Gayla Cairn's Nora, (sired by)
    Ch. Gayla Cairn's Grey Knight, (sired by)
        Ch. Wyesider Grey Knight, (sired by)
            Eng. Ch. Lofthouse Geryon of Mistyfell, (sired by)
                Eng. Ch. Blencathra Redstart, (sired by)
                      Eng. Ch. Blencathra Clivegreen Timothy

Top-Producing Cairn Terrier Sires

1A.   Ch. Cairnwoods Quince - 51
1B.   Ch. Cairmar Fancy Dresser - 51
3.   Ch. Caithness Barnabas - 33
4.   Ch. Cairmar Scot Free - 33
5.   Ch. Caithness Rufus - 32
6.   Ch. Whetstone Halston - 31
7.   Ch. Gayla Cairn's Davey - 29
8.   Ch. Cairndania McBrigand's Brigrey - 27
9.   Ch. Persimmon of Wolfpit - 27
10.   Ch. Sharolaine's Kalypso - 25

Ch. Cairnwoods Quince (Dark Grey
Brindle)
Whelped: February 16, 1968
OWNER
Mr. & Mrs. Taylor Coleman
BREEDER
Luanne Klepps

Eng./Am./Can. Ch. Redletter McRuffie
 Am./Can. Ch. Cairndania McRuffie's Raider
  Can. Ch. Rossmar's Bronda of Cairndania
Ch. Caithness Rufus
   Ch. Unique Cottage Mr Tippy of Caithness
  Ch. Caithness Briar Rose
   Foundation Moss Rose
Ch. Cairnwoods Golden Boy
   Ch. Hillston Jeremy of Braemuir
  Braemuir Jeremy's Sabre
   Braemuir Breacanach
 Crofters Heidre Jarre Sue
   Ch. Peter Mastiff of Westbrook
  Ch. Crofters Saucy Sue
   Bashful Sue
  Eng./Am./Can. Ch. Redletter McRuffie
  Am./Can. Ch. Cairndania McRuffie's Raider
   Can. Ch. Rossmar's Bronda of Cairndania
Ch. Caithness Rufus
   Ch. Unique Cottage Mr Tippy of Caithness
  Ch. Caithness Briar Rose
   Foundation Moss Rose
Caithness Gracenote
   Yeendsdale Feller-Me-Lad
  Yeendsdale Merry Man
   Queensmeade Rebecca
 Lucky Bracken of Yeendsdale
   Fetla Rambler
  Nice-Enough of Yeendsdale
   Queensmead Rebecca

Ch. Cairnwoods Quince (51)
by Ch. Cairnwoods Golden Boy ex Ch. Caithness Gracenote

Bred to Kim-E-Cairn's My Choice produced:
1. Ch. Kim-E-Cairn's Faerie Queen
2. Ch. Kim-E-Cairn's Sandpiper
3. Ch. Kim-E-Cairn's Scotch Rebellion
4. Ch. Kim-E-Cairn's Shadrack
5. Ch. Pennylane's Kara O'Kim-E-Cairn's
6. Ch. Pennylane Kim-E-Cairn's Oliver

Bred to Scotsman Daffin of Wolfpit produced:
7. Ch. Easter Parade of Wolfpit
8. Ch. Greyfriar of Wolfpit
9. Ch. Quince's Spunky of Wolfpit

Bred to Ch. Nightfalls Minute Maid produced:
10. Ch. Nightfalls Harry O
11. Ch. Nightfalls MacDuff
12. Ch. Nightfalls Sundance

Bred to Ch. Craiglyn Christmas Carol produced:
13. Ch. Bayberry of Wolfpit
14. Ch. Boysenberry of Wolfpit

Bred to Ch. Bonnie Vixen of Wolfpit produced:
15. Ch. Bonnie Gidget of Wolfpit
16. Ch. Bonnie Vamp of Wolfpit

Bred to Ghillys Heather of Kilmar produced:
17. Ch. Braemar's MacGregor
18. Ch. Quince the Piper of Cessnoch

Bred to Cairnhoe Fireworks of Wolfpit produced:
19. Ch. Cairnhoe Carronade
20. Ch. Cairnhoe Chantyman

Bred to Ch. Scot's Heather of Ymir produced:
21. Ch. Caries T. C. Jester
22. Ch. Ymir's Kris Kringle of Kishorn

Bred to Crag Valle Cassie produced:
23. Ch. Crag Valley Thistle
24. Ch. Crag Valley Timber

Bred to Ch. Brae Bairn's Flair of Wolfpit produced:
25. Ch. Flair's Flirt of Wolfpit
26. Ch. Jiminie Cricket of Wolfpit

Bred to Ch. Dalwhinnie Gay of Wolfpit produced:
27. Ch. Innisfree's Red Baron
28. Ch. Innisfree's Mr Chipwick

Bred to Loch Ness Nessie of Haverford produced:
29. Ch. Foxy Loxy Vixen of Haverford
30. Ch. Haverford Becky O'Waterford

Bred to Ch. Foxy Loxy Vixen of Haverford produced:
31. Ch. Waterford Quintessent
32. Ch. Waterford Quintillion

Bred to Ch. Milbryan Killarney O'Cairmar produced:
33. Ch. Cairmar's Connecticut Yankee
34. Ch. Tagalong of Wildwood

Bred to Ch. Rossmoor's Nickle Silver produced:
35. Ch. Rockwell's Jubal Early
36. Ch. Rockwell's Quicksilver

Bred to Ch. Justcairns Tally-Ho produced:
37. Ch. Balcoven Bracken

Bred to Quissex of Mayfair at Wolfpit produced:
38. Ch. Balcoven Marksman of Wolfpit

Bred to Ch. Caries Kiss Me Kate produced:
39. Ch. Caries Mod Scot

Bred to Caithness Farthing produced:
40. Ch. Caithness Piper of Bagpipes

Bred to Innisfree's Barbie Doll produced:
41. Ch. Innisfree's Bryan's Song

Bred to Kamidon Cortina produced:
42. Ch. Kamidon's Juniper Jennifer

Bred to Karendale Kricket produced:
43. Ch. Karendale Classic O'Meri-Leigh

Bred to Ch. Londonaire of Wolfpit produced:
44. Ch. London Bridget of Wolfpit

Bred to Ch. Lofthouse Veleta produced:
45. Ch. MacMurrich of Wolfpit (9)

Bred to Rockwells Spark O' Fire produced:
46. Ch. Meriwynds Quincy

Bred to Bagpipe's Paprika of Paisley produced:
47. Ch. Paisley's Kernel Pepper

Bred to Ch. London Chimes of Wolfpit produced:
48. Ch. Quick Trick of Wolfpit

Bred to Ch. Brightridge Sparkle Plenty produced:
49. Ch. Rockwell's Artful Dodger

Bred to Cairndania Brigrey's Miss Trix produced:
50. Ch. Sabal of Overlook

Bred to Caithness Merriweather produced:
51. Ch. Woodmist Bitter Sweet

Ch. Cairmar Fancy Dresser
(Brindle)
Whelped: November 25, 1975
OWNER
Glenna Barnes
BREEDER
Betty Marcum

                                        Ch. Cairnwoods Golden Boy
                        Ch. Cairnwoods Quince
                                        Caithness Gracenote
            Ch. McMurrich of Wolfpit
                                        Eng. Ch. Lofthouse Larkspur
                        Ch. Lofthouse Veleta
                                        Dorseydale Cindy
    Ch. Dapper Dan of Wildwood
                                        Ch. Cairnwoods Golden Boy
                        Ch. Cairnwoods Quince
                                        Caithness Gracenote
            Ch. Quince's Spunky of Wolfpit
                                        Ch. Bonnie Scotsman of Wolfpit
                        Scotsman's Daffin of Wolfpit
                                        Drewfer's Fiona
                                        Ch. Cairndania McRuffie's Raider
                        Ch. Caithness Rufus
                                        Ch. Caithness Briar Rose
            Ch. Caithness Colonel
                                        Eng. Ch. Blencathra Milord
                        Ch. Blencathra Melanie
                                        Ewandale Penny
    Ch. Cairmar Fancy That
                                        Ch. Bellacairn's Bit O'Scotch
                        Caithness Little Bit
                                        Ch. Caithness Rosette
            Ch. Caithness Periwinkle
                                        Ch. Dorseydale Wizard of Oz
                        Caithness Sorceress
                                        Ch. Uniquecottage Holy Terror

Ch. Cairmar Fancy Dresser (51)
by Ch. Dapper Dan of Wildwood ex Ch. Cairmar Fancy That

Bred to Shadow's Sterling Silver produced:
1. Ch. Cairland Bagpipes
2. Ch. Cairland Bobby Dazzler
3. Ch. Cairland Center Fold
4. Ch. Cairland Count Me In
5. Ch. Cairland Count on Me
6. Ch. Cairland Gold Digger
7. Ch. Cairland Hit Parade
8. Ch. Cairland Prime Contender

Bred to Ch. Cairmar's Connecticut Yankee produced:
9. Ch. Cairmar Co Co Chanel
10. Ch. Whetstone Annie Hall
11. Ch. Whetstone Halston (31)
12. Ch. Whetstone Miss Dior

Bred to Ch. Cairmar Misty Storm produced:
13. Ch. Cairland Afternoon Delight
14. Ch. Cairland Atom Action
15. Ch. Cairmar Critics Choice
16. Ch. Cairmar Misty Christmas Morn

Bred to Kiku's Bouncing Bonnie produced:
17. Ch. Terriwood's Artful Dresser
18. Ch. Terriwood's Best Dressed
19. Ch. Terriwood's Dressed in Style
20. Ch. Terriwood's Dressed in Lace

Bred to Ch. Cairmar Carrousel Charme produced:
21. Ch. Criscairn Ms Munchkin
22. Ch. Criscairn Toto Too
23. Ch. Criscairn Wizard of Oz

Bred to Ch. Ms. McD produced:
24. Ch. Cairmar's Tony McLin
25. Ch. McLin's New Decade Diamond Lil
26. Ch. Rocky McLin of Pearland

Bred to Missy Hi Mac Cair produced:
27. Ch. Whipshe Wingtips of Cairland

Bred to Morihas Nike at Cairland produced:
28. Ch. Bramblewood's BMW
29. Ch. Bramblewood's Reebock

Bred to Avenelhouse Martell Brandy produced:
30. Ch. Pattwos Martell Cognac
31. Ch. Pattwos Sherry Brandy

Bred to Ch. Brigadoon's Meg of Sugar Pine produced:
32. Ch. Cairland Mr Fillkatom
33. Ch. Fillkatom's Little Dickens

Bred to Ch. Brightridge Texas Talker produced:
34. Ch. Cairland Fast Talker
35. Ch. Brycairn's Fancy Talker

Bred to Cairmar Chandra Te produced:
36. Ch. Cairmar Caramel Candy
37. Ch. Cairmar Depth Charge

Bred to Cairndania Jeronimo's Jubilee produced:
38. Ch. Cairland Cornerstone
39. Ch. Whipshe Witchcraft

Bred to Windy Gillyflower O St Andrews produced:
40. Ch Billy Bob of Raelain
41. Ch. Fanci Gilliflower of Raelain

Bred to Bobalyne of the Highlands produced:
42. Ch. Fancy Dress of the Highlands

Bred to Ch. Cairmar Charisma produced:
43. Ch. Cairland Talent Scout

Bred to Ch. Cairmar Stormie Dawn produced:
44. Ch. Cairmar Parade at Dawn

Bred to Ch. Caries Fast Lane produced:
45. Ch. Kishorn's Educating Rita

Bred to Gamac Fiddle Stix O'Shadow's produced:
46. Ch. Shadow's Weekend Warrior

Bred to McLain's Merry Lynn produced:
47. Ch. Cairland Money Market

Bred to Ch. McMaggie produced:
48. Ch. Karen's Mr King Brinney Boy

Bred to Roylaine's Bramble Bee produced:
49. Ch. Bramblewood's Cat Dancing
50. Ch. Bramblewood's Kit Kat

Bred to Ch. Tradorohg's Cluny Connamarah produced:
51. Ch. Cairmar Centurion

Ch. Caithness Barnabas (Red Black
  Points)
Whelped: July 22, 1970
Ch. Completed: June 24, 1972
OWNER
Betty Marcum
BREEDER
Rosemary E. Zagorski

BEST OF
WINNERS

                                    Ch. Caithness Rufus
                    Ch. Cairnwoods Golden Boy
                                    Crofters Heider Jarre Sue
        Ch. Caithness Fay's Falcon
                                    Toptwig Thomas
                    Toptwig Fay of Caithness
                                    Toptwig Fiona
Kamidons Country Squire
                                    Ch. Redletter McRuffie
                    Ch. Cairndania McRuffie's Raider
                                    Can. Ch. Rossmar's Bronda of Cairndania
        Caithness Caper
                                    Whimical Rouge of Caithness
                    Caithness Cinnamon Rose
                                    Foundation Moss Rose
                                    Eng. Ch. Redletter McJoe
                    Ch. Redletter McRuffie
                                    Rosefield Rebecca
        Ch. Cairndania McRuffie's Raider
                                    Ch. Redletter McBrigand
                    Can. Ch. Rossmar's Bronda of Cairndania
                                    Rossmar's Ruffican Lass
Ch. Caithness Rosalie
                                    Eng. Ch. Unique Cottage Sir Frolic
                    Ch. Unique Cottage Mr Tippy of Caithness
                                    Uniquecottage Anabladh
        Ch. Caithness Briar Rose
                                    Blencathra McBeth of Rhu
                    Foundation Moss Rose of Caithness
                                    Foundation Mignonette

Ch. Caithness Barnabas (33)
by Kamidons Country Squire ex Ch. Caithness Rosalie

Bred to Ginger Mist of Merriwood produced:
1. Ch. Lakewood's Barnstormer
2. Ch. Lakewood's Charming Betsy
3. Ch. Lakewood's Foxy Lady
4. Ch. Lakewood's Mean Joe Green
5. Ch. Lakewood's O C, TD
6. Ch. Lakewood's Red Raider
7. Ch. Lakewood's Suzy Q
8. Ch. Lakewood's Talking Tilda
9. Ch. Lakewood's Top O' the Mornin

Bred to Ch. Tradorohg's Connamarah produced:
10. Ch. Cairmar Christmas Storm
11. Ch. Cairmar Misty Storm
12. Ch. Cairmar Storm Warning
13. Ch. Cairmar Stormie Dawn
14. Ch. Cairmar Stormie Dream
15. Ch. Era's Dust Storm of Cairmar

Bred to Ch. Metcourt's Orange Marmalade produced:
16. Ch. Metcourt's Bill Bailey
17. Ch. Metcourt's Buckwheat
18. Ch. Metcourt's Butcher Boy
19. Ch. Metcourt's Orange Blossom

Bred to Ch. Metcourt's Dandelion produced:
20. Ch. Metcourt Great Balls of Fire
21. Ch. Cairmar Happicairn's Beckey

Bred to Ch. Gamac Tartan Miss Wags produced:
22. Ch. Gamac Country Squire
23. Ch. Cairmar Tartan Taffy

Bred to Christycay's Good Golly Miss Molly produced:
24. Ch. Chriscay's Heavens to Betsy
25. Ch. Chriscay's I'm Toto Too

Bred to Brightridge Heich Heather produced:
26. Ch. Cairmar Barberry Lass

Bred to Ch. Wicked Witch O'Cairn Cove produced:
27. Ch. Cairmar Barnabas Collins

Bred to Ch. Tradorohg's Kyleigh produced:
28. Ch. Cairmar Royal Brandy

Bred to Nita's Sprig of Holly produced:
29. Ch. Dapper Cairn's Barnaby

Bred to Ch. Milbryan Killarney O'Cairmar produced:
30. Ch. Milbryan K-Mart of Cairmar

Bred to Metcourt's Sweet Jasmine produced:
31. Ch. T'Is Sprout O'Heather Wildfire

Bred to Ch. Ramblewood Stormy O'Moonstar produced:
32. Ch. Ramblewood Barney Brehannon

Bred to Am. & Mex. Ch. Caithness Periwinkle produced:
33. Ch. Vanessa of Cairmar

Ch. Cairmar Scot Free (Brindle)
Ch. Completed: September 26, 1981
OWNER
Betty E. Marcum
BREEDER
Betty E. Marcum

Ch. MacMurrich of Wolfpit
Ch. Dapper Dan of Wildwood
Ch. Quince's Spunky of Wolfpit
Ch. Cairmar Fancy Dresser
Ch. Caithness Colonel
Ch. Cairmar Fancy That
Ch. Caithness Periwinkle
Ch. Whetstone Halston
Ch. Cairnwoods Golden Boy
Ch. Cairnwoods Quince
Caithness Gracenote
Ch. Cairmar Connecticut Yankee
Ch. Milbryan McGillicuddy
Ch. Milbryan Killarney O'Cairmar
Ch. Milbryan Kernal K of Raelain
Eng. Ch. Blencathra Brat
Eng. Ch. Heshe Donavon
Drusilla of Rossarden
Eng. Ch. Robinson Crusoe of Courtrai
Rellerp Arranos Crispin
Courtrai Nimble Nell
Carol Rogue of Courtrai
Ch. Greetavale Golden Vow of Courtrai
Eng. Ch. Unique Cottage Gold Goblet
Eng. Ch. Felshott Wine Taster
Felshott Lonicera
Eng Ch. Greetavale Super Honey
Killearn Kings Ransom
Greetavale Suzette
Greetavale Golden Sun

Ch. Cairmar Scot Free (33)
by Ch. Whetstone Halston ex Ch. Greetavale Golden Vow of Courtrai

Bred to Gayla Cairn's Land Shark produced:
1. Ch. TangleVine's Donnybrook
2. Ch. TangleVine's Doug Flutie
3. Ch. Gayla Cairn's Elvira
4. Ch. Gayla Cairn's Extrafat

Bred to Ch. Ariel Amadan O'Cairmar produced:
5. Ch. Cairmar's Talk of the Town
6. Ch. Cairmar's Tera O'Wildeoaks

Bred to Ariel Windsong of Cairmar produced:
7. Ch. Cairmar Crimson Tide O Ariel
8. Ch. Cairmar Free as the Wind

Bred to Ch. Bonfyre's Early Delivery produced:
9. Ch. Bonfyre's Blackmaler
10. Ch. Bonfyre's Constant Comment

Bred to Ch. Cairmar Captivation produced:
11. Ch. Kilkeddan's Chief Justice
12. Ch. Kilkeddan's Hear Ye Hear Ye

Bred to Ch. Cairmar Courtesan produced:
13. Ch. Cairmar Coquette
14. Ch. Cairmar Courtier

Bred to Ch. Copperglen Fame N Fortune produced:
15. Ch. Copperglen Claim to Fame
16. Ch. Copperglen Great Attraction

Bred to Cragcastle Queen Elizabeth produced:
17. Ch. Cragcastle Great Scot
18. Ch. Cragcastle Royal Scot

Bred to Jesmic Ragtime produced:
19. Ch. Jesmic Duncan of Laurielee
20. Ch. Jesmic Jack O'Hearts

Bred to Ch. Tiffany's Sparkle Twist produced:
21. Ch. T'Is Tornado Stormy Weather
22. Ch. T'Is Oakalley's Thunderstorm

Bred to Ch. Avenelhouse Plain Jane produced:
23. Ch. Cairmar Calamity Jane

Bred to Ch. Bramblewood's Reebock produced:
24. Ch. Bramblewood's Murphy Brown

Bred to Ch. Cairmar Bobby's Girl produced:
25. Ch. Chesapeake Rising Son O'Scot

Bred to Ch. Cairmar Cameo produced:
26. Ch. Cairmar Care Free

Bred to Ch. Cairmar's Tawny Troubadour produced:
27. Ch. Braemar's Yankee Clipper

Bred to Ch. Chesapeake Mary Wilf Rand produced:
28. Ch. Chesapeake Bit O'Scot

Bred to Halston Caryshader's Sugar produced:
29. Ch. Cairmar Great Scot

Bred to Karen's Cash Reward produced:
30. Ch. LaMarc Free Spirit

Bred to Ch. Karengary's Catch the Spirit produced:
31. Ch. Tosaig Emilie O'Karengary

Bred to Rainbow Gilliflower O Raelain produced:
32. Ch. Shajas Rosebud

Bred to Ch. Whipshe Wench produced:
33. Ch. Ollie North of the Highlands

Ch. Caithness Rufus (Red)
Whelped: August 17, 1963
OWNER
Mrs. Ralph Stone
BREEDER
Mrs. Ralph Stone

                                     Eng. Ch. Bonfire of Twobees
                    Eng. Ch. Redletter McJoe
                               Redletter My Choice
        Ch. Redletter McRuffie
                               Eng. Ch. Blencathra Sandpiper
                  Rosefield Rebecca
                               Jenny's Choice
Ch. Cairndania McRuffie's Raider
                               Eng. Ch. Redletter McMurran
                  Ch. Redletter McBrigand
                               Ch. Redletter Miss Splinters
      Can. Ch. Rossmar's Bronda of Cairndania
                               Ch. Redletter McRuffie
                  Rossmar's Ruffican Lass
                               Balkaren Cinders
                               Eng. Ch. Redletter Fincairn Frolic
                  Eng. Ch. Unique Cottage Sir Frolic
                               Uniquecottage Golddigger
        Ch. Unique Cottage Mr Tippy of Caithness
                               Eng. Ch. Uniquecottage McAilenmor
                  Uniquecottage Anabladh
                               Uniquecottage Silver Seal
Ch. Caithness Briar Rose
                               Eng. Ch. Blencathra Elford Chiefton
                  Blencathra McBeth of Rhu
                               Sandrina of Rhu
      Foundation Moss Rose of Caithness
                               Shielling Patrick of Rhu
                  Foundation Mignonette
                               Foundation Marylin

Ch. Caithness Rufus (32)
by Ch. Cairndania McRuffie's Raider ex Ch. Caithness Briar Rose

Bred to Ch. Caithness Shady Lady produced:
1. Ch. Caithness Painted Lady
2. Ch. Caithness Reginald
3. Ch. Caithness Robin

Bred to Ch. KandyKate's Kadence produced:
4. Ch. Bellacairn's Black Bottom
5. Ch. Bellacairn's Lord MacDuff

Bred to Brae Bairn of Wolfpit produced:
6. Ch. Bonnie Brash of Wolfpit
7. Ch. Bonnie Scamp of Wolfpit

Bred to Ch. Blencathra Melanie produced:
8. Ch. Caithness Colonel
9. Ch. Caithness Milady

Bred to Ch. Babeth of the Highlands produced:
10. Ch. Mardi Gras of Tabu
11. Ch. McDuff of Tabu

Bred to Sheigra of Crondall produced:
12. Ch. Shadie Katie O'Windy Pines
13. Ch. Contrary Kerry O'Windy Pines

Bred to Lady Jessica D'Ecosse produced:
14. Ch. Whistle Gate Bit of Caithness

Bred to Ch. Nanlor's Tammy of Rosecairn produced:
15. Ch. Nanlor's Cricket
16. Ch. Nanlor's Merry Kris

Bred to Ch. Topcairn Madrigal produced:
17. Ch. Rocky Knoll's Tiger Lily
18. Ch. Topcairn Mandolin

Bred to Blynman Marag produced:
19. Ch. Accalia's Tempest

Bred to Eldomac Cindy Love produced:
20. Ch. Bonnie Clyde of Innisfree

Bred to Crofters Heidere Jarre Sue produced:
21. Ch. Cairnwoods Golden Boy

Bred to Toptwig Fay of Caithness produced:
22. Ch. Caithness Fay's Fergus

Bred to Caithness Plaidie produced:
23. Ch. Caithness Katydid

Bred to Luckey Bracken of Yeendsdale produced:
24. Ch. Caithness Lyric

Bred to Ch. Red Hackle of Melita produced:
25. Ch. Clary's Sound Off

Bred to Ch. Redletter Miss Romola produced:
26. Ch. Kenmure's Felicity

Bred to Kymry Pudding produced:
27. Ch. Kymry Copper Penny O'Woodmist

Bred to Misty Matilda McGregor produced:
28. Ch. Lil's Rufus MacGufus

Bred to Toptwig Busybody produced:
29. Ch. Mac-Rufus of Honorwyre

Bred to Ch. Piccairn Alban's Merri Whid produced:
30. Ch. Piccairn's Footloose

Bred to Redletter Melicent produced:
31. Ch. Sugarplum's My Robbie (5)

Bred to Ch. Topcairn Barra produced:
32. Ch. Topcairn Sparkler

Ch. Whetstone Halston (Red
  Brindle)
Whelped: February 8, 1978
Ch. Completed: March 4, 1979
OWNER
Dr. Alvaro T. Hunt and Mrs. Joe
Marcum
BREEDER
Mrs. Phillip Wilder

                          Ch. Cairnwoods Quince
            Ch. MacMurrich of Wolfpit
                          Ch. Lofthouse Veleta
      Ch. Dapper Dan of Wildwood
                          Ch. Cairnwoods Quince
            Ch. Quincy's Spunky of Wolfpit
                          Scotsman's Daffin of Wolfpit
Ch. Cairmar Fancy Dresser
                          Ch. Caithness Rufus
            Ch. Caithness Colonel
                          Ch. Blencathra Melanie
      Ch. Cairmar Fancy That
                          Caithness Little Bit
            Ch. Caithness Periwinkle
                          Caithness Sorceress
                          Ch. Caithness Rufus
            Ch. Cairnwoods Golden Boy
                          Crofters Heider Jarre Sue
      Ch. Cairnwoods Quince
                          Ch. Caithness Rufus
            Caithness Gracenote
                          Lucky Bracken of Yeendsdale
Ch. Cairmar's Connecticut Yankee
                          Betcha Boots of Braecroft
            Ch. Milbryan McGillicuddy
                          Ch. Miss McSue of Milbryan
      Ch. Milbryan Killarney O'Cairmar
                          Ch. Caithness Colonel
            Ch. Milbryan Kernal K of Raelain
                          Ch. Khillie of Raelain

Ch. Whetstone Halston (31)
by Ch. Cairmar Fancy Dresser ex Ch. Cairmar's Connecticut Yankee

Bred to Ch. Greetavale Golden Vow of Courtrai produced:
1. Ch. Cairmar Cachet
2. Ch. Het's Christie of Cairmar
3. Ch. Cairmar Scot Free

Bred to Almin's Gusse Who produced:
4. Ch. Almin's Liberty
5. Ch. Cairmar's Boss Man Almin

Bred to Ch. Avenelhouse Plain Jane produced:
6. Ch. Cairmar Simply Smashing
7. Ch. Cairmar Music Box Dancer

Bred to Cairnoaks Cotton Candy produced:
8. Ch. Cairnoaks Maguffin
9. Ch. Cairnoaks Rainmaker

Bred to Copperglen's Caper produced:
10. Ch. Copperglen Cinnabar
11. Ch. Copperglen British Sterling

Bred to Ch. Dorlyn's Easy Lovin' produced:
12. Ch. Cairmar's DeRan Serandipity
13. Ch. DeRan No Can Do

Bred to Ch. McLin's Piper of Loch Morar produced:
14. Ch. Cairmar Bobby McLin
15. Ch. McLin's Hello Dolly O Cairmar

Bred to Ch. Milbryan Delta Dawn O'Cairmar produced:
16. Ch. Milbryan Magic Dawn
17. Ch. Milbryan Misty Dawn O'Cairmar

Bred to Ch. Tagalong of Wildwood produced:
18. Ch. Fashion Tag of Wildwood
19. Ch. Killarney's Image of Wildwood

Bred to Bouncer of Raelain produced:
20. Ch. Cairmar Andrew of Raelain

Bred to Ch. Cairmar Amy Amy Amy produced:
21. Ch. Patter's Tigger of Cairmar

Bred to Ch. Cairmar Shadow Box Image produced:
22. Ch. Glenmores Betsy McCall

Bred to Ch. Cairmar's Taste of Honey produced:
23. Ch. Kishorn's Halston's Honeycomb

Bred to Cairmar Keepsake produced:
24. Ch. Cairmar Lil Gambler

Bred to Ch. Cairn Glen's Pixie produced:
25. Ch. Cairn Glen's Little Vixen

Bred to Ch. Caryshader Seriema produced:
26. Ch. Ariel Amadan O'Cairmar

Bred to Ch. Coralrocks Pippin Maloney produced:
27. Ch. Sandcrest Coralrocks Keeley

Bred to Ch. Daveleigh's Kelley produced:
28. Ch. Daveleigh's Kaparicious Kate

Bred to Ch. Karengary's Sprits Image produced:
29. Ch. Karengary's Dirkson By Design

Bred to Uniquecottage Westwind produced:
30. Ch. Cairmar Light My Fire

Bred to Happicairn Cinnamon produced:
31. Ch. Happicairn Firecracker

Ch. Gayla Cairn's Davey (Red Brindle)
Whelped: June 21, 1966
OWNER
Miss Nancy Thompson
BREEDER
Miss Nancy Thompson

                                                             Eng. Ch. Redletter McJoe
                            Eng. Ch. Redletter Fincairn Frolic
                                            Eng. Ch. Fincairn Gillian
        Eng. Ch. Unique Cottage Sir Frolic
                                              Goldust of Uniquecottage
                        Unique Cottage Goldigger
                                          Jollee Gay Memory
Ch. Pledwick Lord Frolic
                                            Eng. Ch. Redletter Fincairn Frolic
                            Eng. Ch. Uniquecottage Sir Frolic
                                          Uniquecottage Goldigger
        Redletter Miss Frolic
                                            Eng. Ch. Redletter McJoe
                            Eng. Ch. Redletter Elford Mhorag
                                        Foundation Sylvia
                                        Ch. Rob of Blarneystone
                            Ch. Balgrochan Scotch Whisky
                                        Blarney Smiler
    Ch. Tartan of Melita
                                      John of Blarneystone
                      Nesta of Melita
                                      Mandy of Blarneystone
Ch. Gayla Cairn's Hope
                                            Eng. Ch. Redletter McJoe
                            Ch. Redletter McRuffie
                                        Rosefield Rebecca
    Ch. Gayla Cairn's Little Lynda
                                        Ch. Hawk of Melita
                          Ch. B Cube's Gayla Girl
                                      Ch. B Cube's Spunky

Ch. Gayla Cairn's Davey (29)
by Ch. Pledwick Lord Frolic ex Ch. Gayla Cairn's Hope

Bred to Ch. Kenmure's Felicity produced:
1. Ch. Gayla Cairn's Debutante
2. Ch. Gayla Cairn's Doctor John
3. Ch. Gayla Cairn's Earthquake
4. Ch. Gayla Cairn's Enuf-O-That
5. Ch. Gayla Cairn's Et Cetera
6. Ch. Gayla Cairn's Idiot's Delight
7. Ch. Gayla Cairn's Inspiration
8. Ch. Gayla Cairn's Jolly Rodger
9. Ch. Gayla Cairn's Little Sister
10. Ch. Gayla Cairn's O'Tilly

Bred to Gayla Cairn's Maggie produced:
11. Ch. Gayla Cairn's Bridget McKim
12. Ch. Gayla Cairn's Happy Owen
13. Ch. Gayla Cairn's Hi-Hopes
14. Ch. Gayla Cairn's Hooligan
15. Ch. Gayla Cairn's Big Bertha
16. Ch. Gayla Cairn's Hubert

Bred to Bramble Rose produced:
17. Ch. Gayla Cairn's Bramble Rose
18. Ch. Gayla Cairn's Eleanor Fox
19. Ch. Gayla Cairn's Red Fox

Bred to Ch. Gayla Cairn's Eleanor Fox produced:
20. Ch. Gayla Cairn's O'Ruffie
21. Ch. Gayla Cairn's O'Suffie

Bred to Ch. Gayla Cairn's Patty produced:
22. Ch. Gayla Cairn's Honest Abe
23. Ch. Gayla Cairn's Xylophone
24. Ch. Gayla Cairn's Honorable Sam

Bred to Ch. Gayla Cairn's Hope produced:
25. Ch. Gayla Cairn's Quiet Hope
26. Ch. Gayla Cairn's Quite Like Davey

Bred to Ch. Clary's Sound Off produced:
27. Ch. Clary's Charity

Bred to Gayla Cairn's Gypsy Moth produced:
28. Ch. Gayla Cairn's Rosscraggen

Bred to Gayla Cairn's Eagle produced:
29. Ch. Timberlake's Red Baron

Ch. Cairndania McBrigand's Brigrey
(Red)
Whelped: September 18, 1962
OWNER
Mrs. Betty Hyslop
BREEDER
Mrs. Betty Hyslop

```
                                        Eng. Ch. Bonfire of Twobees
                        Eng. Ch. Redletter McJoe
                                        Redletter My Choice
        Eng. Ch. Redletter McMurran
                                        Free Lance of Carysfort
                        Cairncrag Binky
                                        May Moon of Mercrogia
Ch. Redletter McBrigand
                                        Eng. Ch. Redletter McMurran
                        Crowtree Splinters
                                        Redletter Dinah of Bradshaw
        Ch. Redletter Miss Splinters
                                        Blencathra Ruffian
                        Foxearl Goldfinch
                                        Goldilocks of Foxearl
                                        Eng. Ch. Redletter McJoe
                        Ch. Redletter McRuffie
                                        Rosefield Rebecca
        Ch. Cairngorm Clansman
                                        Eng. Ch. Bonfire of Twobees
                        Twobees Fuss of Feltrim
                                        Jane of Feltrim
Ch. Cairndania Clansman's Grey Girl
                                        Eng. Ch. Redletter McJoe
                        Ch. Redletter McRuffie
                                        Rosefield Rebecca
        Cairndania McRuffie's McGay
                                        Ch. Kilmet of Cairndania
                        Ch. Mickey's Pal of Cairndania
                                        Ch. Tam's Grey Girl of Cairndania
```

Ch. Cairndania McBrigand's Brigrey (27)
by Ch. Redletter McBrigand ex Ch. Cairndania Clansman's Grey Girl

Bred to Ch. Cairndania Davey's Dolly produced:
1. Ch. Cairndania Brigrey's Daisy
2. Ch. Cairndania Brigrey's Dorey
3. Ch. Cairndania Brigrey's Dunbar
4. Ch. Cairndania Brigrey's Dumbeg

Bred to Ch. Heshe Idaberry of Nunsfield produced:
5. Ch. Cairndania Brigrey's Barney
6. Ch. Cairndania Brigrey's Berry-Red
7. Ch. Cairndania Brigrey's Red Girl

Bred to Ch. Hillston Geraldine produced:
8. Ch. Cairndania Brigrey's Sir Gerald
9. Ch. Cairndania Brigrey's Gerbrig
10. Ch. Cairndania Brigrey's Gerry

Bred to MerryBrook's Gidget produced:
11. Ch. Brigrey's Brillig of Sullane
12. Ch. Cairndania Brigrey's Brif
13. Ch. Cairndania Brigrey's Brig

Bred to Ch. Cairndania Suffie produced:
14. Ch. Keencairn Gusto O'Cairndania
15. Ch. Keencairn Holly O'Cairndania

Bred to Cairndania Davey's Doll produced:
16. Ch. Cairnlea Katie O'Cairndania
17. Ch. Cairnlea's First Edition

Bred to Clangatha's Mrs. MacIntosh produced:
18. Ch. Cairndania Brigrey's Barkley
19. Ch. Cairndania Brigrey's MacBrig

Bred to Ch. Greysarge Naughty Marietta produced:
20. Ch. Cairndania Perilous Polly
21. Ch. Greysarge Calamity Jane

Bred to Caffrey's Rachel produced:
22. Ch. Drewfer's Decorum

Bred to Cairndania Broc's Sprite produced:
23. Ch. Greysarge Red Man

Bred to Cairndania Dusky Maid produced:
24. Ch. Cairndania Brigrey's Bertha

Bred to Cairndania McBrigand's Brita produced:
25. Ch. Braelog Brigrey George

Bred to Heatherbell of Killybracken produced:
26. Ch. The Scots Grey O'Killybracken

Bred to Jiminy McKiltie's Thorn O'Ri produced:
27. Ch. Brigrey's Simply Smashing O'Ri

Ch. Persimmon of Wolfpit (Dark
  Grey Brindle)
Whelped: November 13, 1975
Ch. Completed: July 2, 1978
OWNER
Lydia C. and Susan T. Hutchinson
BREEDER
Susan T. Hutchinson

                                   Vinovium Dominic
                   Eng. Ch. Vinovium Graham
                                   Glonmar Vinovium Gem
        Vinovium Irwin
                                   Vinovium Gregory
                   Vinovium Saxa
                                   Vinovium Emma
Ch. Vinovium Caius
                                   Eng. Ch. Blencathra Brochter
                   Eng. Ch. Blencathra Elford Badger
                                   Elford Sprat
        Eng. Ch. Pledwick Drusilla
                                   Ch. Lofthouse Sundew
                   Doonrae Elfin Gay
                                   Doonrae Beattie of Waliamor
                                   Ch. Caithness Rufus
                   Ch. Cairnwoods Golden Boy
                                   Crofters Heider Jarre Sue
        Ch. Cairnwoods Quince
                                   Ch. Caithness Rufus
                   Caithness Gracenote
                                   Lucky Bracken of Yeendsdale
Easter Bonnet of Wolfpit
                                   Ch. Bonnie Brash of Wolfpit
                   Ch. Bonnie Scotsman of Wolfpit
                                   Ch. Scotch Maid of Wolfpit
        Scotsman's Daffin of Wolfpit
                                   Ch. Holemil Barley
                   Drewfer's Fiona
                                   Caithness Ailsaveg

Ch. Persimmon of Wolfpit (27)
by Ch. Vinovium Caius ex Easter Bonnet of Wolfpit

Bred to Tammy's Gem of Allendale produced:
1. Ch. Avocairn's Sparkling Gem
2. Ch. Avocairn's Red Ruffian
3. Ch. Avocairns Captivating Cool

Bred to Ch. Bayberry of Wolfpit produced:
4. Ch. Carnoustie of Wolfpit
5. Ch. Gleneagle of Wolfpit
6. Ch. Ravensworth Arran of Wolfpit

Bred to Ch. Sunnyland's Gadget of Wolfpit produced:
7. Ch. Gadget's Gimmick of Wolfpit
8. Ch. Sunnyland Standing Room Only

Bred to Ch. Razzberry of Wolfpit produced:
9. Ch. Baleshare's Meghan of Wolfpit
10. Ch. Berry Special of Wolfpit

Bred to Ch. Biljonblue's Biguine produced:
11. Ch. Biljonblue's Big Time Brucie

Bred to Ch. Weeknowe Walsing Gold Asset produced:
12. Ch. Bonfyre's Tokamar Gold Fanci

Bred to Ch. Bonnie Vamp of Wolfpit produced:
13. Ch. Bonnie Tramp of Wolfpit

Bred to Buccaneer's Bonnie Lass produced:
14. Ch. Buccaneer's Kaitlin

Bred to Ch. Cairn Glen's Pixie produced:
15. Ch. Cairn Glen's Copper Top

Bred to Ch. Cairnhoe Fireworks O'Wolfpit produced:
16. Ch. Cairnhoe Clipper

Bred to Rockwell's Blonde Beauty produced:
17. Ch. Clayridge Priddy McBryce

Bred to Woodmist Chuny II produced:
18. Ch. Foxairn's Pixie of Zomerhof

Bred to Ch. Sherry Berry of Wolfpit produced:
19. Ch. Kerryberry of Wolfpit

Bred to Ch. Marblehill's Kelly Girl produced:
20. Ch. Marblehill's Ice Crystal

Bred to Ch. Mentmore Courtesan of Wolfpit produced:
21. Ch. Mentmore Caraway of Wolfpit

Bred to Oventop Pandora produced:
22. Ch. Oventop Macintyre

Bred to Ch. Pennstone's Lady Cecily produced:
23. Ch. Pennstone's Mist O'May

Bred to Ch. Ragamuffins Sugar Bear produced:
24. Ch. Ragamuffins Trace O'Bagpipe

Bred to Ch. Ragtime's Gypsy Rose produced:
25. Ch. Ragtime Sir Duncan Fitzhugh

Bred to Ch. Rockwell's Quicksilver produced:
26. Ch. Rockwell's Littlechap

Bred to Ch. Quick Trick of Wolfpit produced:
27. Ch. Xroads Quick Like a Bunny

Ch. Sharolaine's Kalypso (Wheaten)
Whelped: October 10, 1984
Ch. Completed: October 26, 1985
OWNER
Elaine D. Eschbach
BREEDER
Elaine D. Eschbach

```
                                    Glenmacdhui Tammy
                      Ch. Tammy of Mistyfell
                                    Penny of Mistyfell
         Ch. Cairndania Tammy's Targon
                                    Ch. Cairndania McBrigand's Brigrey
                      Ch. Cairndania Brigrey's Red Girl
                                    Eng. Ch. Heshe Idaberry of Nunsfield
Ch. Cairndania Targon's Thomas
                                    Glenmacdhue Tammy
                      Ch. Tammy of Mistyfell
                                    Penny of Mistyfell
         Ch. Cairndania Tammy's Eliz
                                    Redletter Santa Clause
                      Ch. Heshe Elizabeth
                                    Bernadette of Nunsfield
                                    Eng. Ch. Blencathra Brat
                      Foxgrove Jeff of Ljekarna
                                    Foxgrove Venus
         Ch. Foxgrove Jaunty
                                    Ljekarna Laurel
                      Foxgrove Jocasta
                                    Foxgrove Venus
Recless Kyley of Sharolaine
                                    Eng. Ch. Craiglyn Stornoway
                      Ch. Ugadale Hallmark
                                    Ainsty Susan
         Ch. Recless Kelly Joe
                                    Eng. Ch. Cairncrag Huntsman
                      Ch. Samantha of Cairncrag
                                    Mouzel Lady
```

Ch. Sharolaine's Kalypso (25)
by Ch. Cairndania Targon's Thomas ex Recless Kyley of Sharolaine

Bred to Ch. Brigadoon's Binnie McBean produced:
1. Ch. Tweedsmuir's Dear Gabby
2. Ch. Tweedsmuir's Miss Daisy
3. Ch. Zigfelds Sweeny Todd

Bred to Ch. CairnAcre's Scottish Nosegay produced:
4. Ch CairnAcre's Primrose
5. Ch Clanranald Highland Fling

Bred to Ch. Copperglen Fame N Fortune produced:
6. Ch. Copperglen Foxtrot
7. Ch. Copperglen Lindy
8. Ch. Copperglen All That Jazz
9. Ch. Copperglen Windwalker

Bred to Ch. Foxairn For Heaven's Sake produced:
10. Ch. Foxairn Heaven's To Betsy
11. Ch. Sharolaine's Kingdom Kome

Bred to Ch. Foxairn Kiss N Tell, produced:
12. Ch. Foxairn Kissmet
13. Ch. Zomerhof's Friendly Lil Ghost

Bred to Ch. Foxairn Little Miss Marker produced:
14. Ch. Foxairn La Bamba
15. Ch. Foxairn Double Trouble
16. Ch. Foxairn Scarecrow
17. Ch. Foxairn Tinman
18. Ch. Foxairn Wizzard
19. Ch. Foxairn Karousel

Bred to Kellicairn's Country Girl produced:
20. Ch. Mistywyns Cooper of Highnoon
21. Ch. Mistywyns Nan Tucket
22. Ch. Mistywyns Polly Anna

Bred to Ch. Loch Katrine Lady Meghan produced:
23. Ch. Sandpiper
24. Ch. Scarlet Tananger

Bred to Ch. Recless Gaelic produced:
25. Ch. Kirkshire's Spice O'Life

Top-Producing Cairn Terrier Bitches

1. Ch. Gayla Cairns' Nora - 22
2. Ginger Mist of Merriwood - 17
3. Ch. Col-Cairn's Ruffy Righinn - 14
4. Ch. Gayla Cairn's Hope - 12
5. Ch. Tradorohg's Connamarah - 12
6. Ch. Lakewood's Foxy Lady - 11
7. Ch. Kenmure's Felicity - 10
8. Ch. Bayberry of Wolfpit - 9
    Ch. Glencairn Molly McNeill - 9
    Ch. Hillston Geraldine - 9
    Kim-E-Cairn's My Choice - 9

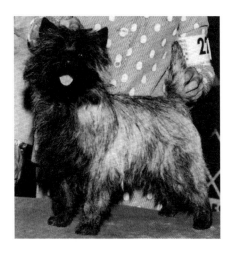

Ch. Gayla Cairn's Nora (Grey Brindle)
Whelped: May 2, 1975
Ch. Completed: May 1976
OWNER
Miss Nancy J. Thompson
BREEDER
Miss Nancy J. Thompson

Eng. Ch. Blencathra Redstart

Eng. Ch. Lofthouse Geryon of Mistyfell

Sadie of Mistyfell

Ch. Wyesider Grey Knight

Eng. Ch. Blencathra Milord

Lordly Greyling

Nightly Snaffly

Ch. Gayla Cairn's Grey Knight

Ch. Pledwick Lord Frolic

Ch. Gayla Cairn's Davey

Ch. Gayla Cairn's Hope

Ch. Gayla Cairn's Eleanor Fox

Ch. Caithness Rufus

Bramble Rose

Lady Jessica D'Ecosse

Ch. Pledwick Lord Frolic

Ch. Gayla Cairn's Davey

Ch. Gayla Cairn's Hope

Ch. Gayla Cairn's Inspiration

Ch. Caithness Rufus

Ch. Kenmure's Felicity

Redletter Miss Romola

Ch. Gayla Cairn's Forget-Me-Not

Ch. Nicholas of the Cantycairns

Ch. Gayla Cairn's Tucker

Ch. Gayla Cairn's Little Linda

Gayla Cairn's Maggie

Ch. Caithness Rufus

Bramble Rose

Lady Jessica D'Ecosse

Ch. Gayla Cairn's Nora (22)
Ch. Gayla Cairn's Grey Knight ex Ch. Gayla Cairn's Forget Me Not

Bred to Ch. Gayla Cairn's Gregor McKim produced:
1. Ch. Gayla Cairn's Jedaiah
2. Ch. Gayla Cairn's Josie
3. Ch. Gayla Cairn's Kaz
4. Ch. Gayla Cairn's Killdear
5. Ch. Gayla Cairn's Kiss My Grits
6. Ch. Gayla Cairn's Kojac
7. Ch. Gayla Cairn's Martha Wurst
8. Ch. Gayla Cairn's Sadie
9. Ch. Gayla Cairn's Sam
10. Ch. Gayla Cairn's Simon
11. Ch. Gayla Cairn's Sinner
12. Ch. Gayla Cairn's Sue
13. Ch. Gayla Cairn's Jennie Rahe

Bred to Ch. Gayla Cairn's Inspiration produced:
14. Ch. Gayla Cairn's Early Bird
15. Ch. Gayla Cairn's Eaststar
16. Ch. Gayla Cairn's Edward McKim
17. Ch. Gayla Cairn's Elmer
18. Ch. Gayla Cairn's Elsie
19. Ch. Gayla Cairn's Endora O'Cairmar

Bred to Ch. Gayla Cairn's Zanzibar produced:
20. Ch. Gayla Cairn's Zeus
21. Ch. Gayla Cairn's Zippi

Bred to Ch. Gayla Cairn's Quarles produced:
22. Ch. Gayla Cairn's Edith

Ginger Mist of Merriwood (17)
Merrywood's Golden Mist ex Gingerbred of Glengary

Bred to Ch. Caithness Barnabas produced:
1. Ch. Lakewood's O C
2. Ch. Lakewood's Red Raider
3. Ch. Lakewood's Foxy Lady
4. Ch. Lakewood's Barnstormer
5. Ch. Lakewood's Suzy Q
6. Ch. Lakewood's Top O'the Mornin
7. Ch. Lakewood's Charming Betsy
8. Ch. Lakewood's Mean Joe Green
9. Ch. Lakewood's Talking Tilda

Bred to Ch. Cuttie Sark Scotch Whiskey produced:
10. Ch. Lakewood's Grey Boy
11. Ch. Lakewood's Tiger Tank
12. Ch. Lakewood's Raggedy Ann

Bred to Ch. Moonbeam of Redletter produced:
13. Ch. Lakewood's Moon Dust
14. Ch. Lakewood's Moon Mist
15. Ch. Lakewood's Moon Shine
16. Ch. Lakewood's Moon Tripper
17. Ch. Lakewood's Moon Flower

Ch. Col-Cairn's Ruffy Righinn (14)
by Ch. Bold Oaks Play it Again Sam ex Bridget O'Winston

Bred to Ch. Cairnwoods Fiver produced:
1. Ch. Tigh Terrie's Buttons 'N Bows
2. Ch. Tigh Terrie's Sadie Sadie

Bred to Ch. Foxgrove Mutt produced:
3. Ch. Tigh Terrie's Rusty Rogue
4. Ch. Tigh Terrie's Callme Casey
5. Ch. Tigh Terrie's Mickey McFinn
6. Ch. Tigh Terrie's Sunny Sideup

Bred to Ch. Graystone Fairborn Flame produced:
7. Ch. Tigh Terrie's Guinnes Stout

Bred to Ch Sulinda Samson of Worrindale produced:
8. Ch. Tigh Terrie's Currie Clown
9. Ch. Tigh Terrie's Chelsea Chimes
10. Ch. Tigh Terrie's Honey Happicairn
11. Ch. Tigh Terrie's Precious Peanut

12. Ch. Tigh Terrie's Sugar 'N Spice
13. Ch. Tigh Terrie's Two Timin' Ted

Bred to Ch. Tigh Terrie's Mickey McFinn produced:
14. Ch. Tigh Terrie's Front 'N Center

Ch. Gayla Cairn's Hope (12)
by Ch. Tartan of Melita ex Ch. Gayla Cairn's Little Lynda

Bred to Ch. Pledwick Lord Frolic produced:
6. Ch. Gayla Cairn's Bonfire
7. Ch. Gayla Cairn's Dapdan Boswell
8. Ch. Gayla Cairn's Dark Star
9. Ch. Gayla Cairn's Davey
10. Ch. Gayla Cairn's Dixie Darling
11. Ch. Gayla Cairn's Drummer Boy
12. Ch. Gayla Cairn's Dunaden

Bred to Ch. Gayla Cairn's Davey produced:
2. Ch. Gayla Cairn's Quiet Hope
3. Ch. Gayla Cairn's Quite Like Davey

Bred to Ch. Cairndania Ruffie's Mister Ruf produced:
1. Ch. Gayla Cairn's Fitzgerald

Bred to Ch. Nicholas of the Cantycairns produced:
4. Ch. Gayla Cairn's Jingles

Bred to Ch. Oudenarde Look Away produced:
5. Ch. Gayla Cairn's Tess

Ch. Tradorohg's Connamarah (12)
by Ch. Milbryan McGillicuddy ex Ch. Megan of Shagbark

Bred to Ch. Caithness Barnabas produced:
1. Ch. Cairmar Christmas Storm
2. Ch. Cairmar Misty Storm
3. Ch. Cairmar Storm Warning
4. Ch. Cairmar Stormie Dream
5. Ch. Era's Dust Storm of Cairmar
6. Ch. Cairmar Stormie Dawn

Bred to Ch. Caithness Colonel produced:
7. Ch. Doss' Modern Milly of Milbryan
8. Ch. Milbryan Milady
9. Ch. Tradorohg's Kyleigh

Bred to Ch. Croftee of Raelain produced:
10. Ch. Cairmar Cantie Croftee

Bred to Ch. Tradorohg's Dunstan Claymore produced:
11. Ch. Cairmar Stormie Surprise
12. Ch. Tradorohg's Cluny Connamarah

Ch. Lakewood's Foxy Lady (11)
by Ch. Caithness Barnabas ex Ginger Mist of Merriwood

Bred to Ch. Moonbeam of Redletter produced:
1. Ch. Lakewood's Cameo
2. Ch Lakewood's Jameson Maloney
3. Ch. Lakewood's Sir Echo
4. Ch. Lakewood's Barwillagin
5. Ch. Lakewood's Gold Trinket
6. Ch. Lakewood's Golden Charm
7. Ch. Lakewood's Foxfyre
8. Ch. Lakewood's Moon Lady
9. Ch. Lakewood's William O'Charbe

Bred to Ch. Lakewood's Spellbinder produced:
10. Ch. Lakewood's Foxy Beau

Bred to Ch. Lakewood's Tiger Tank produced:
11. Ch. Lakewood's Tiger Lady

Ch. Kenmure's Felicity (10)
by Ch. Caithness Rufus ex Ch. Redletter Miss Romola

Bred to Ch. Gayla Cairn's Davey produced:
1. Ch. Gayla Cairn's Debutante
2. Ch. Gayla Cairn's Doctor John
3. Ch. Gayla Cairn's Earthquake
4. Ch. Gayla Cairn's Jolly Roger
5. Ch. Gayla Cairn's O'Tilly
6. Ch. Gayla Cairn's Idiots Delight
7. Ch. Gayla Cairn's Inspiration
8. Ch. Gayla Cairn's Little Sister
9. Ch. Gayla Cairn's Enuf-O-That
10. Ch. Gayla Cairn's Et Cetera

Ch. Bayberry of Wolfpit (9)
by Ch. Cairnwoods Quince ex Ch. Craiglyn Christmas Carol

Bred to Ch. MacBrian of Wolfpit produced:
1. Ch. MacLoganberry of Wolfpit
2. Ch. Spiceberry of Wolfpit
3. Ch. Huckleberry of Wolfpit
4. Ch. Sherry Berry of Wolfpit

Bred to Ch. Persimmon of Wolfpit produced:
5. Ch. Carnoustie of Wolfpit
6. Ch. Gleneagle of Wolfpit
7. Ch. Ravensworth Arran of Wolfpit

Bred to Ch. Gadget's Gimmick of Wolfpit produced:
8. Ch. Cloudberry of Wolfpit
9. Ch. Mayberry of Wolfpit

Ch. Glencairn Molly McNeill (9)
by Ch. Craigly-B Smart Alec ex Glencairn Laurie McNeill

Bred to Ch. Craigly Jamie McFlair produced:
1. Ch. Craigly Jamie McNeill
2. Ch. Glencairn Rob Roy McNeill
3. Ch. Glencairn Britannia McNeill
4. Ch. Glencairn Jenni McNeill
5. Ch. Glencairn Ruggles McNeill
6. Ch. Glencairn Sally McNeill
7. Ch. Glencairn Benny McNeill
8. Ch. Glencairn Missy McNeill

Bred to Ch. Craigly-B Cornelius produced:
9. Ch. Glencairn Bobby McNeill

Ch. Hillston Geraldine (9)
by Greetavale Blondey ex Hillston Bonnie Sweet Briar

Bred to Ch. Cairndania McBrigand's Brigrey produced:
1. Ch. Cairndania Brigrey's Gerry
2. Ch. Cairndania Brigrey's Gerbrig
3. Ch. Cairndania Brigrey's Sir Gerald

Bred to Ch. Lofthouse Davey produced:
4. Ch. Cairndania Davey's Dannette
5. Ch. Cairndania Davey's Denia
6. Ch. Cairndania Davey's Douglas

7. Ch. Cairndania Davey's Lass
8. Ch. Cairndania Davey's Dolly
9. Ch. Cairndania Davey's Dauntless

Kim-E-Cairn's My Choice (9)
by Ch. Bonnie Vandal of Wolfpit ex Lucifer's Scotch On The Rocks

Bred to Ch. Cairnwoods Quince produced:
1. Ch. Kim-E-Cairn's Faerie Queene
2. Ch. Kim-E-Cairn's Scotch Rebellion
3. Ch. Kim-E-Cairn's Shadrack
4. Ch. Kim-E-Cairn's Sandpiper
5. Ch. Pennylane's Kara O'Kim-E-Cairn's
6. Ch. Pennylane's Kim-E-Cairn's Oliver

Bred to Ch. Blondey of Cairn Den produced:
7. Ch. Kim-E-Cairn's Drummer Boy
8. Ch. Kim-E-Cairn's Mighty Shamus

Bred to Ch. Kim-E-Cairn's Mighty Shamus produced:
9. Ch. Kim-E-Cairn's Macho Man

Bibliography

American Kennel Club.	*The Complete Dog Book*. New York: Howell Book House, 1992.
Ash, Edward C.	*The Cairn Terrier. The Dog Owners Hand-books*. London: Cassell and Company, 1936.
Beynon, J. W. H.	*The Popular Cairn Terrier*. 2d ed. London: Popular Dogs Publishing Co., 1929.
Benyon, J. W. H. with Alex Fisher.	*The Popular Cairn Terrier*, 3rd ed. London: M.B.E. Popular Dog Publishing Co., 1950.
Brackett, Lloyd C.	"Planned Breeding," Chicago: *Dog World Magazine*, 1961.
Brown, Curtis M.	*Dog Locomotion and Gait Analysis*. Wheat Ridge, Colo.: Hoflin Publishing Ltd., 1986.
Caspersz, T. W. L.	*The Cairn Terrier Handbook*. London: 1957.
Caspersz, T. W. L.	*Cairn Terrier Records*. Henley-on-Thames, England: Higgs & Co., 1932.
Daniels, Julie.	*Enjoying Dog Agility*. Wilsonville, Ore.: Doral Publishing, 1991.
Dog World Magazine.	1915, 1928, 1929, 1931, 1935, 1936, 1937, 1938, 1940.
Elliott, Rachel Page.	*Dogsteps*. New York: Howell Book House, 1973.
Gordon, John F.	*All About the Cairn Terrier*. London: Pelham Books Ltd., Penguin Group, 1988.
Hess, Gary.	*Cairn Terrier History*. Unpublished.
Jacobi, Girard A.	*Your Cairn*. Fairfax, Va.: Denlinger's, 1976.
Johns, Rowland.	*Our Friend The Cairn*. New York: 1932.
Lee, Muriel P.	*The Whelping and Rearing of Puppies*. Minneapolis: Plantin Press, 1983.
Leighton, Robert.	*The Complete Book of the Dog*. London: 1922.
Lent, Patricia Adams.	*Sport with Terriers*. Rome, N.Y.: Arner Publications, 1973.
Lyon, McDowell.	*The Dog in Action*. New York: Howell Book House, 1974.
Marvin, John.	*The Complete Cairn Terrier*. New York: Howell Book House, 1975, 1986.

McKinney, Patricia A.	*The Compendium of British Cairn Terrier Records.* Shirland, Derby, England: Higham Press, 1994.
Nichols, Virginia Tuck.	*How to Show Your Own Dog.* Neptune City, N.J.: TFH Publications, 1976.
Pfaffenberger, C.	*Knowledge of Dog Behavior.* New York: Howell Book House, 1963.
Rogers, Alice, and Corrine Ward.	"Why We Needed a New Standard for the Cairns," *American Kennel Gazette* (October 1934): 17–21, 152.
Rogers, Mrs. Byron.	*Cairn and Sealyham Terriers.* New York: Robert M. McBride & Co., 1922.
Ross, Florence.	*The Cairn Terrier.* Manchester, England: "Our Dogs" Publishing Co., Ltd., 1925, 1933.
Saunders, Blanche.	*Complete Book of Dog Obedience.* New York: Howell Book House, 1976.
Secord, William.	*Dog Painting, 1840–1940.* Suffolk, England: Antique Collectors Club, 1992.
Smythe, R. H.	*The Dog: Structure and Movement.* New York: Arco Publishing, 1970.
	Terrier Type Cairn Issue, July 1986, publisher, Dan Kiedrowski
Vaughn, C., and D. Fee.	*The Cairn Terrier in America.* Phoenix: C. Vaughn, 1991, 1992, 1993.
Walkowicz, Chris, and Bonnie Wilcox, D.V. M.	*Successful Dog Breeding.* 2d ed. New York: Howell Book House, 1994.
Weber, Shirley.	*Project Breed Directory, Red Book Edition.* Germantown, Md.: Network for Ani-Males & Females, Inc., 1993.
Whitehead, Hector F.	*Cairn Terriers.* London: Rowan Press, Ltd., 1959.
Willis, Malcolm B.	*Practical Genetics for Dog Breeders.* New York: Howell Book House, 1992.
Wilson, Dora Lee, and Judi Hartell.	"Sparring the Terrier," *Kennel Review* 11 (1972): 26-27.

Other Sources for the Serious Fancier

Benjamin, Carol.	*Dog Problems.* New York: Howell Book House, 1989.
Benjamin, Carol.	*Mother Knows Best.* New York: Howell Book House, 1985.
Benjamin, Carol.	*Second Hand Dog.* New York: Howell Book House, 1988.

Davis, Kathy.   *Therapy Dogs*. New York: Howell Book House, 1992.

Fisher, John.   *Why Does My Dog . . . ?* New York: Howell Book House, 1991

Whitney, Leon F.   *Dog Psychology*. New York: Howell Book House, 1991.

Wilcox, Bonnie DVM and Chris Walkowicz.   *Old Dogs/Old Friends*. New York: Howell Book House, 1991.

CTCA Publications

Cairn Terrier Club of America. *CTCA Official Yearbooks.*
Cairn Terrier Club of America. *Interpretation, Clarification, and Amplification of the Cairn Terrier.*
Cairn Terrier Club of America. *Meet the Cairn.*
Cairn Terrier Club of America. *Standard Cairn Terrier Grooming Start to Finish.*